Ra

Teach Yourself®

Raise a Happy Teenager
Suzie Hayman

For UK order enquiries: please contact Bookpoint Ltd,
130 Milton Park, Abingdon, Oxon OX14 4SB.
Telephone: +44 (0) 1235 827720. Fax: +44 (0) 1235 400454.
Lines are open 09.00–17.00, Monday to Saturday, with a 24-hour
message answering service. Details about our titles and how to
order are available at www.teachyourself.com

For USA order enquiries: please contact McGraw-Hill Customer
Services, PO Box 545, Blacklick, OH 43004-0545, USA.
Telephone: 1-800-722-4726. Fax: 1-614-755-5645.

For Canada order enquiries: please contact McGraw-Hill
Ryerson Ltd, 300 Water St, Whitby, Ontario L1N 9B6, Canada.
Telephone: 905 430 5000. Fax: 905 430 5020.

Long renowned as the authoritative source for self-guided learning –
with more than 50 million copies sold worldwide – the **Teach Yourself**
series includes over 500 titles in the fields of languages, crafts, hobbies,
business, computing and education.

British Library Cataloguing in Publication Data: a catalogue record
for this title is available from the British Library.

Library of Congress Catalog Card Number: on file.

First published in UK 2009 by Hodder Education, part of
Hachette UK, 338 Euston Road, London NW1 3BH.

First published in US 2009 by The McGraw-Hill Companies, Inc.

This edition published 2010.

Previously published as *Teach Yourself Parenting Your Teenager.*

The **Teach Yourself** name is a registered trade mark of
Hodder Headline.

Copyright © 2009, 2010 Suzie Hayman

Typeset by MPS Limited, a Macmillan Company.

Printed in Great Britain for Hodder Education, an Hachette UK
Company, 338 Euston Road, London NW1 3BH, by CPI Cox &
Wyman, Reading, Berkshire RG1 8EX.

The publisher has used its best endeavours to ensure that the URLs
for external websites referred to in this book are correct and active
at the time of going to press. However, the publisher and the
author have no responsibility for the websites and can make no
guarantee that a site will remain live or that the content will remain
relevant, decent or appropriate.

Hachette UK's policy is to use papers that are natural, renewable
and recyclable products and made from wood grown in sustainable
forests. The logging and manufacturing processes are expected to
conform to the environmental regulations of the country of origin.

Impression number   10 9 8 7 6 5 4 3 2 1
Year   2014 2013 2012 2011 2010

Contents

Meet the author

What qualifications do I have to write a book on teenagers?
Well – for a start, I have been one. Once we move past that
stage in our lives, especially when we move up to being a
parent ourselves, we often forget what it felt like, what it was
like. That's a pity because we could all do ourselves and our
teenagers a favour if we cast our minds back and used all that
detailed research to inform how you approach your teenage
son or daughter now. One of my light-bulb moments with my
stepson was when I did just that and suddenly saw an argument
we were having from his point of view. I could hear my own
mother in what I was saying – and I didn't like it anymore than
I had when I heard her say it!

Apart from being a teenager myself, I was a stepmother to my
stepson during his teenage years. It was exactly as I have tried
to encapsulate here – a mixture of highs and lows, arguments
and joyful triumphs and discoveries. I learned a lot and I hope
I always tried to do my best, but looking back, I really do wish
I'd had the benefit of a guide like this!

Apart from my personal experiences, my background for writing
this is that I trained as a teacher and worked with teenagers
in school, and later when I worked for the Family Planning
Association and Brook Advisory Centres. Eventually I moved
into being a freelance journalist and used my teaching and
counselling skills to became an agony aunt. I was with *Essentials*
magazine, then *Woman's Own*, BBC Health Online and have
written columns for the Saturday *Guardian* and *The Times*.
I now write a family advice column in *Woman Magazine*.

I trained with Relate to become a counsellor, and Triple P
(Positive Parenting Programme) to become an accredited
parenting educator and I am a spokesperson and trustee for

Family Lives (formerly Parentline Plus), the major UK parenting charity, and a trustee of The Who Cares Trust, for 'looked after' children. I'm one of the founding agony aunts in the Kids In The Middle (KITM) alliance, lobbying for increased support for children caught up in family breakdown, and also edit the KITM website. I make frequent appearances on national and local television and radio, as a counsellor and agony aunt, on programmes such as 'BBC Breakfast', 'Woman's Hour', 'You and Yours' and am a regular on BBC 5Live, BBC Scotland and BBC Wales. I'm also an occasional presenter on my local BBC radio station, BBC Radio Cumbria. I presented my own series on BBC1, *Stepfamilies*.

As well as books I write features, mainly on relationship, parenting, counselling, health and sex matters, for a wide range of national magazines and newspapers – most recently *The Times*, *Independent* and *Guardian*. I have conceived and written leaflets and website material for Family Lives, the NSPCC, Gingerbread, the Family Planning Association, Parenting UK and Brook Advisory Centres and contribute an agony page voluntarily to '*Who Cares?*', the magazine for kids in care produced by The Who Cares Trust. I am regularly asked to give expert comment in national and local media and to speak at conferences and give seminars on a wide range of issues to do with relationships and parenting.

You are the expert of your own children but I know from personal experience that we're often too close to realize what's happening, why it's happening and what we can do to make some helpful changes. That's why a book such as this can be so helpful. It doesn't tell you what to do. It does what I was offered in my counselling training and my parenting training – it opens up understanding and gives skills to put that understanding into action. Parenting is a skill you learn, not an art you're born with, and the more skills you gain, the happier and more confident you and your children are going to be.

Suzie Hayman

Only got a minute?

Parents often dread the teenage years, having heard from family, friends and the media that it's a time of conflict and confusion. What we seldom hear is that in the transition from childhood to adulthood that is adolescence, your young person can be so much fun. They can bring excitement and pleasure to you as well as to themselves, if only we can acknowledge the big changes they are undergoing, and embrace them.

The teenage years can be stormy because teenagers, as apprentice adults, are striving to stand on their own two feet. That process of separation from their parents is an essential part of growing up. A parent's role is to offer support, but resist butting in until asked. The problem is that as the teenager gains their own place in the world, parents can feel rejected and redundant. It is the need to feel necessary and wanted that often fuels arguments.

Teenagers do not behave badly because they have 'gone bad'. Behaviour is a demonstration of needs and emotions. They act out frustration, confusion and distress, either at changes that are happening in the family or in their own lives. A key to dealing with teenagers is recognizing that we may dislike some of their behaviour and want it to change, but we should always love and accept the person. This is why communication is such an important issue.

Communication should always be two-way – listening as much as talking. Teenagers need parents to be encouraging and enabling and to help them to enjoy life when it goes well, and to manage it when it goes badly. Being the parent of a teenager needs different skills to being the parent of a child. It may be hard work, but it is rewarding.

5 Only got five minutes?

Teenagers' years are often stormy and difficult, for both the teenager and their parents. As apprentice adults, teenagers struggle to separate from their parents, to stand on their own two feet and to define who they are and what they believe in. Rebellion is a natural part of this developmental stage, as they pull away in order to say 'I'm different to you – you're no longer the boss of me!' Their anger and confusion as they try to make sense of the changes in their body, their thought processes and abilities, inevitably lead to conflict.

Parents can feel rejected and redundant as their once sweet and obedient little children turn into stroppy monsters. Yet in spite of this, teenagers still need to belong within their family, sharing experiences and time together. What helps is for parents to recognize the need to renegotiate family rules and to keep the lines of communication open.

Teenagers will always need love, support, encouragement, nurture, acceptance and attention from their parents, just as they did when they were children. However troublesome their behaviour, it can also be fun as they explore and discover. Their enthusiasm can widen your world for you again, if you let it.

What can be disconcerting is the fact that the skills you need to parent a teenager are so very different to those needed to parent a child. With a child you are protective and guiding, and the centre of their world. With a teenager you have to learn to take second place to their friends, and to be hands-off and act in an advisory capacity.

When there is conflict, it's often tempting to blame the teenager and to see them as misbehaving or naughty or even bad. But the truth is that teenagers do not behave badly because they have 'gone bad'. Behaviour is a demonstration of needs and emotions.

They act out frustration, confusion and distress, either at changes that are happening in the family or in their own lives. A key to communicating with teenagers is recognizing that we may dislike some of their behaviour and want it to change but we should always love and accept the person. This is why communication is such an important issue with teenagers.

Communication should always be two-way, where you listen as much as you talk. Teenagers need parents to be encouraging and enabling and to help them to enjoy life when it goes well, and to manage it when it goes badly. Being the parent of a teenager needs different skills to being the parent of a child. It may be hard work, but it is rewarding.

It's helpful to prioritize and pick your battles. Some issues you can stand firm on, but it helps to know which issues you want to negotiate and which you'll leave alone. Letting go on the small things can help you to be able to stand firm on what really matters. Bringing the same intensity to insisting they keep their rooms tidy or wear clothes you find acceptable, as to whether they smoke or drink or get in a car driven by someone under the influence, can lead to them rejecting everything you say.

Having realistic expectations of what you can and cannot do can help you and your teenager. What you're aiming to be is a 'good enough' parent, not a perfect one. There's no such thing as a perfect parent or a perfect teenager. Recognizing you can be a 'good enough' parent, with 'good enough' teenagers' allows you to relax and enjoy them.

10 Only got ten minutes?

Teenagers' years are often stormy and difficult, for both the teenager and their parents. Parents often approach these years with anxiety, having heard from family and friends and the media that it's a terrible time. Which is a pity, because it can be a time of fun and discovery, as your teenagers take on the world with the gusto that only teenagers can have.

Parents can manage better if they understand what is going on and why. Teenagers are not argumentative or awkward simply for the fun of it. They have a job to do in these years and it's the clash between what they had to do as children and what they have to do now as adolescents that produces the conflict. As apprentice adults, teenagers need to separate from their parents, to stand on their own two feet and to define who they are and what they believe. Rebellion is a natural part of this developmental stage, as they pull away in order to say 'I'm different to you – you're no longer the boss of me!' Their anger and confusion as they try to make sense of the changes in their body, their thought processes and abilities, may lead to clashes.

Arguments can be about major issues such as education and qualifications, sexual exploration, drinking and driving or drugs. Or it can be about lesser ones such as being tidy about the house, their clothes and musical tastes and who their friends are. A lot of the time, the arguments with a teenager are not really about a particular issue, even though that sparks off the row. They come from the teenager's need to do their own thing, and the adult's own feelings of rejection and loss. It's the process of separating from family and home and starting out on a journey to their own self-sufficient adult life that causes the pain, the anxiety and the upset.

Parents can feel rejected and redundant as their once sweet and obedient little children turn into stroppy monsters. Yet in spite of this, teenagers still need to belong within their family, sharing experiences and time together. What often needs to happen is for parents to recognize the need to renegotiate family rules and to keep the lines of communication open.

Teenagers will always need love, support, encouragement, nurture, acceptance and attention from their parents, just as they did when they were children. What they want to hear from their parents is an acceptance of their complex emotions at this time. This is a time when both parents and teenagers are learning new skills – one for a parent is to know when to stand back and let the teenager practise theirs. Teenagers are battling to define themselves, to developing empathy and some interest in outside society. They are finding out who they are, what they believe, which group or role model they admire, what their sexual identity is and what they want, or need, to rebel against.

It is true that teenage behaviour can often be troublesome, but it can also be fun as they explore and discover. Their enthusiasm can widen your world for you again, if you let it. What can be disconcerting is the fact that the skills you need to parent a teenager are so very different to those needed to parent a child. With a child you are protective and guiding, and the centre of their world. With a teenager you have to learn to take second place to their friends, and to be hands-off and in an advisory capacity.

When there is conflict, one way of dealing with it is to recognize it is their *behaviour*, not the teenager, which is the problem. They express needs and feelings through the way they act – acting out – and understanding this can help you to find out what your teenager is really trying to tell you – and what they really need.

Teenagers do not behave badly because they have 'gone bad'. Behaviour is a demonstration of needs and emotions. They act out frustration, confusion and distress, either at changes that are happening in the family or in their own lives. The argument may flare over their forgetting to clear up after themselves, with accusations from them of 'You're always on at me!' and you of

'You're so messy!' At the bottom of it all may be their stress over schoolwork, and your distress at the fact they're soon going to leave you. A key to communicating with teenagers is recognizing that we may dislike some of their behaviour and want it to change but we should always love and accept the person. This is why communication is such an important issue with teenagers.

Communication should always be two-way, where you listen as much as you talk. There are some skills that can help you practise good communication – ways of making it clear you are listening, of using body language, tone of voice and praise more often than criticism. Negotiation and compromise always work better with teenagers than laying down the law, even though they do still need and appreciate firm boundaries. Although the rules you might have had in place when they were children will largely no longer be appropriate, family rules are still important. The best way to enforce them is to discuss them together during a family conference, negotiating and compromising to achieve agreement.

Teenagers need parents to be encouraging and enabling and to help them to enjoy life when it goes well, and to manage it when it goes badly. As a parent there is a natural tendency to think that you must sort out all of your children's problems. When it comes to teenagers we need to resist the temptation of trying to fix the problem, in favour of standing back and letting them do it for themselves.

It's helpful to prioritize and pick your battles. Some issues you can stand firm on, but it helps to know which issues you want to negotiate and which you'll leave alone. Letting go on the small things can help you to be able to stand firm on what really matters. Bringing the same intensity to insisting they keep their rooms tidy or wear clothes you find acceptable, as to whether they smoke or drink or get in a car driven by someone under the influence, can lead to them rejecting everything you say.

Being a parent can be a complex and tiring job and when it involves teenagers, it can become even more so. Parents need to think and look after themselves as well as everyone else in the family, occasionally putting their needs and wishes first. You can't care for other people if you are exhausted and running on empty. Every parent needs to refresh and recharge now and then.

Having realistic expectations of what you can and cannot do can help you and your teenager. What you're aiming to be is a 'good enough' parent, not a perfect one. There's no such thing as a perfect parent nor a perfect teenager. Recognizing you can be a 'good enough' parent, with 'good enough' teenagers allows you to relax and enjoy them.

Introduction

The problem with a kitten is that
One day it becomes a cat.

Ogden Nash

You have a child – adorable and adoring, sweet and biddable – and then they grow up. Benjamin Franklin said, 'In this world nothing is certain but death and taxes' – but he was wrong. A third certainty is that children eventually become teenagers. From the days when they smelled of talc and only wanted to please you, they enter the realm of slammed doors and the witheringly scornful 'Oh, Muuuuuuuuum/Daaaaaaaaaaaaaad!' Overnight, it seems, it changes from 'I love you!' to 'I hate you – you're ruining my life!' You're no longer the person with all the answers who can solve anything; you're now the person who knows nothing and '…is not the boss of me!'

What happened? How have you suddenly become a uniquely awful person with the only out-of-control adolescents in the world? Is it all doom and gloom?

A few facts

For a start, it's worth knowing that you certainly aren't unique or alone. There are some four million teenagers in the UK, over 25 million in the US, and every one of them will give their parents grief at some time or other. All parents find the teenage years difficult. It's the nature of adolescence to rebel against the people who care, and many of us are unprepared for the changes that happen within our relationships as our children morph from kids to adolescents. We are all – both adults and young people – likely to find the process a puzzling and painful time. Just about every parent – before or during this period in their children's lives – will need support, explanations and ideas for how to cope. It's a strength, not a weakness, to recognize you could do with some help, and that's what this book is all about.

The way things are

When you've got a teenager in the house your life may begin to feel as if it's full of conflict – of misunderstandings and stand-offs, of disagreements and tussles. When parents and teenagers argue, parents usually imagine something has gone terribly wrong. You may well think that you've failed as parents, or your teenager is especially awful. What have you done, you may wonder, to turn your sweet, obedient, charming child into such a monster? In fact, what you're probably experiencing may be no more than par for the course for this time in your life and theirs. While teenage–parent conflict can clearly get out of hand and be a real concern, it's actually perfectly normal for parents and their children not to see eye-to-eye during the teenage years.

The reason for this friction is that teenagers have a job to do – to learn to stand on their own two feet. They need to explore their own needs and voice their own opinions and become themselves, rather than their parents' children. A teenager is an apprentice adult, and apprentices have to learn, struggle and find out for themselves how to do the job in their own right. Teenagers need to separate from their parents – to draw a line and say, 'That is you, and this is me and we aren't the same.' They need that boundary, but in the process of drawing it they may say and do things they know will upset you. It doesn't necessarily mean that they hate you or will forever disown you or have different opinions or beliefs from you; it simply means that they need to try things on for size before settling on their own identity.

These disagreements can be painful because they tell us that we are growing old and that our children may soon no longer need us.

Faced with the demands and protests of a teenager in the throes of adolescence, we may feel overwhelmed and find ourselves drawn into arguments, reacting like teenagers ourselves, rather than as responsible adults. Forewarned is forearmed; what I intend to do is explain what is happening and why, and to show you how to avoid conflict. The trick is to be able to act, not *react*.

Unlikely as it may feel when we're in the middle of adolescence, young people still want and need their parents' approval and care. Once they have moved beyond this period, they tend to share many beliefs and attitudes with their parents. Parents need to know that they are not alone – most families with teenagers go through the same difficulties. We need to trust that when a situation does get out of hand, there is help. *Raise a Happy Teenager* will guide you through the teenage years, explaining what to expect and why, offering some tips and tricks of the trade to cope with conflict, and to support you in managing your parent–child relationship better.

Ten top tips discussed in this book

1 *Keeping an eye on your teens – showing you care and are prepared to set some limits, but trusting them and not interfering or trying to control them. Parents may resist the idea of negotiating and compromising with their teenagers because they fear they will lose control or lose face, but what worked for a child may not be appropriate for an adolescent. Teens need, and respond better to, more communication and negotiation and less direct supervision and guidance. By respecting and listening to them, you give them the confidence to run their own lives, and they will respect and listen to you in return. Research suggests the stronger the bond between parent and teen, the less likely they are to go off the rails.*

2 *Prioritize and choose your battles. Parent–teenager arguments tend to revolve around a common set of disagreements: loud music, the wrong sort of friends, staying out late, provocative or unsavoury clothes, untidiness, sexual activity, drug taking.*

Don't expend the same intensity on whether your teen can wear a particular T-shirt as to whether they have sex or take drugs. Decide which issues to stand firm on, which to negotiate and be flexible about, and which to let go.

3 *Understand why your teen may be behaving badly. Many of us find it hard to put our worries into words and act out problems with moodiness, anger or misdirected aggression. Conflict can often be about a reaction to something that has happened that you have not recognized or been made aware of. The loss of someone who has died or left the family, or change, such as a move of home or school, can all lead to feelings of guilt, anxiety or anger which in turn can result in bad behaviour. So, too, can arguments with friends, fear of falling behind at school, worry over the physical and emotional changes that occur during adolescence and many more reasons. Talking over what has prompted the reaction, rather than focusing on the bad behaviour, can often help.*

4 *You may be hurt by what your teenager is doing or saying, but you need to avoid taking it personally. Adolescents often hit out at the people they most love and trust, not because they hate you, but because they feel confused, stressed and uncertain. Growing up is hard work. And they target you with their anger because they trust you to cope with it.*

5 *Parents often use insulting and damaging words to describe their teenagers. However angry or upset you feel, remember that it's what they do that you dislike, rather than them.*

6 *Remember your own teen years and what you and your own parents clashed over. You also challenged your parents by wearing clothes and having friends they did not like, and pushed boundaries for exactly the same reasons as your teenagers – as part of the same struggle for identity, separateness and difference.*

7 *Look at what's happening in your own life. Young people tend to enter adolescence at the same time as their parents enter middle age, a time of crisis and reassessment. You may be striving to get what you want in life personally, emotionally, romantically and professionally. You may feel that your children are in competition, deserting you – or seem to be*

throwing it all away. Conflict between parent and teen often comes about because of jealousy, anxiety or anger over your own issues, rather than theirs.

8 *Accept that your children can't live your life by fulfilling your ambitions or making up for your lost chances. You may have particular high hopes for them in education or work, marriage and family. Disagreeing with you or going their own way doesn't mean that you have worked in vain.*

9 *Look after yourself. Parenting teens is hard work at the best of times and you may need time and space to recharge. Organize your own support networks so you have people to talk to and share problems with. Every parent needs help at some time and asking for it is not a sign of weakness, but of strength.*

10 *Parents often worry about especially challenging behaviour: aggression, drug and alcohol abuse, sex and pregnancy. Sometimes, their anxieties are out of proportion to their teenager's actual behaviour. In some cases, their fears may be justified and more specialist help could be needed for themselves and their teenagers. This book will help you to manage the usual, common, normal issues of teenage–parent conflict; if you do need further help, signposts of where to go for specialist support will be given.*

1

The change from child to adolescent

In this chapter you will learn:
- *about the physical changes that precede and accompany adolescence*
- *about the mental, emotional and social changes that also go with adolescence*
- *how to understand and work with your teenager.*

The physical changes

As children become teenagers they change. Children grow – from helpless babies to sturdy toddlers – and if you stood a photograph of your eight-month-old beside one of your eight-year-old, you'd see a clear difference. But the degree of alteration seems far greater in a few months of adolescence than years of childhood. Teenagers do not only alter physically, they develop mentally, emotionally and socially. This section will outline what these changes may be, why and how they happen and what parents can do to understand and cope with the way these changes affect the teenager, the parent and the family.

The physical changes that happen to our children before and during their teenage years are probably the first aspect we think about, and perhaps worry about, when we consider adolescence.

Both teenagers and their parents and carers may be waiting and watching nervously for these, but often with different anxieties. The young person may be apprehensive and embarrassed, and sometimes even dreading the ways their bodies will alter and their self-image adjust. But equally, they may be longing for them and be on the look out for every new sign of change. Parents may also be on the alert, with a mix of anticipation and apprehension.

The actual changes are one thing, how your teenager interprets and makes sense of them is another thing entirely. What for one young person may be the exciting signs of the entrance to a new life that they eagerly anticipate, could for another be a depressing signal of loss. Becoming an adolescent means accepting responsibility – it means starting on the road to eventual adulthood. It means entering the exhilarating but scary arena of sexual potential. It means losing your status as carefree child who can be looked after, and who doesn't have to think about such complex things.

Insight
The physical changes of adolescence signal a transition from childhood to adulthood. As such, they can be a source of excitement and anticipation, and of fear and anxiety, for both parent and child.

WHAT PART CAN PARENTS PLAY?

Where do parents fit in here? You might expect schools to take far more of a role in explaining puberty and sexual development than perhaps happened in your day. Or you may feel that this is entirely your responsibility and be anxious about what schools may teach. Sadly, you may be right to fear that some schools renege on this role. Neither British nor American schools have a good record on sex education, although it is improving in Britain. But on the whole, the teaching is too little, too late, and far too mechanistic. Young people do need to know the facts about sex education; but far more than that, they need to be reassured, to be permitted to discuss the emotional aspects of their development and given the opportunity to ask questions. Both schools and parents are sometimes so frightened of the Pandora's Box this may open, of being overwhelmed by questions they feel they cannot answer, or of triggering impulses they cannot control, that they fudge this issue.

DO TEENAGERS WANT TO TALK TO THEIR PARENTS ABOUT PHYSICAL CHANGES?

Parents may shy away from raising the subject of physical changes out of a fear that they may be shouted down with the classic teenage 'Eeeeuuuww! Gross! And anyway, I know all about *that*' (said with withering scorn, rolling eyes and frantically flapping hands!). You may indeed encounter such a response at first. Persevere because all the evidence shows young people really do appreciate being able to talk to their parents, and would like you to be available to them for this. And whatever they say, often they don't 'know all about *that*' and have plenty of questions that could do with answering.

DOES TALKING ABOUT SEX ENCOURAGE SEXUAL ACTIVITY?

You shouldn't and needn't be worried that raising the issue of sex and sexuality will in any way be harmful to your teenagers. There is absolutely no evidence to suggest that talking about sex promotes curiosity or initiates activity. On the contrary, there is plenty of evidence to suggest the opposite. Countries that have had explicit sex education for some years, such as Sweden and Holland, have far lower pregnancy rates than the UK and the US, and even more importantly, their teenagers become sexually active at a later age than ours.

HOW MUCH SHOULD PARENTS KNOW?

You're a parent, not a university lecturer, teacher or medical professional. You do not need to know all the details of physical development to help your son or daughter through the changes that happen in their teenage years. All you need is confidence, and the most important thing you may need to say with confidence is,

'I don't know, let's go and find out together.' Above all, perhaps the area young people most need to discuss is not the physical details themselves, but their feelings about them. It's opinions, attitudes and emotions around sexuality, sexual development and sexual relationships that we all primarily have to sort out, understand and learn to negotiate.

What your children most need to know is that it's okay to ask questions, and that you won't fob them off with a lie, a change of subject or make them feel bad for being curious and asking questions. When parents do any of these things, young people don't recognize you're avoiding the issue because you're embarrassed or scared of appearing ignorant. They think that there is something wrong with them for asking such questions, and feel guilty and humiliated for doing so. Sooner or later, they stop coming to you, which may be a relief, but it doesn't mean the questions go away; it means they have to go elsewhere. And if the elsewhere is a well prepared and enlightened school or well written books and magazines, that at least means they have their questions answered. Unfortunately the elsewhere could also be friends who are just as confused, or a media that specializes in shock-horror and celebrity sex-scandal stories – not to mention pornography on the internet.

Insight

You don't need to be an expert. What your teenager needs from you is for you to be an 'askable parent' – someone who makes them feel comfortable in being able to ask questions even if you can't immediately answer them.

WHAT DO YOUNG PEOPLE WANT TO HEAR FROM THEIR PARENTS?

Your teen may need to have some specific questions answered about the developments they are experiencing, or hope to experience soon. You can help by remembering back to your own transition from child to teenager. What worried you? What happened to you? It will also help for you to have a refresher course on what does occur in adolescence (see Getting prepared for physical changes, below).

What teenagers most need is an acceptance of their complex emotions at this time. A common feature in many cries of help from teenagers is the feeling that they are utterly out of control – of their lives, their families and their relationships. This feeling may well come from the fact that, as puberty advances, they feel utterly out of control of their bodies. Perhaps it is why films about alien possession and zombies are so prevalent and such a favourite with young people. They are not, as some people suggest, a political statement but a perfect metaphor for what is happening to them.

TEENAGERS CAN BE SELF-ABSORBED

Teenagers also need understanding and acceptance for their sometimes annoying self-absorption. Most young people during this period become quite self-obsessed and introspective. They indulge in endless navel watching, both literally and metaphorically. Many will spend hours behind locked bathroom doors staring at themselves, or in their bedrooms writing diaries or blogs. Such intense introspection is likely to throw up all sorts of issues they may not have otherwise noticed. When they look at themselves, they are likely to become intensely aware of their bodies and see marks on the skin or floating specks in the eyes. They may become hyperconscious of obsessions, repetitive thoughts and short-term enthusiasms, as everything around them comes under a spotlight. Anyone who looks intensely at themselves will always find something they have not seen before; it is human nature – instead of realizing it is simply a fact of your not having noticed it before – to assume it is a new development and a problem. Teenagers may become convinced they have cancer, brain tumours and all sorts of incurable diseases, or are going mad. You may find it funny or exasperating, but their distress can be very real and the resulting stress significant.

What helps your teenager?
Teenagers benefit from having parents who understand what they are going through. If you can cast your mind back to when you were a teenager, you might recall going through just the same dilemmas, and having just the same needs. It can help to drop into the conversation that 'I remember when...' But go carefully. You know how annoying

it can be for someone to take something over from you – to be forever butting in with, 'You think you've got problems! Well, I...' Sharing your own experiences can be powerful, if used sparingly.

The trick is to be ready with a reassuring word or hug, and to only step in when asked. Your teenager doesn't want lectures and doesn't need you to second guess how they may be feeling or why. Ask an open question; that is, a question that cannot be answered with 'Yes' or 'No' (such as 'Are you feeling okay today?') Instead, try 'You look down in the dumps. Tell me about it.'

Having helpful books, leaflets or an internet site to hand to point to when a query arises, or to show that you are trying to keep up, can be useful.

The physical changes – be prepared

Periods and wet dreams may well be issues that you, or the school, do discuss, either before they occur or when they have begun, since they are, after all, the most obvious changes that occur during adolescence. What sometimes gets missed out is the variety and number of the other small changes that occur at the time. Teenagers may be ready for the big changes, but be utterly undone and left overwhelmed by the sheer number and accumulation of all the little ones. Many teenagers are still not quite prepared for the scale and the speed of the way their bodies will transform. Letters to agony aunts and despairing appeals to nurses or doctors make it clear that as far as many teenagers are concerned, they wake up one morning and their slim, neat, small, trim and clean bodies have suddenly been transformed into fat, shambling, sweaty, hairy, smelly monsters with the most embarrassing and ugly bits sprouting out of everywhere.

So what does happen in the process that takes a young person from child to budding adult? We often think of puberty as a specific event: the first period for a girl, the voice breaking or the first wet dream for a boy. In fact, puberty is a process and often takes several years with those landmark events coming along some years after the process gets under way. The process commonly starts for girls around their tenth or eleventh year and for boys around their eleventh or twelfth year. But it is just as usual for the process to start a year or so earlier, or later, in both sexes.

Boys and girls experience similar changes – human bodies have more similarities between the sexes than differences. It's useful for parents and teenagers to be aware of this, and of the particular differences; even if you have only daughters or sons, it helps to brush up on the full range.

Insight

Once we grow up, and particularly once we become a parent, we often forget what it felt like to be a teenager. It can be helpful to talk over with your partner or a friend what you experienced and what your worries were at this time in your life. Remembering your anxieties can help you put yourself in your teenager's shoes.

FIRST THINGS FIRST – EARLY DEVELOPMENT

What comes first? In girls, it's likely to be a sudden increase in height, often closely followed by the budding of the breasts. The areola, the area around the nipples, will enlarge and darken slightly. This area will bulge outwards and develop into distinct breasts.

In boys, the first sign is usually the appearance of pubic hair and then the growth spurt. Teenagers can grow as much as an inch or a couple of centimetres in a month. They may shoot up, almost overnight, so that parents used to looking down fondly on a child, may soon find them looking them eye to eye.

WHY TEENAGERS ARE SO CLUMSY

The immediate result of the growth spurt can be that young people of both sexes become extremely clumsy. There are two main reasons for this. The first is simple mechanics. Hands and feet that four weeks ago were one distance from their body are now a tiny bit further away. The simple act of reaching for a cup or walking across a room is complicated by the brain not having caught up with that fact. Teenagers have to make constant adjustments to their new size and thus the new centre of gravity of their bodies. This is frequently not easy.

Their awkwardness is made worse by the second reason: the fact that this new body often embarrasses them. Early starters may find themselves towering over classmates, which can be awkward. Late starters may look a year or so younger than their contemporaries, which can be humiliating. Teenage girls may hunch over to hide developing breasts, walk with their arms crossed or insist on wearing coats or baggy jumpers, even in summer. Boys trying to control their new gangling arms may shove their hands in pockets, fiddle with things and, rather than standing in the open, will slouch and lean against walls or furniture. It is why teenagers are often to be found sitting on pavements or steps or leaning against lampposts. They're shy, they feel awkward and their new body simply won't obey them as it once did.

The more these displays of clumsiness are criticized or drawn attention to, the more convinced the teen will be that everyone is looking at them, and the more they may stagger from disaster to disaster. Criticism does not help them to slow down or be careful and deliberate in their movements. It only convinces them that they are stupid and at fault and since they cannot control themselves now, may never be able to do so again.

WEIGHT GAIN

Another early sign of the onset of adolescence is a gain in weight in both sexes. Boys and girls will find their silhouettes altering. The weight should redistribute itself very quickly, as long as their diet is healthy and their lives are active. Girls' hips become wider and padded with a layer of fat, and their thighs will fill out. The face will often become fuller and the voice may drop a little.

Boys become heavier in the shoulders and the muscles over their body will thicken. Boys' voices will not deepen until puberty is well under way, and the Adam's apple grows. Around the time that their body hair has thickened, boys will go through a phase when their voices break. They may find they cannot stop themselves wavering between a younger, high-pitched treble and a deeper tone, especially when they are excited, angry or nervous.

Boys as well as girls will find the areola, the area around the nipples, enlarges and darkens slightly. While for girls the development of breasts is an early and expected sign of puberty, as many as one in two boys will also find their nipples pushing out and heavier breast tissue developing, to their acute embarrassment. This is called gynaecomastia and is a perfectly normal, passing phase. It certainly does not mean that the boy is turning into a woman or has anything amiss in his physical development. It usually recedes after a few months, although it can last for up to 12 to 18 months.

Insight

It's not unusual for teenage boys to develop moobs (or 'manboobs') at this stage but it could be a signal for all the family to think about and act on a healthier lifestyle with a better diet and some fun exercise you could share as a family.

'PUPPY FAT'

Girls are often particularly alarmed at the reserves of fat that accumulate. In our society, slim has become synonymous with beautiful. Even young girls can be intensely fashion-conscious and are horrified when their previously svelte body begins to fill out. You may remember being told when you were a teenager that this is puppy fat and will soon go away, and be tempted to do the same. Think back; did that offhand description reassure you, or convince you that your parents simply didn't really understand how you were feeling? To a young person whose whole lifespan is measured in less than 15 years, a period of years quite genuinely seems like a lifetime. Even puppies are only cuddly and plump for a few months. Calling it puppy fat is dismissive and trivializing and does not adequately describe a major alteration that a teenager might feel singles her out and makes her ugly and cumbersome at a time in her life when she longs to be acceptable.

It might be more useful to explain the reason for the new shape. Adult women have greater subcutaneous or under-skin stores of fat than children or adult men. It is a survival trait to ensure that even in times of food shortage, the female body will have put something aside to be able to nourish a breastfeeding baby. It is also the reason that women have greater stamina than men. Men may have greater speed and instant strength, but when it comes to trials of endurance, such as very long foot races over 50 miles, a fit woman matched against an equally fit man will come out on top. Understanding these facts might comfort a teenage girl who is waiting for her body to gain the height that gives the extra padding proportion, or for the extra pubertal fat to melt away.

AN OPPORTUNITY TO ADDRESS LIFESTYLE CHOICES IN HEALTHY EATING AND EXERCISE

Your child's change in body shape can also give your whole family a chance to consider important issues around healthy eating and exercise. There is a difference between healthy adolescent padding and being overweight. Overweight children become overweight teenagers and become fat adults. Many schools are now trying to reverse a cycle that saw regular and routine exercise being reduced at the same time as fatty, sugary food became freely available to pupils in school canteens, on school premises or from nearby shops they could access during the school day. But offering healthy food – and healthy exercise – in school can have little effect if what happens at home encourages patterns of behaviour that work against such initiatives. If this healthy lifestyle issue is something you've struggled with yourself – and feel you could and should address – having a teenager in the house might be an ideal opportunity for all of you. We'll look at this in more detail in Chapter 7.

What helps your teenager?
When young people become adolescents, you can no longer get away with 'Do as I say, not as I do.' Teenagers need you to practise

what you preach, not to have double standards. Parents who are having affairs may find their teenagers engaging in premature sex; after all, if it's okay for you, why shouldn't it be okay for them? Similarly, it's no good giving lectures on drugs if you smoke or drink in an unconsidered way. Having a teenager might, in fact, be a good – if uncomfortable – opportunity for you to consider your position on all sorts of things; it may prove valuable to discuss these issues with them, so they can see how much you respect them and wish to do the best for them. For example, you may begin with a hard line on sexual activity for teenagers, because that was the attitude your parents passed on to you. But if you rebelled and didn't actually keep to their strictures – having sex before marriage, for example – you might like to consider why and how, and whether you might have benefited from a more realistic approach. You may want to say to your teenager that a sexual relationship is best when it's with someone you care for and who cares for you, and when you both use contraception. That may not fit with what you have been brought up to believe, but if it squares with how you actually behaved, your child will know you are being honest with them. They will be far more likely to listen to your opinion than if they suspect you're passing on a double standard.

SKIN AND BODY HAIR CHANGES

At the same time as their bodies gain height and weight, a young adolescent will find that the texture of their skin will change and become rougher. The fine, downy hair that covers our whole body, and can look like peach fuzz on a small child, will darken and coarsen. It becomes noticeable under the arms, around the genital organs and down the insides of the thighs. Legs and arms may also acquire a thatch. Both sexes can find hair on their cheeks and upper lip – often too little for boys' tastes and too much for girls. Both sexes may find hair growing on their chests, and most girls find a fine ring of long hair developing around the nipples.

The amount of body hair we develop is usually related to our racial group, as well as individual differences. Those with Mediterranean, Asian or Jewish ancestry will have more obvious hair growth than those with Negroid or Caucasian genes.

The presence of body hair is probably one of the few developments to provoke a different response in the sexes. We tend to associate body hair with masculinity, rather than seeing it as an aspect of most mature human bodies, both male and female. While girls will accept the growth that covers their genitals and tolerate hair under the arms, any other growth may be greeted with horror. Hair on the back or buttocks, on the legs and thighs, between the breasts and around the nipples, and a fine growth on the upper lip or sides of the face are often seen as abnormal. A girl with such a natural pattern of body hair growth may be too embarrassed to undress in front of friends, family or medical personnel, and be terrified that something is wrong with her – especially if her friends are developing to a different timetable to her, or are from different cultural backgrounds.

Boys on the other hand may be trying everything they can to encourage facial hair growth and proudly showing off body hair – or shyly concealing what they think is a lack.

What helps your teenager?
Treating your teenager as an equal is the best way to build trust and foster communication. That doesn't mean treating them as your best friend. Teenagers have friends their own age. What they need is for you to be a parent, but one who respects them and listens to them – without criticism or judgement. This can often be hard. We may be used to condemning and disparaging our child's behaviour or attitudes, very clearly stating our opinions. Whatever the rights or wrongs of that approach, the point is that it simply isn't effective with teenagers.

> ## Insight
> 'Do as I say not as I do' is a motto that simply won't work with teenagers. If you want to pass on a message, you first have to do it yourself.

A WORD ON TEASING

Teasing is one of those words that often means one thing to the person doing it, and quite another to the person having it done to them. The person teasing usually believes that they are being playful and simply trying to ruffle feathers, and maybe puncture solemnity using gentle ribbing. The person being teased may see it as more than annoying – it can be considered provocative, irritating and humiliating. They may feel ridiculed at best, bullied at worst. Teasing doesn't, as you might hope, make a difficult situation easier. Instead, it can often convince a teenager that they aren't understood and are being criticized. If teasing is a family trait, and adults and other children use it within your family, see what happens if you ban it for a month or so. You may find that the amount of conflict within family relationships reduces.

WHY TEENAGERS THINK THEY SMELL

Once puberty is underway, skin becomes a far more active part of a young person's body. Your skin is the largest organ of your body – a 1.5 square metre sense organ, which also protects and insulates you. Teenagers find sweat becomes an issue – often, a big issue – in their lives. Not only do they sweat, especially around the genital organs, under the arms and on their feet, but sweat acquires a distinct odour.

Adolescent and adult sweat contains chemical substances called pheromones. Pheromones are messengers – they use the sense of smell to attract attention. We may not consciously realize it, but human beings are aware of other people's aroma, and attraction to a particular person often starts or is made sharper through the nose rather than through the eyes. As teenagers begin to sweat more, their bodies produce pheromones and these can arouse sexual feelings. Unused to this new development, young people may become aware of both their own and other people's odour, and become alarmed or repelled by it. Sweat is also an ideal growth medium for bacteria. While most teenagers usually become fanatical about personal hygiene, for some there may be an overlap between being a carefree and bath-averse child and a stronger-smelling adolescent. With a few exceptions, most teenagers are not nearly as damp or as ripe as they imagine. It's not that suddenly they shed moisture or smell at an abnormal rate, as they often fear; it's the change from perspiring and smelling as a child to an adult that makes them become so hyper-aware.

You sweat when you're hot or doing exercise. Teenagers also sweat for a very wide range of reasons, completely beyond their control. The hormones racing through their system can bring about sudden flushes and the various excitements and embarrassments of adolescence will turn on the taps. The sebaceous glands, tiny glands under the skin which produce oil called sebum, can also cause problems at this time.

SPOTS, ZITS AND ACNE

Sebum functions as a built-in moisturizer, lubricating the skin and keeping it supple and healthy. The oil is supposed to ooze up out of minute pores and spread over the surface of the body. However, during the teenage years, the production of sebum can be so vigorous that minute flakes of skin can break off inside the channels and block the pores. This leads to the greatest horror of teenage life – acne. If the blockage is under the surface, it produces a white lump, or a white head. If the flake of skin is forced to the surface, it will blacken on exposure to air and become a blackhead. If the pressure of sebum trying to escape continues, it will rupture the wall of the channel and become infected – a spot, a pimple, a zit. Sebaceous glands are concentrated on the face, chest and back – hence these being particular sites for spots.

Teenage acne can be physically and emotionally disfiguring. Many young people become hyper-conscious of their own zits and fail to notice that it is a common difficulty – nine out of ten teenagers suffer from spots at some time. The over-vigorous production of sebum that produces acne is a reaction to the hormonal changes of puberty, which is why it is almost an occupational hazard of being an adolescent, and why it will pass in time.

Insight

A few spots are a natural result of growing up, but some teenagers can suffer outbreaks that leave physical as well as emotional scars. It may well be important to encourage them to visit and talk with the family doctor if their spots depress them.

More boys than girls get acne; boys tend to have a more severe reaction since it is the production of testosterone, the male sex hormone that encourages spots. You could reassure your son that the more zits he has, the sexier he is, but that would hardly reassure a daughter – even though both sexes do perfectly naturally produce a range of these hormones.

Because infection and black marks are associated with dirt, many teenagers worry that having acne means they are unclean. Spots and blackheads can be used by some young people as an excuse to tease and bully, as if the young person who has them is in any way different from dozens of their school mates. In fact, the colour of blackheads has nothing to do with dirt. It is caused by a chemical reaction. The same way as skin tans in the sun, the flake of skin blocking the pore turns a dark brown when it comes into contact with the air. Washing too often and with strong soap isn't helpful at all. Rather than cleaning up the acne, it over-stimulates the sebaceous glands to turn up their oil production. Soaping and rubbing leads to more sebum, and leads to a greater chance of having spots.

There are no easy ways to prevent or cure acne in a teenager – unless you can send them into hibernation until they reach 20. Acne is not caused by eating fatty foods, chocolate or other junk food. Neither is it encouraged by late nights or masturbation. It will not go away under a regimen of cold baths and dawn runs either. A wholesome, healthy diet, good exercise and sufficient sleep will certainly make for a fitter, healthier and possibly happier young person – who may still have teenage spots. Young people have enough misery to contend with over acne, without being told that they cause it, or could cure it if only they tried harder. Neither is true. Bad acne can drive a young person into a depression and severely damage their self-esteem. And, of course, how you define bad is entirely subjective. What, to you, appear to be no more then a few undetectable pimples can be enough to drive your teenager into taking up sackcloth and ashes.

MARKS ON THE SKIN

The natural coarsening of the skin at this age produces other fears. Most teenage girls find fine red or silver lines appearing on their breasts, stomachs and thighs, and teenage boys find such lines on their arms, shoulders and backs. These lines – called stria – are also known as stretch marks. We usually associate them with pregnancy or old age and they can come as quite a shock to the young person. Stria are not actually on or in skin itself, but are the result of minute bundles of fibres under the skin breaking apart. In spite of advertising promises, no amount of oil, cream or massage can prevent this happening or banish the lines once they are there – although pampering with oils and massages may help the young person feel better about themselves. The only consolation is that the lines fade to a faint silver and are far less visible to other people than the person who has them thinks. Far from being a sign of old age or weight gain, they are simply a common side-effect of adolescence.

CHANGES IN THE GENITALS

As fat accumulates on the hips, thighs and breasts of girls, and boys' shoulders fill out, so the genitals of both sexes also grow. As puberty advances, the skin covering the external genitals in both girls and boys darkens in colour and coarsens in texture as hair appears.

Girls will find the opening between their legs will change shape. As a child this area, called the vulva, has been a narrow slit, clearly visible when she stands up. Now, the slit will be gradually concealed by hair and will move gradually downwards as the mound above it – the *mons veneris* or 'hill of love' – fills out.

In between their legs, women have three openings. Through the front opening, we pass waste water or urine, and this passage is called the urethra. The middle opening is the vagina, or sex or birth passage. The back opening – the anus – leads to the back passage or rectum, through which solid waste matter is excreted.

Two folds of skin stretch from the front of the genital slit back towards the anus. During this period, these folds – the labia or genital lips – thicken and round out. They can hang down quite some way. The inner set – the *labia minora* or small lips – are hairless and the skin that covers them is shiny and darker in colour than the outer lips. *Labia minora* are often frilly or wrinkled and look very untidy indeed, especially in comparison with the neat, smooth vulva the young woman would remember from her childhood. The outer lips – *labia majora* or large lips – are usually covered by a growth of hair. The outer pair can hang down lower than the inner pair, or the other way round. And, indeed, some women find one side longer or thicker than the other. Labia come in all shapes and sizes and can vary in colour too, from dark plum to pale pink.

In front of the urethra, the *labia minora* come together to form a protective hood covering the most sensitive part of a woman's body – the clitoris. This too will have developed during puberty, although it has been present and sensitive since before the child's birth.

Insight

The size, shape and colour of labia are as varied and individual as your face or the colour of your hair. Teens often fear they are too big, too hairy, too textured. They won't be. Whatever they are, it's normal for them.

CHANGES TO A GIRL'S INTERNAL ORGANS

When the time is right, some one to two years after the pubertal process has begun, and when a young woman's body has the right proportion of fat to weight, internal organs develop as well as external ones. The pituitary gland at the base of the brain starts sending hormones or chemical messages into the bloodstream and the uterus – or womb – doubles in size to become a pear-shaped and sized organ, situated in the pelvic cavity. The best way to visualize its position is to clench your fist and place it against your lower stomach below the navel. If you could move 10–15 cm back into your body, that would be the position of the uterus. The ovaries which are suspended on either side of the uterus also begin to work. The ovaries are two plum-shaped and sized glands situated in a woman's pelvic cavity on either side of her uterus.

Each ovary contains as many as 100,000 microscopic egg cells. Given the proper stimulus, each could grow into an egg or ovum. Each one of these, given the optimum conditions, could be fertilized and grow into a baby. In practice, only 400 or so ova are released in any woman's lifetime.

THE FIRST PERIOD AND WHAT HAPPENS NEXT

The signal that a first period is about to begin is often the appearance of a white or creamy discharge on a young woman's pants. This can happen for few months before a show of blood. Some adolescent girls get warning cramps or feel tired and aching – again, sometimes for a few false alarms before the first period. The actual flow can be a bright red colour, but it is just as likely to be brown or black.

Insight

Daughters tend to start periods at around the same time as their mother started. So it's really helpful for a mum to remember when she began and make sure she prepares her daughter in advance for it to happen around then. The more advanced the preparation, the less the chance of trauma.

A BOY'S SEXUAL DEVELOPMENT

In pubescent boys, the physical development that enables them to contribute to a pregnancy starts a few years later than in girls. The signal for pubertal changes, as in girls, comes from the pituitary gland at the base of the brain. In boys, these hormones get to work on the testes – the two glands suspended below the penis, outside the body. After pubic hair has begun to grow, hormones cause the male sex organs to enlarge, boy's height and weight to increase and their muscles to become heavier. The testicles will also begin to manufacture sperm – the male cells. Unlike ova in girls, sperm are not present in a finite number from birth, but are made anew each day. As many as 300 million sperm may be present in each ejaculation. The advantage of such conspicuous waste is that even the loss of one testicle will not affect a man's ability to start a pregnancy; and, indeed, if a woman loses an ovary, the other will take over. Another advantage is that there is safety in numbers – only one sperm gets the prize and fertilizes an egg, but the other millions aid it on its way.

A tube connects each testicle to two small glands called seminal vesicles, which are connected in turn to the prostate gland. Sperm is passed up these tubes into the seminal vesicles where it combines with seminal fluid from the prostate. The resultant mixture, which is about 98 per cent fluid and two per cent sperm, is called semen. Semen can remain in the seminal vesicles and eventually be absorbed back into the body as new, fresh sperm – mature and ready to travel up from the testicles. More often, it is expelled during masturbation or during erotic or wet dreams.

Boys have erections from the time they are born. How often a boy masturbates or has wet dreams depends entirely on individual factors. However, it is neither abnormal nor unusual for a teenager in the throes of adolescence to have frequent emissions – as many as several each day. Boys are also constantly bedevilled by spontaneous erections. An erection is the *first* response to male sexual excitement. The body often reacts to a trigger – the sight, scent, sound or thought of something stimulating – even before the mind recognizes it, and certainly before the penis is touched or manipulated. Adolescent boys can find themselves becoming excited in the most public of places and at the most inappropriate times, without meaning or trying to become so.

LOPSIDEDNESS

Another area of potential confusion arises from the fact that human bodies are very rarely symmetrical. Young people of both sexes are likely to find various parts of their body growing out of proportion to others. Most of us have an arm or a leg longer than the other, and a hand or a foot bigger than its twin. Boys may find that one testicle hangs down lower than the other, and girls that one breast outweighs its companion. It is common for a woman who has completed her development to find one breast is as much as a whole cup-size larger than the other. In developing girls, this lopsidedness is all the more likely, as the growth of one side outstrips the other and it can take months before things more or less even out.

BREASTS

Breasts are a particular source of pain and pride for young women. These secondary sexual characteristics are on show, perhaps more than at any time in recorded history in our society and culture. In newspapers, magazines and on the internet, bared breasts are visible every day, so it's hardly surprising that both boys and girls are very breast conscious. They acquire a standard by which they judge their own or other people's breasts, without realizing it is a very inaccurate one. Breasts come in all shapes, sizes and textures. Some are small, firm and pear-shaped. On some, the nipples point up and on others they droop downwards. But whatever their appearance, they are *normal*. In most published nude pictures, various tricks are used to idealize the body. Invisible tape supports the breasts, ice cubes make the nipples stand out and the blue veins or stretch marks are concealed by make-up, or neatly airbrushed out of the completed photograph. And of course, many, many models and celebrities who bare their bodies have cosmetic surgery before doing so.

Because commercial pictures are often the first introduction teenagers have to the naked human female form, they may be convinced that it's normal for nipples to stick out constantly, and do not realize that this part of the body is designed only to react to stimulus. The nipple is made of erectile tissue. It fills with blood, swells and stands out if triggered to do so – by direct touch, by cold, by an emotional reaction such as fright or sexual excitement, or by exertion. At other times, the nipple can lie flat or even dimple inwards. Boys may expect an erect nipple, and girls may be confused at seeing themselves apparently different – and therefore inferior – to the models in the pictures.

MASTURBATION

During puberty both sexes discover, or rediscover, the delights of self-pleasuring – masturbation. Both sexes soon learn that touching their genitals is pleasant; even before boys' bodies manufacture semen to produce an ejaculation, or girls start menstruating, both can experience arousal and orgasm. Girls and boys find comfort and pleasure in touching themselves from an early age, but it is perhaps during the teenage years that masturbation becomes special. Both sexes will enjoy erotic daydreams, fantasies and dreams and may use hands, pillows or objects to help give themselves satisfaction, either consciously or while asleep.

Adolescents will find that their sexual organs grow. During sexual excitement, a girl's clitoris, labia, breasts and nipples swell and become tender and sensitive. A boy will discover that his testicles and penis undergo the same transformation. It's hardly surprising therefore, that many connect the permanent changes and growth with the temporary increase in size during excitement, and conclude that these alterations are freakish and a result of abnormal or forbidden practices. This is especially likely if they have been warned against 'self-abuse' and told it would harm them.

ALTERED GENITALS – SHAPE AND SIZE

Girls often have particular problems in coming to terms with their altered genitals; not only is this often a forbidden area for them, it is also a hidden one. Our fingers are such sensitive organs, that feeling an object you cannot see often makes it appear rougher and larger than it actually is. Few girls are supple enough to see their own genitals, or self-confident enough to use a mirror. Their fingers 'do the walking', and with nothing to compare themselves against, many girls become quite depressed and worried about what they find. A pre-pubescent girl's genitals are smooth, neat and tidy. Adult genitals, in comparison, are quite untidy – wrinkled, bushy and irregular. Unless the young woman understands this transformation *is* normal, she may well feel that her new genitals are horribly unattractive and no man would ever want to touch or see them, as this letter highlights.

From the mailbag

Please don't tell me off but I've been touching myself – I hope you won't be shocked – and I've found something that really scares me. Inside my body I can feel a lump. It's about a finger length inside me and I'm sure it's cancer or something. What can I do?

I'm not shocked – touching and exploring yourself is entirely natural. All teenagers do it, and it's perfectly normal to get great enjoyment from pleasuring yourself. And I can be totally reassuring about that lump; no, it's not cancer or anything problematic. It's actually your cervix, the entrance to your womb. You probably thought, as most people do, that it's at the end of your vagina. In fact, it juts into the passage about two thirds up. Nothing to worry about! But it may help to get a better idea of what your body looks like, so you don't have any more scares. I'd recommend a really good book such as *Growing Up: All about Adolescence, Body Changes & Sex* by Susan Meredith – it has photographs and diagrams that will reassure you.

Conversely, boys can suffer from the fact that they *can* compare themselves with friends. As with any part of the body, a wide range of size and shape is normal, but most boys quickly assume that big is beautiful. The lads who are late to grow may feel, or be made to feel, that their masculinity and future sexual prowess are in question. Boys' fears are fed by two important factors. First, the range of penis size is greater in the flaccid or non-erect organ than it is in the erect article. The average flaccid penis is 7–11 cm (2–4 inches) long; the average erect penis is 14–18 cm (5–7 inches) long. Most men will find themselves to be around 10.5 cm (4 inches) in the normal state and 15.5 cm (6 inches) when excited. But a penis that is smaller when limp is likely to swell *more* than a larger one, so that a group of men with a range of sizes will end up roughly equal when ready for intercourse. The boy admired in the showers for his size may well show little difference to his apparently smaller friends when it comes to lovemaking. Second, when boys do compare themselves, they always look downwards at themselves and across at their friends. A cylindrical object hanging down will always look shorter when viewed from above than from the side. This foreshortened view gives the owner a false impression of the actual size of his own body and that of his friends. If a boy wants to compare realistically, he has to do so by viewing himself and others in a mirror, side by side.

Insight

Size really doesn't matter! It's what you do with it that matters. Love, care and skill count for far more than size but that's a reassuring message that few teachers or parents seem to feel able to give.

SIZE DOES MATTER TO THE TEENAGE BOY

Of course, size is *not* everything, but it would be unrealistic not to recognize that this is, always has been and probably always will be, a major preoccupation with young lads... and of older men, too! There are very few adult men who can honestly say that they have never worried about whether their penis was adequate or not. Rather than dismissing such worries, it is probably better to help youngsters tackle them, before going on to explain that penis size has less to do with sexual prowess than love, care, understanding and knowledge. As well as size, the shape of their organ, both in its flaccid and erect state, can cause heartache. It is common for the penis to bend to one side or the other, and curve up – or even downwards – both when limp and erect. It is equally common for one testicle to be suspended lower than the other. The scrotum – the bag in which they are held – can feel taut or quite loose, allowing the testicles to hang down except when sexual excitement, fear or cold pulls them up against the body.

Reading the sort of literature, or viewing the sort of internet sites that tend to circulate among teenage boys, leads many of them to despair if their erections are not 'ramrod straight' and at an angle of 45 degrees. (For something better, I've recommended a couple of books – see Taking it further at the back of the book.) Such material can also give young men the mistaken belief that their bodies' reaction should be under their control – that a penis should become erect with – and not without – its owner's permission. A boy who becomes visibly excited at the flimsiest excuse can often be terrified that he is growing into an uncontrollable sex fiend. He may feel that everyone can see his shame and be laughing at him. He may go to great lengths to avoid certain situations or people, or wear baggy clothing or carry objects to hide behind, to conceal what is happening to him.

GIRLS AND THEIR PERIODS

If boys are obsessed by the sexual development displayed by the size of their penis, girls are especially absorbed with their menstrual cycle. Periods, how to manage them and how to conceal them, can form a major concern in the early teenage years. Period blood is not diseased or dirty, but as natural as any other normal discharge from the body. Like blood from a wound however, it does decay and start to smell as soon as it comes into contact with the air. Girls wearing sanitary pads or towels are bound to find they become a bit whiffy, however frequently they change. The fault is not in any bad hygiene on their part, but in a simple biological reaction.

Girls may find the idea of wearing internal protection very attractive, since it does make menstruation far less obvious, but come up against a new set of problems in this. Tampons are difficult to use if a young woman feels unhappy at touching herself intimately, and if she is afraid at the thought of anything entering the private parts of her body. Many women are unsure of the size and shape of their internal organs and so fear that a tampon could harm them, or become stuck or lost deep inside them. Many parents are unhappy at the thought of their daughters using tampons in case it encourages a precocious sexual knowingness. They also fear that tampon use will 'break' a young woman, robbing her of her virginity. Even when these fears have not been voiced, your daughter may well pick them up from you, or believe that is how you feel. She may be afraid to broach the subject, even if using a towel rather than a tampon means she stands out from her school friends and makes her a target for unkind teasing.

VIRGINITY AND FIRST SEXUAL EXPERIENCE

Being a virgin is not just a question of having an intact hymen or maidenhead – the thin tag of membrane that partially closes off the vagina or sex passage. Virginity means not having had complete sexual intercourse with a member of the opposite sex. Some girls do not even have a hymen, and in many it is stretched or broken long before puberty, by normal movement or by self-exploration. A tampon is far smaller than an erect penis, so is highly unlikely to be a substitute.

It is one thing for parents to feel that a girl should save her first sexual initiation for a man for whom she has a permanent and loving relationship, but quite another for them to insist that the first object to breach her body must be a rampant male penis, and to ask that she endures perhaps years of discomfort, embarrassment and teasing to support their views. If your fears are that she might hurt or harm herself in trying to insert a tampon, the best help you can offer is a pack of the smallest size – about the dimensions of a very slim little finger – and a tube of KY or any other water-based, soluble lubricating jelly (not Vaseline or petroleum jelly). Add a mirror, a good light and your supportive guidance in getting the angle right and relaxing while doing so. So long as tampons are changed at least three times each day, even when the flow is slight, and as long as ordinary hygiene is observed, there is no real risk of infection from using them.

Insight
I'd personally recommend tampons to teenagers for several reasons. One is that, used as per instructions, they are safe and hygienic. Another is that they put a girl not only in charge of her period but of her body. Using a tampon gives her the opportunity to explore and know her body and so gives her self-confidence and self-esteem.

Parents and sex education

Parents give their children a pretty comprehensive sex education from the day they are born. If yours is a family that has always been open about physical and emotional matters, the result is likely to be a young person who finds the changes of adolescence relatively easy to manage, and who can and will bring any problems to you or other trusted adults. At the other end of the scale, parents who find this an area of pain, confusion and fear, will teach their youngsters to be anxious and silent. There is no such thing as a parent who does *not teach* on this matter. The choice is between whether your lessons are constructive or not. Most of us are probably somewhere on the line in between the two extremes, and happy to work at doing better all the time.

What helps your teenager?
Teenagers need you to be there and to love them, no matter what they do. With all the changes happening in their bodies, it is very easy for them to feel isolated, in the spotlight and to blame. They may feel bad about themselves, so the last thing they need is for anyone to add to that. You may be fed up with something they do and have every right to say so. What parents and teenagers can find helpful is to separate the undesirable behaviour from the person itself. Try this approach: 'I love you – always, whatever. I may not like what you're doing...'

Sadly, secrecy and embarrassment tend to multiply and create more misery in their wake. Boys and girls left in ignorance of their own physical development – and particularly of the changes happening in the other sex – can become both intrigued and angry at the apparent mystery. Boys, for example, often take a special delight in teasing girls about their periods, or in shouting out or writing on walls the code names associated with this event: 'jam butties', being 'on the rag', 'aunt flo' or 'showing the flag'. Schools that make the mistake of segregating sex education classes – believing that giving boys more information can encourage this behaviour, and letting the secret out of the bag may embarrass and humiliate the girls – often make this worse. It is this insistence that a period is a taboo – a dark and terrible secret – that gives the harassment its spice. Every woman menstruates for a large part of her life; that is 52 per cent of the world's population sharing a normal, healthy event. Hardly something to be ashamed of.

The more that young people understand their own bodies and the normal changes and reactions they will be experiencing during adolescence, the happier they will be. Since many of us parents were not helped in our own youth to see these matters as anything but embarrassing, it can be difficult to approach them with ease. Young people will shy away from asking us questions, not because they do not have them, but because they know they are unwelcome. They need our permission to raise these subjects. We also need to accept that we do not always have to know the answers, and we certainly do not have to keep our composure, to be doing a good job. You need grounding in the facts to recognize what may be happening to your teenager and what may be worrying them. But more than that, you need the willingness to say, 'I don't know the answer to that... let's go and find out!'

Essential points to consider

▶ *You do not have to be a teacher or a medical professional to help your child. You just need to develop the confidence to say 'I don't know that. Let's go and find out together', and have your child feel safe with this.*

(Contd)

> ▶ *What your child needs to know is that it's okay to ask questions and that you won't fob them off with lies or evasion.*
> ▶ *Most of all, teenagers need your acceptance of their complex emotions at this time and for you only to step in when asked to.*
> ▶ *Appreciate the difference there can be between your teen as a person and their occasional bad behaviour. You will always love your teen, whatever, but have a right and a parental duty to speak out against any unacceptable behaviour.*

The law and your teenager

You might think that the law gives some guidance on when a young person is considered a child and when they cross over into being adults. The significant figure parents and teenagers often fix on is the age of consent – when a young person can legally consent to sexual intercourse. However, laws across the world show quite a lot of variation in this:

> ▶ *In the UK, a young person can consent to sex with someone of the same or opposite sex at 16. The only exception is if their partner is someone who is in a position of trust, such as a teacher or youth worker and is over the age of 18. In this event, an individual is guilty of committing an offence if they have sex or engage in sexual activity with a person aged 16 or 17 in their care.*
> ▶ *In France, the age of consent with someone of the same or opposite sex is 15.*
> ▶ *In Austria, the age of consent is 14 but it is illegal to have sex with someone under 16 by 'exploiting their lack of maturity'.*
> ▶ *Paraguay sets the age of consent at 14 within marriage and 16 outside of marriage.*
> ▶ *In Nigeria, the age of consent for heterosexual sex is 13, but same-sex sex is illegal.*
> ▶ *Although the age of sexual consent in Japan is 13 years of age, prefecture law usually overrides federal law, raising the age to 18.*
> ▶ *In the USA, as with some other countries, state laws and federal laws sometimes clash. Quite a few states have laws*

*against same-sex sex which are invalidated by federal law –
Florida, Michigan, Tennessee and West Virginia to name a
few. Others such as Hawaii and Idaho have repealed laws
against same-sex contact so it is now the same as for straight
sex. In the majority of states the age of consent is 16;
in Arizona and North Dakota it is 18; in Nebraska and
New Mexico it is 17. In some states, a lower age applies
if the partners are the same age, or with a small age gap and
the older partner is under 18 or 21; in South Carolina it is
16 or 14; in Washington, 18 or 16; in New York, 17 or 15.*

In keeping with the fact that adolescence is a process, not a hurdle,
there tends to be plenty of variation within each country as to the
other things teenagers can do, and when they can do them.

In the UK
At 12 a young person can:

▶ *buy a pet*
▶ *sign their own passport*
▶ *be sent to secure accommodation if convicted of an offence*
▶ *see a 12A-rated film without an adult and buy or rent a
  12-rated DVD or game.*

At 13 a young person can:

▶ *have a part-time job, with restrictions laid down in local
  by-laws. Usually, it can't be during school hours, before 7 a.m.
  or after 7 p.m., for more than two hours on a school day or
  Sunday, or more than five hours a day, or more than 25 hours
  a week in the holidays.*

At 14 a young person can:

▶ *go into a bar or a pub, but can't buy or drink alcohol*
▶ *own an air gun or rifle, but must be supervised by someone
  over 21*
▶ *if a boy, be convicted of rape, assault with the intent to
  commit rape and unlawful sex with a girl if she is under 16.*

At 15 a young person can:

▶ *see a 15-rated film without an adult and buy or rent a 15-rated DVD or game.*

At 16 a young person can:

▶ *have a full-time job if they have officially left school (they can't work full-time until the last Friday in June – even if they have turned 16 before this), but they can't work in a betting shop or in a bar during opening hours*
▶ *live independently, subject to certain conditions being met*
▶ *get married with their parent's or guardian's consent*
▶ *ride a moped of up to 50 ccs*
▶ *pilot a glider*
▶ *consent to medical treatment*
▶ *join the armed forces with their parent's or carer's consent*
▶ *apply for their own passport*
▶ *have beer or cider while eating a meal in a restaurant or an eating area of a pub, but not in the bar*
▶ *buy liqueur chocolates!*

At 17 a young person can:

▶ *hold a licence to drive most vehicles*
▶ *pilot a plane*
▶ *emigrate*
▶ *donate blood without their parent's or carer's consent*
▶ *buy or hire a firearm.*

At 18 a young person can:

▶ *vote in general and local elections*
▶ *get married*
▶ *join the armed forces without their parent's or carer's consent*
▶ *buy cigarettes and tobacco and buy and drink alcohol in a bar*

- *open a bank account in their name, without their parent's or carer's signature*
- *ask to see their birth certificate and have their name added to the Adoption Contact Registrar if they are adopted*
- *change their name*
- *be called to serve on a jury*
- *buy a house and make contracts*
- *sue or be sued*
- *make a will*
- *place a bet and work in a betting shop*
- *have a tattoo*
- *buy fireworks and sparklers.*

But they still can't adopt a child, become an MP or supervise a learner driver until they are 21.

Insight

21 used to be the age in the UK at which you were considered to be an adult which is why 21st birthdays were, and still are, celebrated as special. Yet it is 18 now that is the key age when most adult privileges are gained – to vote, to marry, to make contracts.

Emotional changes

We can see the alterations in a young person's body when he or she passes from child to adolescent in preparation for becoming an adult. Every extra gram or centimetre, every pimple or hair, every new pair of jeans or T-shirt needed to replace those outgrown makes it clear that we're chartering new territory. Physical changes are obvious and cannot be denied. What is less visible – but far more significant and far more of a shock to you, the teenager, the family and possibly society at large – are the emotional changes that are bubbling underneath the surface.

Linda spoke for many parents when she wrote to me about
her two teenage children, Joe and Kerry:

*What happened to my sweet little children? They used to be
so biddable, so nice, so loving. They'd do as I asked – well,
not every time but most of the time. And now it all seems to
be arguments and shouting. It seems as if I ask them to do
something and they'll do the opposite for spite. They pour
scorn on everything I hold dear and sneer at me all the time.
If I say I like anything – a bit of music, a film, a new
dress – they laugh at me and tell me how lame it is; I'm so
uncool, it seems. And don't get me started on what happens
when I try to kiss them or suggest anything. They pull away
from me, push me off, they don't want me or anything
from me. I just don't recognize them anymore. And I feel so
useless and awful. What did I do to deserve this? I thought
I was a good mother.*

WHAT ARE THE SIGNIFICANT DIFFERENCES
BETWEEN CHILDREN AND TEENAGERS?

Children model themselves on their parents. If they see you cooking,
cleaning, ironing, driving a car, answering the phone, they love to
pretend they're doing it too. If you chat and listen and play, if you
eat healthily and do exercise, they will too. If parents smack and
shout, smoke and drink, then that's the pattern children will see as
normal behaviour to be copied. Children want your approval and
will seek it and accept your guidance, your rules, and your example.
You are the centre of their world – the most important people in
their lives. If they feel you approve of them and accept them, love
and care for them, they will be full of self-confidence and self-esteem.
Children who feel that their parents reject them or do not care for
them, or are not there for them (either physically or emotionally)
will blame themselves, instead of blaming their parents for their

inadequacy. Since their parents are their centre and the example against which they measure themselves, they take the responsibility for what is missing and feel at fault. Children also transfer parental authority to other authority figures, so will tend to believe and respect people such as teachers who come with their parents' stamp of approval. Of course, if parents themselves are anti-school or anti-police or anti-anything, their children will follow suit. Children tend towards happiness, as long as what is going on in their background makes them feel loved and secure, approved of and accepted.

Teenagers are another kettle of fish entirely. As Linda discovered, teenagers rebel, reject and pull away, and it's easy to begin to feel that you've done something wrong – that you are a uniquely incompetent and incapable parent, with uniquely awful children. But here's the secret: teenagers are meant to be like that!

Insight

Parents shouldn't take teenage rebellion personally. Teenagers will do anything and everything in their power to make it clear you are separate and different. It's not about you – it's about them. It's about the teenage task – to cut the apron strings.

TEENAGE REBELLION

Teenagers are meant to rebel against you, to reject you and many of your beliefs, to pull away from you. That's what being a teenager entails.

When they rebel, reject and detach, they are only doing their job, because the job of an adolescent is to learn how to be themselves, to learn how to stand on their own two feet and to learn how to be an independent adult. In short, to separate.

What helps your teenager?
Teenagers may still love the family outing – a meal out, a visit to the cinema, shopping (as long as it's for them!) and even a Christmas pantomime. But adolescence is usually the time when they prefer to be with their own peer group, showing solidarity with them and separation from you. This may manifest itself as

total embarrassment at even the idea of walking down the same street as you, let alone side by side. Teenagers need for you to include them in family events – to assume they will be there and be happy to welcome them along. But at the same time, they need you to understand, and let them off the hook if they don't want to join in. Give them the choice to opt out and you may well find that when they grow up a bit, they'll be happy to return. Make it a battle and they may exclude themselves for good.

Children are connected to their parents. They learn how to be children with your guidance because part of their job is to learn how to take direction and fit in. But to be an adult, an individual has to sever that connection to become independent, and to learn the skills it takes to do this, your teen has to stand alone. If you show them how, they are never going to learn themselves.

Case study – Kim's story

When Kim's eldest daughter was 15, and since the girl had expressed an interest in working with animals, she fixed up a week at a local vet. Kim made all the arrangements – writing letters, agreeing a timetable, checking out travel to and from the surgery. Kim's daughter was unenthusiastic and non-committal about the experience and Kim was horrified to hear later from a teacher that she had been late on all but the first day, had missed the last day altogether and her final report was highly critical – of her attitude, behaviour and commitment. Two years later, Kim's younger daughter wouldn't say what she wanted to do, until announcing she had arranged work experience in an old people's home with the support of the school, but basically on her own. Her final report was glowing. Kim later said: 'It took me some time to recognize that it isn't that the two girls are so different – the main difference was that I snatched the whole thing away from one and let the other do her own thing. They're both young people I respect and admire and both are doing really well now. The behaviour my older daughter showed at that time was totally uncharacteristic and really more about her protest at the way I behaved. I had some growing up to do.'

LEARNING NEW SKILLS

The teenage years are hard for everyone for this reason. All of us
are learning and perfecting new skills. As a parent, you have to get
used to standing back and letting your teen get on with it – sitting
on your hands as they make mistakes and biting your lip as they
go their own way. They are learning to take over the reins,
to think and feel and act as the adults they want to be. Of course,
it doesn't happen overnight. One moment, your teen will be telling
you 'You're not the boss of me!' The next moment, they will be
expecting you to fill in forms or make calls for them. Swinging
between child and adult mode, they need you to respond as is
needed at the time, to show patience and to curb the temptation
to say 'I told you so!' as they make mistakes.

Part of the separation process is that teenagers will often deliberately
flirt with behaviour, appearance, friends, and interests that they
know are divergent to, or will upset, their parents. It may also be
totally contrary to anything they may have done before. So a tidy,
organized, quiet child from a tidy, organized, quiet family may
become a noisy, messy and shambolic teenager. They may turn Goth
or Punk or flash gang colours. Instead of looking to you to set the
pace for their beliefs and opinions, their friends and peer group
will become the touchstone and it will be 'So-and-so says...' and
'So-and-so thinks...' What their friends feel and think about them
will become all-important and they may feel under tremendous
pressure to fit in, to wear the 'right' clothes and do the 'right'
things.

Since it will be their friends' opinions that they value most, the
influence of any authority figure will be challenged and seen as
fair game. Teenagers can become frighteningly cynical, questioning
what you and their teachers, what the media and politicians say
and believe. But on the other side of the same coin, they can
become forcefully idealistic, caught up in the need to tackle
injustice and issues, such as world poverty and environmental
change.

What helps your teenager?

Teenagers benefit from having close contacts outside their own
family. In the battle to discover and refine themselves, they need to
measure themselves against as many different standards as possible.
Teenagers who come through adolescence well are often those
whose parents have supported and encouraged them to have close
friends, even when those friends were people they weren't entirely
happy about. You're not condoning a bad influence or colluding
with a poor choice when you support a teenager in having the
friends they want. What you're doing is respecting their decisions,
and standing back to be the safety net if they need it – or to
recognize that they had it right and you were wrong.

It's also very helpful if teenagers know you're okay with them seeking
out and listening to other adults: family friends, parents of their
friends, older siblings, aunts, uncles, grandparents, teachers, youth
workers. You may feel a bit jealous and wish your child relied on you
instead of them, and feel it's a little insulting for them to say they need
to go elsewhere. However, think about your own support network; if
you have a good one and use it, you'll know that you don't go to one
person for everything. Teenagers need to know there are other adults
who have faith in them and will be there for them. And as you will
remember from your own teenage years, sometimes we need someone
other than our parents to speak to, either to have confirmation about
what our parents have said, or to bitch to about them.

DEVELOPING EMPATHY

An interest in moral, ethical and social issues is the inevitable
result of the development of empathy. It is futile to expect a
young child to empathize with someone else. Telling a four-
year-old not to hit a playmate using language the child cannot

understand: 'How would you feel? Look, you've hurt them. Don't you feel sorry?' is pointless. They are simply not capable of feeling another person's pain as their own. They are fully able to see that you disapprove, and children want your approval so may well amend their behaviour to please you, which is how we socialize and train children to fit in. They will develop the ability to sympathize – to recognize when another person is in pain and to feel compassion for them. But it is not until the teenage years that they become capable of making another person's feelings their own, to fully understand and identify with them. Teenagers feel other people's pain; indeed they often feel the pain of the planet. Hence, the admirable and idealistic teenage championing of causes, from the environment to animal suffering. They may feel frustrated and angry at what they see as adult apathy – after all, if we all worked together...

This is also why teenagers tend to ponder the deep issues of the 'meaning of life', and suffer from general emotional angst. You can point at hormones for some of the emotional highs and lows; the sweeps from intense joy to deep depression that characterize adolescence. But as much as it might be their body's development that contributes to this, so too does their emotional development as they try out powerful feelings for size. Love, hate, anger – all are feelings children have, but about which they may feel confused and overwhelmed.

WHO AM I?

Teenagers are in the throes of finding out who they are. They will try on clothing styles, insisting on copying the fashion of their particular friends which could be expensive high-street labels or charity-shop rags. They'll try out music which may get your foot tapping, or sound to you like gangster manifestos or dirge-like misery. They'll try out friends; you may be convinced that they've gone out and chosen the one person in school or college who you'll hate, and you may be right!

They may also be struggling with their sexual identity. Some of this is part of the separation process. Recognizing that they do have sexual feelings underlines the point that they are no longer a child – your child – but near adults, with the potential to make allegiances of their own and to make choices that you cannot control. This may be the time that your child feels able to indicate: 'I have sexual desires and sexual curiosity and it's time, or soon will be, for me to exercise that.'

EARLY SEXUAL YEARNING AND LEARNING

As adolescents' bodies change, it tends not to be their own peer group they first notice. Young people commonly focus their early sexual yearnings and learning on the unobtainable: music and film stars, figures at a distance. Initial obsessions may involve someone of the same sex. Boys may become fixated on a footballer, girls on boyish music stars with an almost genderless appeal. There are reasons for this.

Falling in love with someone you don't, and are unlikely ever to, know feels safer – far safer – than making your first attempts at sexual connection with a real person. Young people experiment, running through the strong sensations triggered by thinking about their idols, but at a distance and in dreams. Such involvement in fantasy can be as intense and as real to them as genuine relationships. They are an important and healthy way of practising before doing it for real.

The reason the first icons for many young people tend to be androgynous or same-sex is not necessarily a signal they may be gay. Early sexual awareness is often more about self-identification than desire. Young people may run through a variety of looks in their clothing, music and interests, trying to align themselves with the tribe they wish to be a part of and the person they want to be. Similarly, they may practise their emotional and sexual feelings on someone they might like to model themselves upon, rather than someone they might like to attract. This may be why music groups and films for young people are often ensemble affairs, offering a variety of physical types and apparent characters – so that there's someone for everyone.

Insight
Early sensual yearning is far more about 'who I want to be' than 'who I want to have'.

WHAT DOES YOUR TEENAGER NEED?

Having heroes and heroines, people whose achievements they aspire to, or bad behaviour they'd love to descend to, is a normal and healthy part of being a teenager. When the house is covered with posters or the air split with loud music, you may be tempted to clear the walls, refuse to pay for one more DVD and pick apart what you see as a talentless, shiftless waste of time. Hold your tongue. That was exactly what your parents thought about your heroes, and did it make you say: 'Goodness Mum, you're so right! I shall mend my ways at once!' No? Then it's unlikely that your saying so will make them feel good about themselves, you or their heroes. The point about having heroes that achieve something in life is that they often inspire young people to do better for themselves, and the point about heroes that are destructive or express an anti-authority, anti-everything you hold dear attitude is that they often function as a stand-in; they do the rebellion for the young person, so they can get on with doing their chores and homework.

ARE THEY REALLY GAY?

Of course, adolescence may indeed be the time for a young person to come out as gay. It may be easy as an outsider to confuse the testing nature of much of adolescent sexuality with a belief that gay feelings during the teenage years are 'just a phase.'

From the mailbag

My 18-year-old son has just told me he is gay. I can't get my head around this. He's always got on well with girls – his best friend at school is a girl. Surely it must just be a phase they all go through? I can remember idolizing a girl at my school when I was that age. He says he's always known and that I need to listen to him but he's far too young to be making up his mind about something like this. He wants to tell his father, he says he has a boyfriend and wants to introduce us. I told him he should think it over further. I'm right, aren't I?

(Contd)

Many young people go through a stage in the early teenage years where they may have feelings for people of the same sex and may even experiment with them. It's a natural part of the process of finding your own sexual identity, likes and dislikes, tastes and eventual personality. Being drawn to someone of the same sex is less about sex itself and more about seeking to model upon and identify with someone they want to imitate or even become. But that's a very, very different thing to being 18 and coming out. That's not reacting to a developmental stage that is temporary. That's becoming aware of who you are, and seeking to be comfortable and honest with it. It's interesting that he says he's always known – most people do become aware, if only unconsciously, of both their gender identification and their sexual orientation at quite a young age. Sexual orientation and gender identification are two different things, by the way. Your gender identity is whether you feel male or female, and children become aware of that as early as two or three years old. Your sexual orientation is whether you are attracted to men or women, and many young people say that happens before puberty too. Your son has a male gender identity and he is attracted to men and that's not really something he can change by making up his mind; it's how he is. You mention his best friend – perhaps feeling that gay men don't like women and so this proves he's straight? No – male homosexuals don't hate women. If anything, perhaps he found her company preferable to that of some boys in his class who might have been going through the aggressive 'All I'm interested in is girls' phase that he wouldn't have identified with. He's trying to be honest with himself and you. He needs you, and his father, to listen to him and accept him for who he is. He's your son and no different to the person he's always been.

Finding their own beliefs

Teenagers need to establish a belief system and a set of values for themselves, as part of becoming fully independent and self-responsible and preparing for a lasting adult relationship and family life. They will spend much of their time questioning your and other adults' beliefs to do this and may aggressively challenge all the things you accept or stand for, including your spiritual beliefs. Teenagers frequently distance themselves from their parents' political and religious attitudes, become right-wing to your left or vice versa, taking up or rejecting a faith you hold or exploring a new one. Some parents can remember they did something similar. Sometimes, recalling your own feelings you can smile and step back, letting them find out for themselves. Sometimes, your own embarrassment at having done this or the fact that you can't recall doing anything of the sort, may lead you to argue with or tease them. The fact is that families tend to pass on beliefs and behaviour from generation to generation. Your children are a product of you, so they are more likely than not to end up with much the same moral code and live their life as you do. The teenage years are simply the time that they shake it around, try it on for size, find if they can make some nips and tucks and improvements and change the style a little to make it fit them.

Insight

Don't despair if your teenager seems to be the very opposite of you. Whatever they do or believe as teenagers, most young people come to agree with most of their parents' belief system.

RITES OF PASSAGE

One of the problems facing many young people in our society is that we don't maintain formal rituals – rituals still practised by some cultures – to clearly signal the end of childhood and the passage into adulthood. Rites of passage allowed children not only to leave childhood and enter into the privileges of adulthood, but also to recognize and take on the responsibilities that came with their new status. Jewish children have the Bar (for boys) and Bat (for girls) Mitzvah. It's not only a celebration, as an 18th or 21st birthday may be, but also something for which you have to work and think, and during the ceremony the 12- or 13-year-old commits to becoming a responsible being, now liable for their own behaviour. In contrast, many western teenagers do not have such an opportunity. And if there is no formal rite of passage, young people tend to invent their own. American college fraternities have 'hazing' rituals, often elaborate and painful. Gang members beat up new recruits or set them challenges. Other teenagers see learning to drive, having a first alcoholic drink or cigarette or having sex as being the entry ticket, grabbing the privilege without grasping the accountability that should go with it. Not having formal rituals means that in their desire to be considered old enough, western teenagers may grab at risky and harmful signifiers of what they see as maturity.

Essential points to consider

▶ *Teenagers are meant to rebel against you – to learn how to be independent and themselves. In short, to separate from you and stand on their own two feet.*

▶ *The separation process will be easier if both parents and teens learn the necessary new relationship skills together.*

▶ *Part of the 'letting go' process is to let your teens know that it is okay for them to seek out and listen to other adults. It does not mean you are no longer needed.*

Social changes

Children – even toddlers – have friends, and these friendships are often deeper and more important than we sometimes realize. However, it is during the teenage years that their peer group becomes more important than their family. Parents may find this difficult. It might seem dangerous that teenagers look to other teenagers for answers and a yardstick against which to judge themselves and their actions. Occasionally it might even seem that immediate considerations – the need to be part of a group and at a social event – takes precedence over long-term necessities, such as having to stay in to study for a test. But young people are really only doing what their seniors do too, except on perhaps a smaller scale; establishing a place in, and being accepted by, their community. You may feel that by ignoring your guidance they are being selfish or throwing over the reins of acceptable behaviour. But what they are often doing is exploring the boundaries of their own social group, and coming to their own understanding about what it means to be socially responsible. Having set their own boundaries and rules, most teenagers go on to broaden it and align their code with society at large.

Insight

Criticizing friends and putting barriers in the way of friendships is likely to result in your teenager resenting and resisting you and allying themselves even more strongly with the people you dislike.

NEW FRIENDS, NEW ALLEGIANCES

Adolescents need to fit in, but they also develop more mature relationships with friends of both sexes – friendships that they test and assess. Allegiances, especially among girls, can be intense and characterized by great loyalty and passion, but also may shift, break up and reform quickly and regularly. Someone quoted at length and described as a best friend one day may be a deadly enemy the next – and back to being a best friend a week later. It may be hard, but it's inadvisable to criticize someone you dislike, or either leap to the defence of/try to do down anyone who is blacklisted today. Because friendships are the testing ground of how your teenager manages their new maturity, it's really important to them that this is their own territory, not yours. Trying to influence their relationships will probably be met with by violent resistance, not necessarily because they disagree with you, but because it's their ability – and right – to make their own choice that is at stake. One mother said to me:

> I had a boyfriend when I was 16 who my mother simply hated. She thought he was a complete loser and she was really horrible about him – she'd call him The Shrimp because he was quite small. She just made fun of him and was patronizing and unpleasant. I went out with him until I went to college at 18 and to be frank, it was at least a year longer than I would have liked to stay with him. He was a lovely guy – which she never appreciated – but she was right in saying he wasn't what I needed. What she couldn't see was that I chose him and he was right for me for that time because he was so kind and caring. But I stayed with him because I was damned if I would give her the satisfaction of telling me she told me so. When my daughter started going out with someone I wasn't keen on at the same age, I thought back. I was nice about him to her. I invited him in. I could see what she saw in him and I knew it wouldn't last. So what? Relationships at that age don't and what does it matter? But when she was ready to leave she could and didn't see it as losing face as I had.

TEENAGE TRIBES

Teenagers have many ways of showing they are part of a new tribe (whether this is their age group, their friendship group or a particular clique such as Goth, Punk or Emo) and no longer part of yours, 'normal' society and their family. As well as the music they play and the clothes and make-up they wear, teenagers may acquire body piercings – in the tongue, eyebrow or navel – which have the double effect of showing their friends and the public at large where they stand, and of horrifying, annoying and frightening the life out of their parents. As well as wearing their allegiances on their sleeves and bodies, young people use language to draw a line between them and their seniors. Slang has always been a divider between teenagers and their parents, and there is very little point in parents trying to catch up and get it. Slang is there so that kids can converse in their own language, which you cannot understand – that's the point if it. It says: 'We belong and understand and you don't.' You can try to keep up, but not from written books; usually, by the time they are published the common words used have evolved yet again. For example, at the time of writing, while 'cool' was still the perennial way of saying something was good, the latest word is 'mint', as in 'Thanks for my birthday present. Mint!' Go figure. By the time you read this, it will probably be way out of date. But keeping up may be something you do to reassure yourself that in fact, they're only discussing going to a club, not an orgy; adults trying to join in are usually met with disdain, not admiration.

Insight

Internet sites such as gotateenager.org.uk and urbandictionary. com can help you keep up with teenage slang. But remember – read it to understand, don't use it to try and fit in.

Essential points to consider

▶ *Exploring boundaries is an essential part of teenage development. This will mean new friends and allegiances. Try to see these for what they are – a part of the learning process, not an attack on you.*

▶ *Teenagers see their testing ground of new friendships as their territory, not yours. They resist your intrusion, not because they necessarily disagree with you, but because it threatens their new found right to choose for themselves.*

MENTAL CHANGES

Far more is demanded of young people when they move from childhood to adolescence, from early education to a school system that prepares them for further education or employment. This is not because they suddenly become more intelligent as teenagers – basic intelligence is present from their beginnings. But what do develop are certain mental and emotional capabilities.

As well as the ability to empathize, teenagers become able to think things through to a conclusion. Children will do homework or chores because they can see an immediate reward: to please parents and teachers, to avoid punishment, and sometimes even because they are interested in the subject. Teenagers are capable of appreciating the overview, that certain actions have long-term advantages as they make choices for their lives after school. This is the key time for them to prepare for practical and financial independence and to learn how to look after themselves in all sorts of ways. Young people may appear to want the easy life, to be looked after, to have everything done for them and for pocket money to appear magically, as if it grows on trees. But not only is that entirely unhelpful for their future, it's actually not very satisfying. Teenagers will appreciate being asked to pull their weight around the home. If they're not already doing their fair share of chores, now is the time to introduce a rota. If they are doing some work, then now is the time to make it more of a responsibility; ask them, perhaps, to assume total control over the welfare of a family pet or to be in charge once a week of an evening meal, from deciding on the meal to buying, cooking and serving it. Teenagers could also be encouraged to take a holiday or weekend job, for the opportunity to earn money of their own.

YOUR TURN

Teenagers often behave in ways that make it difficult for us to give them what they need most – love and acceptance. When you find yourself in conflict with them, it helps to remember that it's the behaviour, not your teenager, that you dislike and that they are just doing what is normal for their age and development.

Your teenagers need to come to you to ask questions about their changing bodies and emotions. So what do you know about sex and sexuality?

Which of these statements do you think are true?

1 *Sex education at school leads to early experimentation.*

2 *Over half of teenagers have sex before the age of 16.*

3 *A doctor can give contraception to a person under 16 without their parents knowing.*

4 *In a class of 30, between two to six teenagers are likely to be gay or lesbian.*

5 *Masturbation is harmful.*

6 *Only dirty people doing dirty things get sexual infections.*

7 *You should wait to talk about sex with your children until they need to know.*

8 *Even if it doesn't last, young love is important.*

9 *Teenage crushes are a waste of time.*

10 *Teenagers can give blood at the age of 17.*

ANSWERS

1 *False.* In fact, the evidence suggests that young people given early sex education not only make better, safer choices when they do begin to have sex, but delay their first sex until later than young people given no or inadequate sex education.

2 *False.* Actually, the real figure – in spite of what the media would have you believe – is one in three boys and one in four girls.

3 *True.* Both boys and girls can ask for help from their own family doctor or a doctor in a clinic and the advice must be confidential.

4 *True.* All the evidence suggests young people who are gay know so from quite an early age, and may need help and support from family and friends.

5 *False.* It's normal, natural and a good way of getting to know your own body – and giving you pleasure.

6 *False.* Anyone having sexual contact with someone who has an infection is at risk.

7 *False.* The earlier they can have their questions answered the better. Children start asking about sexual matters as soon as they can talk. You need to tailor what you say to fit their age and understanding but leaving it until too late makes them vulnerable; it doesn't protect them.

8 *True.* Early relationships may be short lived but they are powerful and often set the tone for later entanglements. It can affect them profoundly, regardless of whether the teenager is left feeling that it was a good or bad experience.

9 *False.* The heroes and heroines they yearn after are role models and their first experiments in love and longing. However much you dislike them, it pays to respect your teenager's choice and interest.

10 *True.* And buy a gun, pilot a plane, drive a car and emigrate.

How did you do? You may want to review the chapter before moving on. You don't need to know everything to be a 'good enough' parent to your teenager. You do need to be an 'askable parent' – someone your child will want to come to, to get questions answered. If you don't know the answers you need to have the confidence to say 'I don't know – let's go and find out.'

THINGS TO REMEMBER

Teenagers are helped by having parents who:

▶ *understand and take action only when asked for help*

▶ *practise what they preach – no double standards*

▶ *listen without judgement or criticism*

▶ *treat them as an equal*

▶ *are there for them and love them no matter what*

▶ *include them in family activities but give them the choice to opt out*

▶ *encourage them to go to other adults for advice, such as family friends, their friends' parents, older siblings, aunts, uncles, grandparents, teachers and youth workers*

▶ *encourage them to have close friends and curb their natural jealousy at no longer being first in their hearts*

▶ *encourage them to have heroes and heroines, such as athletes, pop idols or actors.*

2

....

What do teenagers need?

In this chapter you will learn:
- *about the new situation you are facing*
- *what teenagers need in order to enjoy a successful adolescence*
- *what will help your teenager*
- *how to negotiate and agree what the new rules are to be*
- *how giving 'helpful attention' will benefit both of you*
- *what your teenager needs to make the best of their life.*

Teenagers may seem so very different from the people they were as small children. They're bigger for a start – all too soon they meet you eye-to-eye or loom over you, instead of looking up to you. That change in point of view is significant. It's harder for an adult to exert control over someone who is of the same height or looking down on them than it is to dominate a small child. Where they once looked to you for comfort and guidance and accepted your direction and discipline, an adolescent may appear to want nothing and say they don't need you. The child that was compliant and enthusiastic may suddenly be defiant and moody. You can be forgiven for thinking that you've lost control.

The new situation

But loss of control doesn't accurately define the situation. Understand that adolescence demands different rules for interaction. Instead of exerting control over your teenager as a parent, what you can reach is agreement through discussion and negotiation. Instead of being in charge, you're now looking at power sharing. The important thing to note is that this struggle is neither unusual nor abnormal, nor is it a rejection of you; the underlying needs your teenager has are still the same.

Young people going through the process of adolescence need what they have always needed from their parents. They want your love, your support, your encouragement, your nurture, acceptance and attention. The difference is that while children need their parents to take the lead, guiding them along, directing their steps and making the important decisions, teenagers need to stand side-by-side with their parents. Teenagers need 'helpful attention', rather than 'protective attention'.

When children are little, it is true to say that parents often know best. I'd say that even when they are small, it's still important to listen to and respect the opinion of a child. But when crunch time comes, it is the parent who does – and should – draw the line and say what goes.

There are particular skills that support children in learning how to manage for themselves, to trust their own judgement, and in turn develop their own life skills. When it comes to dealing with teenagers, we may use much the same skills as we did when they were younger, but from a greater remove. These skills include: being encouraging and enabling, allowing them to learn from their mistakes rather than showing them how to do it; accepting that they might do something differently from you, acknowledging and respecting their choices; following your teen's lead rather than jumping in with ideas; being in the present and spending time focused on your teenager. This section will discuss these skills and explain how to utilize them.

WHAT DO TEENAGERS NEED?

All of us need to feel safe and protected, to have our physical requirements for food, clothing, warmth and healthcare met.

A potential flash point may be a conflict between a parent's wish to fulfil these needs and a teenager's apparent desire to frustrate or be unrealistic about them.

Teenagers may defy your attempts to keep them safe, by staying out late, running around with bad company or taking what you may consider risks with internet use. They may go head-to-head with you on the nutritional guidance you try to offer, refusing healthy food and demanding chips and fizzy drinks with everything. Perfectly good clothing may be rejected on the grounds that their friends will laugh at them; they have to have the latest styles. And routine appointments like dental and health checks may be something they suddenly turn their noses up about.

Insight

Parents and teenagers often clash on what teenagers might need. On some aspects – their health or educational needs – you may be right. But it's far more effective with teenagers to listen and negotiate than to insist.

What helps your teenager?

The fact that your adolescent becomes contrary, however, doesn't mean that they don't want you to continue caring and acting on their behalf. What they want is for you to enter into a dialogue about these issues and to reach a consensus. When you are clear about what your concern is and what you'd like to happen, but are also prepared to hear their point of view, you can get somewhere. We'll look at this key skill later on.

What teenagers want – as much as when they were little – is your love, your care, your respect and your attention. They want to be noticed by you. Too often, because teenagers become moody and withdraw into themselves, we respond by ignoring them. Ignoring bad behaviour and not rising to it is one thing; ignoring the person who is annoying us is another. It can also become a pattern: they mope so we ignore them, so they mope even more, convinced we don't care.

Family time

Teenagers still want to spend time with their parents. Yes, of course they'd like to be on their mobiles or computers, playing games and communicating with their mates, all hours of the day and night. Given the chance, they want to be with their mates too – either at each other's homes or out together. But they also still value family time – eating together around a table, watching television as a family, even going out with you.

This is why one core aspect of family life, that seems to have slipped away, may be something you need to defend or bring back – the family meal. For many families, shared meals have become a lost luxury. A contributing factor may be the pace of life – you and your children have so many competing demands that it's really hard to find an hour each evening when you can all be together. If you feel pressured and short of time, opting for meals that can be put together easily, you may also be offering dishes that can be prepared and eaten individually; there doesn't seem to be any reason why you should all be at the table at one time. Also, if preferences and food fads mean that family members eat different foods anyway, it can seem just as sensible for people to get their own meals, as and when they wish.

BRINGING BACK MEALS TOGETHER

If this has happened in your house, it may be time to turn back the clock. Sharing a family meal may seem problematic and difficult to arrange, but it's worth it. Nothing quite brings a family together – and promotes understanding and unity – as eating together. You may come up against opposition when you suggest it. You may have to rearrange timetables, come home earlier, and your children may have to reschedule when they see their friends or study. You may all even have to give up certain things to do it. But the benefits will outweigh these hassles.

One of the side effects of sharing family meals is that it allows everyone around the table to feel valued and appreciated – another core need for teenagers. It means that you can talk in a relaxed way, asking about their day and telling them about yours. Aim to eat together as a family every day – but if that really is impossible, then aim for at least four times a week. When you do get together:

▶ *ask everyone to contribute to the meal by laying places, preparing or cooking or taking something to the table*
▶ *encourage everyone to talk – go around the table asking everyone to tell the family about something they did that day they enjoyed, something they were pleased and proud about or something they could have done better*
▶ *use mealtimes to discuss plans to spend time together: outings, nights in playing games, shared time on the computer*
▶ *don't harp on about table manners – you can encourage chewing with the mouth closed, holding cutlery properly and not leaning on elbows once everyone has begun to enjoy having shared meals.*

Insight

A good way to encourage table manners is to let teenagers eat with friends. Invite their mates over for a meal or support them in going out for a pizza together. They soon learn how unpleasant it is to chew with mouths open or slump all over the table!

TEENAGERS NEED BOTH STIMULATION AND ACTIVITY, AND REST AND RELAXATION

Teenagers today seem overloaded by things to do and information to absorb. It's not unusual for a young person to come home late from school because of an after-school activity, turn on the TV and computer and be messaging friends while watching a programme with one eye, texting on the mobile with the other, somehow managing to play a computer game as well while eating a hasty meal, before dashing out to another club or meeting with friends – where they'll text friends who are not there, at the same time as listening to music, chatting and maybe watching one screen or other and playing computer games.

The use of technology

We do need to get this apparent overuse of technology into some perspective. We'll address how and why parents do need to be up to speed on internet use, and why our children need us to be involved in this later. For now, the important issue is how, and to what extent, technology fulfils our teenagers' needs. And it often does. Watching programmes on TV can be an excellent way of acquiring information. It is also a form of social networking, in that teenagers – by watching the same programme – not only have something to talk about with friends, but reinforce the bonds they have with each other by doing so. TV programmes can also raise important discussion points – issues of relationships, sexuality, politics, the environment – and can trigger your teenager to ask questions, or allow you to check out their knowledge and opinions, enabling you to make your own opinions felt.

Using the internet and mobile phones keeps teenagers connected, not only to their friends but to a broader range of people, which widens their horizons. So on the surface, stimulation doesn't seem to be a problem, except, as with anything, too much of something and you wind up in a rut. Some young people become stuck in repetitive actions; rather than learning new things from technology, they're simply repeating the same thing over and over. Also, if internet access and TV is available in their bedroom, what happens is that although the teenager may be connecting with people outside the home, they are not doing so with their nearest and dearest.

Keeping fit and healthy

Teenagers also need stimulation from activities – and that doesn't just mean activities such as meetings or clubs, but physical exercise. Young children tend to keep fit by rushing around in school breaks; teenagers often need support in keeping active so that it becomes a part of their adult lifestyle, ensuring they stay fit and healthy. If they're not attending after-school sports activities (and even if they are…) it's important that exercise is something the family does together. This has the added value of giving you another opportunity to share time with them – try running, cycling, swimming or going to a gym.

What helps your teenager?
Recognizing the value of their technological know-how, whether on the computer or mobile phone, raises their self-esteem. Teenagers are often unaware of their skill in this area, and it's important that you give them positive feedback. However, as a parent you need to be the one to make some rules about sensible use. You might like to insist, for example, that all mobiles – including your own – are off or on silent during shared family meals; maybe use the answer machine to screen landline calls too. TVs and computers should be off too, and meals taken around a table, not on laps. And your teenager may moan and groan, huff and puff but they need you to set some guidelines about physical activity, and to lead the way in making regular exercise something you all do, together. Apart from doing your best for your child as a parent, you'll be doing yourself a favour too!

REST AND SLEEP

As well as stimulation and activity, teenagers need rest and relaxation; sometimes this can be the hardest thing for them to fit in. With all the rushing around from after-school clubs to weekend activities, with all the games, websites, TV programmes, mobile calls, texts and instant messages calling to them, some are on the go from the time they get up until the time they go to sleep. Parents often complain that teenagers do nothing but slump and sleep, and are impossible to wake up in the morning, but that can be for several reasons. One is that growing up takes energy and is exhausting. Growth spurts and hormonal upheavals do take it out of your teen. Another is that school days can be as tiring as full-time employment; their attention is demanded from the first lesson to the last and – even with breaks – they probably have less time off the hook than most workers do in an average day.

Another reason is all that addictive stimulation from screens and headphones, with very little let up. Teenagers with TVs and computers in their bedrooms can often end up with a sleep deficit. No wonder they can be difficult to wake in the morning – they might have had six, five or only four hours of sleep when they need at least eight.

Teenagers often feel that part of growing up means staying up until the adults go to bed – which has probably been an ambition since the age of two. It's often hard to argue with someone your height that being under 18 still means an earlier bedtime is advisable. If they have a TV and computer in their bedroom, you can also lose control over what they do when the door is shut. And of course, they may be sending texts and emails or chatting on networking sites into the early hours. Your adolescent is likely to pass on to you the pressure they are under to allow all this. Or they will insist that you don't have the right to interfere and set boundaries. But you do – and that's actually what they need from you.

Insight

Make bedrooms tech-free zones – no television, no game consoles, no mobile phones – and that means you too. Hard as it may seem, this will pay off in a reduction in tiredness, stress and tension. The family that plays together stays together.

The need for new rules

Building in recognized chill out time in your schedule, and acknowledging it as such, can be vital. Designate a sacrosanct quiet time when everyone comes home, when you can share a drink and a snack, discuss the day's events and anything that comes to mind, and where the aim is to kick back and relax with no TV, no phones or mobiles and no computers. By scheduling it and recognizing it, this time becomes a period when your kids – and you – know you can slob around doing nothing, simply being, which is a luxury we all need and can afford. It's not being lazy or irresponsible to have that built-in down time.

Another rule could be having TVs and computers only in public spaces, not bedrooms, and setting agreed times when they are used, rather than it being a free-for-all at all times. If there are no rules, it's easy to become addicted to the quick-fire and quick response interaction with a game, and to chatting with an online community. It takes more time and more effort to interact with real people, which is why your teenager needs you to put your foot down and insist they do so. Young people may object, but may also be secretly relieved you've taken the burden off them by making it a rule: 'No, can't chat now. I have to go. It's a house rule set by my boring old folks,' is easier than 'No, can't chat now. I want to go.'

HOME TIMES AND BEDTIMES

Your teenager also needs you to decide and keep both times for being in at night, and times for going to bed. It's essential for their health and wellbeing that you know where they are in the evening, that they are home at a reasonable time and that they go to bed at a reasonable time. Once they become teenagers, it seems harder to enforce but that's actually an illusion. Home times and bedtimes are two of the many issues you will clash over, but they need to know that you care enough for them and think enough about them that you will hold firm on the things that matter. As with limiting time spent online, it does help at a time when they might come under pressure from friends, for them to be able to sigh and roll their eyes and blame you for a curfew. We'll talk later about how to do this.

Another chill-out time could be the half hour before people go to bed. Sending kids – or yourself – off to bed still buzzing from watching TV, having been on a computer or mobile makes it hard for them to 'come down' and relax. This can be why young people find it hard to settle at night; they're still 'up' when they go to bed, can't sleep immediately and think that means they're still wide awake and should go back to what they were doing. Insisting on half an hour's quiet time to read, and allowing books but not machines in bed, can help them.

AGE-APPROPRIATE CHOICES AND RESPONSIBILITY

Teenagers need us to give them choices and responsibility appropriate to their age. Obviously they can become stroppy, insisting they are perfectly capable of running their own lives and making decisions for themselves. Some parents may be tempted to throw up their hands and to opt for a peaceful life, allowing their children to stay out late, do the things they want – even leave school early or not take up a challenging college course. Other parents may come down hard, and take over all responsibility for everything: what they study at school, who they see, when they are home.

What may be more effective, and certainly what teenagers need, is for a gradual process of emancipation where teenagers learn how to make decisions, and gradually assume control. It's the most effective option because part of being a teenager is a desire to take on the role; if they have no opportunity to do so progressively, they will seize it in an uncontrolled way. When adolescents act irresponsibly and foolishly, it's often because they have been denied some control over their lives. The answer is neither to let this behaviour continue nor clamp down on them, but to work together to decide the responsibilities they could and should take on, increasing them as they prove their maturity. Young people tend to rise to responsibility when it is transferred to them.

Insight

Teenagers are apprentice adults – they're learning the ropes and gradually taking over the reins.

'Helpful attention'

One of the ways we meet our children's needs as parents is by giving them attention. This is as true of teenagers as it is of youngsters.

What teenagers, even more than youngsters, need is 'helpful attention'. Giving our children helpful attention helps us to develop close and cooperative relationships with them and builds their confidence and self-esteem. It's a way of showing that we care and that they matter.

Helpful attention means:

▸ *enjoying and being interested in who they are and what they're doing*
▸ *being responsive – listening to them when they want to talk, even when it might be inconvenient*
▸ *being guided by the young person rather than always taking charge and imposing our will on them (although sometimes this is necessary, for example in situations involving safety).*

A key element in dealing with teenagers is to enjoy them. This can sometimes be hard if they seem to spend a lot of their time defying you, arguing with you and ignoring you. However, from the teenager's perspective, they sometimes get the impression that all parents want to do is criticize and control. Both of you can be on a negative default setting. You can often tackle their defiance, argumentativeness and disregard by switching to a positive setting; look at aspects that you *do* like. Take an interest in who they are at this moment, which will not be the child they were some time ago, nor the adult they will be in a few years' time. Don't quiz or interrogate them, but ask open questions about their interests and enthusiasms, and accept them without judgement.

BE RESPONSIVE, TAKE YOUR CUE

Being responsive means sometimes dropping what you're doing to pay attention. Tonight's meal, the cleaning, ironing or maintaining the car really are not as important as making that connection with your child. It may also mean simply giving them an ear while doing something else; but make sure it is a listening ear. We all sometimes want to raise important issues at a time when the person we're talking to might not be able to turn round and give us eye-to-eye contact.

It's a way of keeping the issue at some arm's length and within control. Similarly, teenagers will sometimes pick the moment you're driving or washing-up to ask about sex – or whether they can attend an all-night party!

On the whole, helpful attention also means taking your cue from your teenager. This can mean talking about important issues when – and only when – they raise them, or give you some indication that they would be receptive. It also means avoiding the impulse that we all have to fix problems for them. This may involve talking things through, enabling them to arrive at a solution they can put in action, rather than jumping in and doing it for them. Occasionally, we might have to intervene – for example, if your teenager is planning to attend an all-night party and you decide this is not on or if they want to make their own way home late at night and you feel they have underestimated the risks involved. But frequently it is most effective to listen and support, rather than take charge.

Helpful attention does not mean:

▶ *ignoring or denying your own needs or letting them have their way all the time*
▶ *spoiling them.*

SATISFYING PEOPLE'S NEEDS

When you set out to identify and satisfy people's needs, you often have to make a choice. One individual's need to be listened to can conflict with another's. Your need for peace and quiet and a chance to read your paper may clash with your teenager's need to tell you all about an argument with a friend RIGHT NOW. Giving your child helpful attention does not mean having to drop everything every time, and putting yourself second. What it does mean is making a judgement call about when you do have to put down what you are doing and focus on them, and when you can say: 'Give me a moment to finish this/Just let me deal with your brother first and I'll be with you.' As long as you do make time for them when you have said you will, your teenager reaps the benefit of helpful attention. And as long as you show you are fairly balancing up both your and other people's needs against theirs, your teenager learns two valuable lessons: that you are there for them when they need it, but the world does not revolve around them and sometimes they have to wait.

We may have some beliefs about what happens when we make an effort to give our attention to children and young people. One of these is that it spoils children if they ever get their way or if we listen to them too much. However, research shows that children are not spoiled by helpful attention. On the contrary, they are spoiled in the real sense of the word when they are ignored or only given negative attention which criticizes or punishes, but never praises. Children with the most challenging behaviour have been shown to get less of this kind of helpful attention; a key way of changing such behaviour is to increase the amount of helpful or responsive attention. Disruptive behaviour is a way of getting attention. From a child's point of view, any attention is better than no attention at all. So if a child or a teenager is not getting positive attention, they will react by pushing all your buttons until you explode. Negative strokes are preferable to being ignored.

Insight

Never getting what they need and always getting what they need are equally destructive to children and teenagers. It's a tricky balancing act but one that as parents we need to manage – getting the balance right between always and never saying 'Yes'.

HOW DO YOU GIVE HELPFUL ATTENTION?

The elements of helpful attention that can make a difference with your teenager are:

▶ *using encouragement and being enabling*
▶ *allowing children to learn from their mistakes rather than showing them how to do it*
▶ *accepting that they might do it differently from you*

- *acknowledging and respecting their choices*
- *following the young person's lead rather than jumping in with ideas*
- *being in the present and spending time focused on your teenager.*

USE ENCOURAGEMENT AND BE ENABLING

Using a soft voice, showing interest, noticing and describing what your teenager is doing are all encouraging and enabling. When your teenager does something you like, that pleases you, the most effective way of ensuring that they repeat this behaviour is to use descriptive praise.

When we're pleased with someone, we often tell them that they are 'good' or say 'well done'. This is great, but often it doesn't actually tell the person what they've done, why we like it and what we would like them to continue doing. It tells them about us, that *we* are happy, but it doesn't tell them about *them*, that they are capable and competent. Descriptive praise does exactly this. So, when you come home and find your teenager has washed up after having a snack and fed the cat, instead of 'Aren't you good!' say 'You fed the cat and washed up. You cleared the deck so now I can get on with preparing a meal. That was really helpful. Thank you!' Instead of thinking 'Yeah, well, whatever... but what did I do?' the teenager thinks 'Yeah! I'm really helpful! I can do that!' and has every incentive to repeat the behaviour, and a clear idea of what you appreciate.

Let them learn from their own mistakes

When they were young, you might have striven to hold back as your child tipped over drinks, fumbled with blocks, blundered through jigsaws. The temptation to leap in and say 'No! No! Watch me – this is how you do it!' can be irresistible. It's important to realize that standing back and letting your child learn by trial and error is an important part of being a parent, in order for them to become skilled. Children learn more quickly and more thoroughly if they are allowed to do something for themselves, rather than by observing you do it for them. This can be harder to accept if the lessons involve anything that can harm them – hot stoves, electric plugs, busy roads. But the principle remains the same – we need to respect the struggle, and let them figure out some things on their own or with minimum direction and supervision.

And the principle remains the same with adolescents. Obviously, there are some issues that we can't let them discover for themselves. We can let them find out for themselves that they need to plan their homework and submit it on time; if part of this learning process means that they fail a test or get a bad mark, it's usually more effective in changing their behaviour than constant reminding. However, we can't let them learn from experience that it's a bad idea to get into a car with a friend who has been drinking – in this scenario, the lesson they learn could prove fatal. But on a continuum from the utterly trivial to the downright dangerous, there are plenty of lessons they can learn for themselves. It's one of the skills that we as parents need to appreciate: that holding back, gently guiding, but ultimately saying 'That's your business – work it out yourself' is the most effective way for your adolescent to discover how to manage.

Insight

While teenagers learn to make their own choices, the parents of teenagers may need to learn how to prioritize. Putting your foot down about their getting a qualification is far more important than insisting they don't blow their entire allowance on a pair of trainers. Let the small stuff go and you can fight your corner about the important issues when you need to.

ACCEPT THEY MIGHT DO IT DIFFERENTLY FROM YOU

Just as when they were little, there may be a great temptation to jump in and say 'No, that's not the way you do it; watch me – this is how!' Bite your lip and sit on your hands – this is the time to listen and observe. Whatever the issue at hand, whether it's a practical skill, a mental puzzle or a discussion over beliefs and moral codes, the important thing is that it's all part of your adolescent finding their own way. They may do it differently from you. They may have beliefs, opinions and ideas that differ from yours. That does not mean that they are rejecting you, or that they are heading for hell, or that they are being stupid. They may not have thought the issue through fully, and debating it – with your spirited championing of your point of view – will help them do so. But denying them entitlement to have another point of view also denies them the privilege of being an individual in their own right.

Sweeping away their positions or telling them they've got it wrong won't lead them to say, 'Oh, yeah, thanks – you're right and I'm wrong.' It may end up with them angry with you and distrusting everything you say. After all, if you won't listen to and respect them, why should they listen to and respect you? It also can result in them distrusting themselves and losing both self-respect and self-esteem. If you want them to trust themselves and you and to build up their confidence, you need to acknowledge difference and accept it. If you think you're right, defend your position – and be prepared to change your opinion too.

ACKNOWLEDGE AND RESPECT THEIR CHOICES

Adolescence is the time for choices. It's when young adults have to decide what path to take, at least for their early life – college or a job. But they also have so many other decisions to make: how to appear, whom to identify with, befriend and be loyal to. Parents and teenagers can argue over so many of the options that the young person decides upon. Parents may say this is because the young person is making choices based on inexperience and on temporary and trivial deciders, for example, choosing a school because friends are going there, rather than because it's the best teaching environment for them.

One underlying factor that you need to consider is how much this conflict is affected by the process of separation, and how much by the issues you focus on. Adolescence is, after all, a painful time of life for many parents. It's the time when your children slowly – and sometimes very suddenly – tell you they no longer need you, no longer want to be guided by you and that they are closer to other people than you. It's the time when they appear to cease to look to you and up to you. Every choice they make on their own – and every choice they make that is different from the one you made – underlines this separation. You may find yourself in opposition, not necessarily because of the choice itself, but because it was made by someone who is no longer a child, and not by you.

Acknowledging and respecting their choices doesn't mean you have to sit back and entirely lose control. Maybe the choice is one you feel you simply cannot allow, or one you feel is short-sighted – such as a promising student leaving school at 16, or a teenager insisting on following a friend to a particular school. Acknowledging and respecting their choices means saying that you can see why they feel it important, explaining your thoughts on the matter and discussing the issue in a mutually respectful way. The result may be compromise or you both agreeing on one course of action. You are more likely to reach a satisfying – and safe – result if you begin by seeing they have a point of view that deserves an audience.

Insight

Teenagers tend to see issues in passionate black and white, rather than the more nuanced grey that adults see. Listening to them and their ideas can sometimes have the wonderful effect of giving you back the rush of excitement and discovery you may have lost.

FOLLOW YOUR TEENAGER'S LEAD RATHER THAN JUMPING IN WITH IDEAS

A parent begins the difficult job of parenting by being the one who has to come up with all the answers. If a baby is hungry, has a dirty nappy, is feeling in need of comfort, you're the one to fix it; it's all down to you. As they get older, you pick them up when they fall, feed them when they are hungry, console them when they cry.

So you tend to continue considering yourself the fixer; the one not only with the solutions, but the one whose whole reason for being there is to lead with ideas and answers.

But sometimes, jumping in can be less than helpful. You miss an opportunity – and often, you miss the point. Consider the following sequence of interventions to the same scenario by a parent:

> **John:** Had a good day, dear?
> **Nicci:** Well, not really, Dad. Mrs Brown got on my case and...
> **John:** Oh, teachers. I had some terrible ones when I was at school.
> **Nicci:** No, she's usually OK but today...
> **John:** Sometimes the ones you like are the worst because you expect too much of them.
> **Nicci:** Yes but the point is...
> **John:** You've just got to hang in there and be firm.
> **Nicci:** Yeah, but Dad, I had this...
> **John:** Don't let it get to you, that's what I say.
> **Nicci:** Oh, forget it!
> **John:** Hey, was there something you wanted to say to me?

Dad is loving, caring, keen to sympathize, but constantly interrupting. Is it any wonder Nicci gave up?

> **John:** Had a good day, dear?
> **Nicci:** Well, not really, Dad. Mrs Brown got on my case and told me off for not doing the science project the way she'd said we should.
> **John:** Well, I wouldn't stand for that. If you had a good idea you should stick with it and tell her where to get off!
> **Nicci:** Yeah, but Dad, she sort of had a point...
> **John:** You should talk to the Head of Department and see what other people think about this. I mean, showing a bit of initiative, that's admirable.
> **Nicci:** Yeah, well thanks, Dad, (mutters) for nothing!

John tries to help, but by imposing his own ideas on what he thinks his daughter should do, gives her no real support or understanding of the situation and her feelings about it.

John: Had a good day, dear?
Nicci: Well, not really, Dad. Mrs Brown got on my case and told me off for not doing the science project...
John: ...in time?
Nicci: No, the way she'd said we should. The thing is Dad, she said we had to...
John: ...do it the way it was in your books, is that the problem?
Nicci: No, we had to do it in groups. The problem was...
John: Oh, you wanted to do it on your own and she made you pair up.
Nicci: No, I wanted to do it with Debbie...
John: Oh, she split you up from your friends. Well, I'm sure she had a good reason for doing that, love.
Nicci: Yes (sighs), thanks Dad, (mutters) for nothing!

In this case, her father's constant interruptions mean he can't hear what Nicci is trying to tell him.

John: Had a good day, dear?
Nicci: Well, not really, Dad. Mrs Brown got on my case and told me off for not doing the science project the way she'd said we should.
John: Uh-huh?
Nicci: Yes. She said we had to do it in groups and I wanted to do it with Debbie and Beth.
John: Ummm?
Nicci: Well, Debbie was away all last week and Beth and me, we thought she was coming back so we did it together, 'cos we thought she'd be back in time to catch up.
John: You thought Debbie would be back in time for the three of you to finish the project together.
Nicci: Yes, but she's got flu so she isn't even going to be back this week. But Mrs Brown just ripped us off for doing it in a pair, she said it needed at least three of us and

why hadn't we joined up with someone else.
That wasn't fair, was it?

John: I can see you feel upset about this.

Nicci: Well, I suppose we should have told her last week that we were waiting for Debbie.

John: Uh-huh.

Nicci: It was a bit silly not to let her know, wasn't it?

John: You think it was silly not to let her know.

Nicci: Well, maybe the best thing would be to talk to her tomorrow and explain and say we're sorry for not having told her sooner.

John: So you're going to talk with Mrs Brown tomorrow.

Nicci: Yup. Thanks for helping, Dad.

Result! And what has John done? He listened. In Chapters 5 and 6 we'll look more at the skills used by John, to make communication with teenagers more effective, productive – and enjoyable.

> ## Essential points to consider
> ► *In the teenage years, the total parental control used in childhood needs to be replaced by negotiation and discussion.*
> ► *Teenagers need 'helpful attention' rather than the protective attention they were given in their earlier years.*
> ► *Teenagers, for all their appearance of forever trying to escape from it, still need family time and we should encourage and create this for them.*
> ► *Teenagers' use of technology – phones, the internet, video games – needs to be kept in perspective. It can be helpful but overuse, misuse or dependence can isolate a teen from connecting with their family or even real life.*

Spend time focused on your teenager

Because children grow up so fast, and because their development seems to be one milestone after the other, it can be easy to forget to concentrate on the present. You can forever be looking back – to when they were sweet and charming and biddable, or forward – to when they will be grown-up and gone. Adolescents themselves often say the teenage years seem to be a period of waiting until they can do this, enjoy that, that it's all about preparation for the future and very little about enjoying what is happening at that moment.

Focusing on what your teenager used to be like, or may soon be, can mean you forget to appreciate them as they *are*. It can mean you actually don't see them as they are, but keep confusing the picture with what they were, or could be. On a simple level, this can mean that you are still convinced your child wants to be a vet, when this was three 'career fantasies' ago. On a wider level, it means you're not only out of touch with their dreams and thoughts, their tastes and preferences, but also their very personality as it emerges and firms up.

What they are now, this moment, may be confusing, annoying, contradictory, confrontational… but it's also likely to be amusing, exciting, inspirational. If you're forever looking back to when they didn't argue with you, or forward to when they might have it all sussed out, you'll miss the challenge they set you and themselves as they strive to find out, to sort out, to work out who they want to be. Teenagers are enormous fun; we can miss that if we're longing for how they were, or what they soon may be.

Insight

An important skill for all of us is to be in the present – focusing on the here and now and what is good and enjoyable about it. Every parent of a teenager should practise that skill as often as possible.

NOT FOCUSING

Getting into the habit of not focusing on the person in front of you has more drawbacks than simply not realizing who they actually are at present. It means you may also become accustomed to having only one ear and eye on them. Take this situation, with John and Nicci:

John:	Had a good day, dear?
Nicci:	Well, not really, Dad. Mrs Brown got on my case and told me off for not doing the science project the way she'd said we should. Dad, are you listening?
John:	Hmmm? Yes, of course sweetie. Mrs Brown gave you a bad mark.
Nicci:	No. She told me off.
John:	Uh-huh.
Nicci:	It's not fair. She never listens to me. Dad?
John:	Well, I'm sure she had a reason. Have you seen my car keys? I'm sure I put them down somewhere around here.
Nicci:	Oh, Dad!
John:	What? Look, I'm in a hurry. What was it you wanted?
Nicci:	Never mind.

John might be there in body but he is hardly available to his daughter. Helpful attention requires us to accord our children the concentrated attention we'd like to be afforded. Giving attention in such a way is enabling – it allows your teenager to share their thoughts and needs with you. More important, it has a positive effect on the young person's self-esteem and on the closeness and trust you have between you.

SEIZE THE MOMENT

Teenagers, because they do want to draw a line in the sand and insist on being self-determining, will often pull away from wanting to share time with their parents, or will prefer to take their worries or queries to other people. This is why it's so important to seize the moment when they do make an overture to you. When they ask a question, sit down with you, offer an opinion or insight, or suggest they might like to do something together, grab the moment with both hands. These opportunities may not come very often. And if you turn one down because you're too busy, have your hands full, can't take a moment just now... they may not come again.

Look at it this way. What, in the end, is more important than your teenager? Which are you more likely to say on your deathbed: 'I wish

I'd written another work report/done more ironing/cleaned the house better/served meals right on time every night' or 'I wish I'd had more time with my child as a teenager and built a really good relationship with them then'?

Relationships between teenagers and parents – indeed, between any of us – are not built by one or two grand events. Of course going on an epic journey together can cement bonds and create understanding, but on the whole, relationships are built little by little, by thousands of small acts. That's why taking advantage of tiny moments and apparently unimportant exchanges can make a great difference.

FITTING IN WITH YOU

Teenagers need to know that you are human and have a life too. One of the tricky balancing acts is the need to be responsive and there for them, and to seize the moment, yet with an acknowledgement that sometimes we can't give our children all our attention because we're exhausted, busy with other things or have other members of the family that need us at that time.

When a child always comes second they conclude that they are unworthy or bad. At first, they may become angry and bitter at the people who always concentrate on something or someone else; in the long-term it is their own self-confidence and self-esteem that is damaged. Conversely, a child who is always put first becomes demanding and needy. They do need for you sometimes to look after yourself and look after other people. It's okay to say 'No, wait. Not now,' as long as you give an explanation, and go back and give them time later on.

COPING WITH THE UPS AND DOWNS OF LIFE

Teenagers need to develop the ability to enjoy the ups and cope with the downs of life. They best learn this from you, both by example and by experiencing a mixture of having their needs for attention satisfied, and by being asked sometimes to wait or stand aside. Author Karen Joy Fowler, in her book *The Jane Austen Book Club*, says: 'All parents wanted an impossible life for their children – happy beginning, happy middle, happy ending. No plot of any kind.' And she is right. We often want the impossible – that our children will always be happy and always do well and never suffer shocks and alarms. Our teenagers need us to avoid putting unrealistic expectations on them. Not just because it's unlikely that they could find a life with no plot of any kind, but because such a life could make them entirely vulnerable. Not being able to deal with crises and unhappiness actually makes it difficult to enjoy the good times. Teenagers are more likely to have a positive experience of adolescence and adulthood when they realize they can enjoy it when it's going well, but manage when it's going badly.

Insight

What teenagers most need from their parents is the message that they are deserving and worthwhile, competent and capable.

ARE SOME HOPES MORE FOR US THAN FOR OUR TEENAGERS?

Teenagers need us to be able to separate our own dreams and ambitions from any hopes we have for them. It's understandable that we may want them to have the things we didn't achieve, or perhaps to share the things we did. But it doesn't help for us to be driving them on because, underneath it all, we are trying to live out our frustrated ambitions through them and wanting them to achieve it for us, by proxy.

It is helpful for us to encourage and suggest on the basis of our own experience, either based on what we managed to accomplish or feel we missed out on. But, as in all cases, the best tactic is to discuss and listen as well as advance our own ideas, and to ask ourselves, 'For whose benefit is this – mine or theirs?'

Communication skills – listening and talking in ways that build our relationship with our adolescents – are what we need to help us to help them. These are the building blocks that create an awareness of what teenagers need, and what we as parents can do to meet these needs. We'll deal with these skills in more detail in

Chapters 4 and 5. As we practise helpful ways of relating to our children, you can ask yourself to:

▶ *think about what your teenager needs to be able to make the most of life*
▶ *talk about what you can do as a parent to help make this happen.*

WHAT DOES YOUR TEENAGER NEED TO BE ABLE TO MAKE THE MOST OF LIFE?

The Government's aim, in their 'Every Child Matters' agenda is for every child, whatever their background or their circumstances, to have the support they need to:

▶ *be healthy*
▶ *stay safe*
▶ *enjoy and achieve*
▶ *make a positive contribution*
▶ *achieve economic wellbeing.*

This is an excellent framework for us, as parents, to recognize what our teenagers need.

They need to be healthy
They need to enjoy good physical and mental health and live a healthy lifestyle. It's your responsibility as a parent to offer them healthy food at home, to encourage them to make healthy choices when outside the home, and to set a pattern of doing exercise and keeping fit. It's also your responsibility to foster their mental health, by loving and accepting them, by setting appropriate boundaries and by helping them enjoy life when they are happy and deal with problems when they are not.

....

Insight
Standing up for your teenager isn't the same as defending their bad behaviour. When a child misbehaves they need you to be there for them, making it clear you love them. But they also need you to be there on the side of whoever pulled them

up about their behaviour, and making it clear you think the behaviour is unacceptable too.

They need to stay safe
Teenagers, just as much as small children, need your protection from harm and neglect. You need to give them your attention and time, even when they seem to push you away, and you need to stand up for them when anyone within or outside the family could harm them in any way. This may mean being unpopular with your teen when, for example, you say no to alcohol being served at a party or insist on driving them from an event. It's worth braving their anger or upset to keep them safe.

They need to enjoy life and achieve something
Your teenager needs you to encourage them to get the most out of life and to develop the skills for adulthood. This may mean your having to stand back and give them responsibility, and hold your tongue when you think they are not as competent as you might be in the task. It could mean being on their case occasionally to challenge them in school work and other assignments and you need to see how important it might be to court your short-term unpopularity for their long-term gains.

They need to make a positive contribution
Teenagers need to know that you expect them to behave – not to be drawn in to antisocial or offending behaviour but more important, to be positively involved with their family, their community and society as a whole. A positive contribution starts in childhood with children helping their parents with chores around the house. It extends in the teenage years to not only taking full responsibility for some aspects of this – dealing with the rubbish or being in charge of composting or caring for the family pet – but also doing something outside the home. Most schools offer opportunities for teenagers to do voluntary work and this can be encouraged by parents.

They need to achieve economic wellbeing
Teenagers should not be prevented by lack of money from achieving their full potential in life. But your teenager needs you to show them that this doesn't mean you have to go all out for

funds simply to enjoy yourself. It means having enough money and knowing how to use it; your teenager needs your support in learning how to manage finances – to earn, to budget, to save.

Teenagers need self-respect and self-esteem, and both come from having your respect and attention. They need the opportunity to learn skills, not just to get them educational or vocational qualifications for a job, but for life. And life skills start with you, their parent. So perhaps what your teenager needs most is for you to do exactly what you are doing – to brush up on some skills yourself!

YOUR TURN

Teenagers need helpful attention and support. Which of the following would you say helps or hinders you and your teenager?

	Does this help?	Does this hinder?
Having regular meals together as a family		
Being allowed to stay up late most nights		
Having a TV and laptop in their bedrooms		
Being encouraged to do physical exercise		
Having an agreed time to come home		
Being told what exams they should be taking		
Knowing you'll be there if they need you		
Always having you drop what you're doing to attend to them		
Being allowed to learn from their own mistakes		
Being asked to do it your way		
Spending time with you		
Being protected by you at all times		

Consider your answers and review the chapter to see how you might have done.

THINGS TO REMEMBER

▶ *The rules of interaction change when a child becomes a teenager. Try to replace earlier total parental control with a new agreement reached through mutual discussion and negotiation.*

▶ *Teenagers still need family time and you need to celebrate and enjoy the core component of family – the shared family meal.*

▶ *Teenagers' use of the new technology needs to be kept in perspective. The new technology can be a great aid to communication and learning, but its overuse or misuse can be a dangerously isolating influence on a young person.*

▶ *Negotiating and agreeing new rules as early as possible will help the family to stick together and stop your teenager from becoming or feeling separated from their home and family.*

▶ *The process of a teenager taking control of their choices and responsibilities should be a gradual, not an extreme one. As a parent, try to take a middle course between the two extremes of either fighting to keep total control or completely abdicating your own responsibilities.*

▶ *Learning the 'helpful attention' approach and becoming encouraging and enabling can be your best guarantee of a successful relationship with your teenager.*

▶ *In deciding choices, you are more likely to get a satisfying and safe result if you begin by accepting that your youngster has a point of view that deserves an audience.*

▶ *Teenagers live now, so concentrate on the present and stop looking back to earlier, and perhaps easier, times – the way things might have been in their childhood.*

▶ *Teenagers are not meant to achieve their parents' frustrated ambitions for them, and should not be driven or coerced into trying to do so.*

▶ *Your teenager is more likely to have a successful adolescence and passage into adulthood if they have been shown how to enjoy life when it goes well, and how to manage it when it goes badly.*

3

Understanding teenage behaviour

In this chapter you will learn:
- *how to identify the link between feelings, needs and behaviour*
- *how to recognize that the behaviour, not your teenager, is the problem*
- *how to show your teenager ways of expressing needs*
- *how to use 'I' language*
- *how to understand your own feelings and behaviour.*

Children are dogs, teenagers are cats.

Anon

I realized that while children are dogs, loyal and affectionate, teenagers are cats. You feed your pet, train it, boss it around. It puts its head on your knee and gazes at you as if you were a Rembrandt painting. It bounds indoors with enthusiasm when you call it. Then, around the age of 13, your adoring little puppy turns into a big old cat. When you tell it to come inside, it looks amazed, as if wondering who died and made you emperor. Instead of dogging your footsteps, it disappears. You won't see it again until it gets hungry... then it pauses on its sprint through the kitchen long enough to turn its nose up at whatever you're serving. When you reach out to ruffle its head, in that old affectionate gesture, it twists away from you, and then gives you a blank stare, as if trying to remember where it has seen you before.

(Contd)

You, not realizing that the dog is now a cat, think something must be desperately wrong with it. It seems so antisocial, so distant, sort of depressed. It won't go on family outings. Since you're the one who raised it, taught it to fetch and stay and sit on command, you assume that you did something wrong. Flooded with guilt and fear, you redouble your efforts to make your pet behave. Only now you're dealing with a cat, so everything that worked before now produces the opposite of the desired result. Call it, and it runs away. Tell it to sit, and it jumps on the counter. The more you go toward it, wringing your hands, the more it moves away.

Instead of continuing to act like a dog owner, you can learn to behave like a cat owner. Put a dish of food near the door, and let it come to you. But remember that a cat needs your help and your affection too. Sit still and it will come, seeking that warm, comforting lap it has not entirely forgotten. Be there to open the door for it. One day your grown-up child will walk into the kitchen, give you a big kiss and say: 'You've been on your feet all day. Let me get those dishes for you.' Then you'll realize your cat is a dog again.

Why do teenagers misbehave?

There is always a reason why people behave the way they do. It may seem out of character and out of proportion and you – and the person themselves – may have no idea what their actions are all about. But there is always a reason, even if it is difficult to understand and apparently has nothing to do with what is going on in the here and now. If you want to create a situation where you and your adolescent cooperate and avoid conflict, the first important strategy is to recognize there are always reasons for their actions – not because they want to upset you – and to seek to understand them.

WHAT IS BAD BEHAVIOUR REALLY ABOUT?

Sometimes, it isn't bad behaviour at all; it might be inappropriate or it might be puzzling to you, but most of it is about your teenager's desperate desire to separate from you, to stand out and stand up for themselves. Sometimes that might involve having to take an opposite position to yours, simply to become disconnected. But it's not personal and it's not malicious.

In their behaviour, teenagers are usually acting out the emotions and dilemmas they find hard to understand or explain. So-called bad behaviour is often the only way they can express their feelings and reactions. They might do it by defying your rules, by being argumentative or by constantly doing things their way rather than doing what you have asked. They may do it by being aggressive and foul-mouthed or by simply ignoring you. This is why one issue often comes to the fore when young people become teenagers: discipline.

HOW DO YOU DISCIPLINE A TEENAGER?

This is a bit like the joke: 'How do hedgehogs make love?' Answer: 'Very carefully.'

If your way of enforcing rules and boundaries when your child was young was to lay down the law, to insist 'Because I say so...' to use your size, age and authority to have your way, you may find you're in trouble now. It's far easier to exert pressure on a small child who looks up to you – in every sense of the phrase – and feels that it would be positively scary to find Mum and Dad were not in charge, than it is over a teenager. Children have a vested interest in maintaining the security that comes from them feeling you know best, and what you say goes. Teenagers aren't like that.

For a start, one of the tasks of adolescence is to take over that job – to become their own arbiters of what is right and wrong. But the other reason is how much weight you have to throw around. One of the first things your adolescent may realize is that the sanctions you can impose are not that powerful. They may be almost your size, or bigger. What keeps them in their room when sent there, or in the house when told they're grounded, is mutual consent and mutual respect alone. The only thing that makes them do what you say is the thought of what it may do to your relationship afterwards if they defy you. But if the relationship is already going downhill, if their sense of rebellion and defiance is greater than their need for your approval, this control has a limited life. So what does work? While rules and boundaries are important, it's often more effective to enforce them by considering the various needs being expressed when you clash. This can mean swallowing your pride, and your need to be in control.

Insight

Children need your approval; good behaviour tends to follow when they strive to win it, and so do the things you have made it clear you like. Teenagers want your approval too, but also your respect.

WHY KEEPING IN CONTROL CAN FEEL IMPORTANT

The apparently runaway changes that happen to your teenagers – the physical, emotional, mental and social changes they will be going through – can have such profound and dramatic effects on all of the family. You might feel in desperate need of some still, small centre of stability and calm. Trying to keep some things the same, one of them being your leadership, may feel important. Adults also often wish to be seen in control, to be acknowledged as doing the right thing – to be acting as good parents. And an element of good parenting is often seen as being in a position of authority, the person giving the orders.

To teenagers, this may be a red rag to a bull. At the time when they are altering, developing, looking to new ways and a new self, having you try to put the brakes on and harking back to the way things were done, and always have been done, can provoke even more defiance than they might have shown anyway.

So when a teenager defies you, the impulse might be to reach for a way of exerting discipline. On hearing the word 'discipline', most of us think about punishment. It's about keeping our children in line and doing the right thing. But the original meaning of the word is 'to teach'. Discipline is something we do to help young people learn. Indeed, the best way to get teenagers to behave in ways that please us is to help them understand what they actually want and need, and to see how they can get those needs met in ways that don't upset other people. Respond to the underlying need rather than the bad behaviour and the young person's reason for behaving that way usually melts away.

ALL BEHAVIOUR IS A WAY OF GETTING WHAT YOU NEED

Bad behaviour is a way of trying to show bad feelings. When you as a parent can understand what your teenager needs and why they do what they do, you can help them to help you. It's better to dive under the behaviour to understand what's going on than get into a head-to-head fight. Parents of teenagers need to identify the link between feelings, needs and behaviour. Understanding the needs that may be underneath a young person's behaviour is a key tool in resolving frustrating situations.

Understanding what is underneath the behaviour

Everyone has feelings and needs, and teenagers communicate them through their behaviour.

Your teenager might be fighting with you: shouting, slamming doors, swearing, hitting younger siblings, refusing to do their homework or staying out later than agreed. All very rude, worrying and disturbing behaviour that you'd rather they didn't demonstrate. You're probably both at loggerheads about this, with you trying your best to insist they stop. This conduct, you quite rightly might be saying, is unpleasant and unacceptable.

The question you might ask is 'How can I change my teenager's behaviour?' But the reality is that asking a different question is likely to get you a better result. What must be uncovered are the needs and the feelings that trigger these unacceptable outbursts.

It's not discipline in the form of punishment or control that your teenager needs when struggling with their conflicting emotions. What underlies their behaviour is often a need for attention, acceptance, appreciation and independence. They are often fighting to get these when they act up. You can help them by:

- *talking openly about the changes they are experiencing*
- *helping them to show their feelings*
- *sharing your own feelings with them*
- *using 'I' language – 'I feel', 'I need'*
- *telling them it's okay to feel bad, although not okay to act badly*
- *giving them plenty of time and attention*
- *keeping them busy doing things they enjoy*
- *giving them love, reassurance and support.*

Insight

Instead of asking yourself 'How can I change my teenager's behaviour?' ask yourself 'What is this behaviour trying to tell me?' Once you can understand and address the need underneath the action, you can find a solution.

WHAT IS THE LINK BETWEEN BEHAVIOUR, FEELINGS AND NEEDS?

Behaviour, feelings and needs are a three-part puzzle. Think of it as three layers: the first, top layer is the behaviour – the obvious, visible piece of the puzzle; the second layer is the feelings – which are perhaps hidden by the top layer; right at the bottom, the third layer, is the needs – often completely obscured. The best way of imagining this behaviour/feelings/needs puzzle is to visualize it as a fountain. Above the fountain are the jets of water shooting into the sky and sparkling in the light. That's the first thing you see, that's behaviour. Behaviour can be laughing and dancing or shouting and crying – it's what you see and respond to.

But behaviour is driven by feelings, just as the fountains are driven by the water in the pipes. You can often tease out and recognize the feelings if you look hard enough – some of them will be hidden, like the water still in the pipes. Some will be evident, like the water just gushing out. The needs may be the layer you miss entirely, as it's hidden like a reservoir of water underground. But that reservoir drives the water in the pipes to create the fountains in the sky. That reservoir is what behaviour is all about. We often need to dive under the behaviour to try to understand not only the feelings but the needs – to listen to the tune not the words. Behaviour is the signal to look for feelings, which are what can help us work out the need.

Remember, it is the behaviour, not your teenager that is the problem – they are expressing their feelings and needs through their behaviour.

THE FEELINGS BEHIND THE BEHAVIOUR

So, the question more effective than 'How can I change my teenager's behaviour' is 'What are the feelings behind their behaviour?' Asking this will help you take action together to meet the need that is causing the behaviour.

Feelings are not right or wrong, they are just a normal part of being human. There is nothing wrong with feeling angry, jealous, frustrated or rejected. Sadly, we do sometimes judge people or blame people for what they are feeling. When a small child expresses jealousy for another sibling, we might try to control or banish what we see as something negative – or even destructive – by denying it 'Oh no, you don't mean that!' or making them feel bad for feeling that way 'What a horrible thing to say!' What the child hears is 'What a horrible little boy you are to feel like that!' They feel confused, because they can't control their feelings, so they start feeling bad about having them.

Feelings are not right or wrong, good or bad; they simply are. What matters is what we do about them. While making someone feel bad about feeling angry, jealous or frustrated might curtail the immediate behaviour which could be directed against someone else, it doesn't deal with either the underlying feelings or needs adequately. When someone feels bad about having an emotion, it doesn't go away. Instead, the feeling might be directed against themselves, as they blame themselves for feeling that way. Or it might come out later, in more disguised or indirect ways: self-disgust, depression, eating disorders, self-harm. Either way, bad feelings emerge. And of course, denying or blaming themselves for their feelings doesn't deal with the underlying need. Understanding and accepting needs – both ours and other people's – cuts through blame and judgement and copes with them.

What are your teenager's real needs?
What might be the real needs? For teenagers, it might be part of the confused and confusing process of pulling away from their parents and developing their own place in their peer group. They may need to be liked, looked up to and accepted by people their own age. They may need some control over their lives and some sense of identity. They may need to feel they can and should be allowed to try to manage without their parents' close direction, but still want their approval and attention. They may want to feel safe and secure, but need to take some risks. They may need to test the boundaries of what they feel being an apprentice grown-up is all about.

What's the need?
> ▶ *It is probably for comfort, security, reassurance, approval, a sense of self, some control over their life.*

What might a teenager be feeling if their needs aren't being met?
> ▶ *They may be feeling overwhelmed, angry, confused, rejected.*

What might they be saying?
> ▶ *'I hate you!'; 'You don't understand me!'; 'You can't tell me what to do!'*

What might their behaviour be?

▶ *Shouting, slamming doors, arguing and coming home late.*

DOES ACCEPTING FEELINGS AND NEEDS MEAN THAT YOU'RE ACCEPTING BAD BEHAVIOUR?

Understanding and accepting the feelings and needs that underlie behaviour doesn't mean that you shouldn't challenge the behaviour itself. What it *does* do is allow you to do it in a constructive way that doesn't bring about a defensive or angry reaction. The best way of disciplining children is often to set out to help, not punish them. Teenagers don't do what they do to upset you. They may be doing it to get a reaction – to prove to their own satisfaction and your edification that they are in the driving seat, not you. But hurting you is not their aim, however much it seems so at times. If you punish a teenager for acting up or acting out, you may be punishing them for doing their job – learning and trying to be their own people. That's not exactly fair, nor useful. But most of the time, the upset and the arguments are an unintended side effect. Your teenager is acting the way they do without really thinking about how it affects you.

It may not seem like it sometimes, but all children, whatever age, want to please their parents and the adults they live with, and win their approval. When they feel you have understood what they need, and can understand you in turn, they have the incentive to change. If you can tell them clearly what you want and why, and respect and listen to them, you'll get a better result than simply coming down hard on them. Whenever you find yourself feeling fraught, the best strategy is to be very clear about what seems to be going wrong and what you'd like to happen instead.

ONE WAY TO GET YOUR TEENAGER TO COOPERATE

This is a four-part strategy to help you both. It requires you to be clear about the problem. You must take a deep breath and describe what is going on that you don't like. For example:

1 *Define the problem:* 'Kirsty, **when** *you come home late without ringing me to say you'll be delayed...*'
2 *You say* **what** *you feel:* 'I **feel** *really upset/angry/scared.*'
3 *You then say why you felt like that:* '**Because** I *had a meal ready/I was worried something had happened to you...*'
4 *And finally explain what behaviour is acceptable:* '**What** I *would like is for you to ring and tell me if you're coming home later than expected*' *or* '**What** *are we going to do when this happens again?*'

Insight

It's important to separate the person from the behaviour. Anybody would be hurt and their self-esteem damaged if they were told 'YOU are unacceptable'. But equally, it doesn't help teenagers or children to have bad behaviour go unremarked. The trick is to be clear that it's what they *do*, not who they *are*, that you don't like.

This flow diagram succinctly illustrates this four-part strategy for cooperative behaviour:

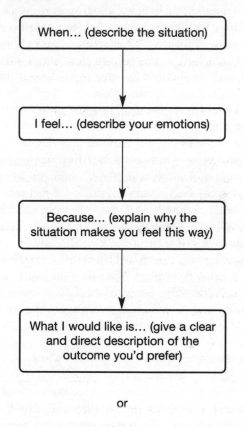

When... (describe the situation)

I feel... (describe your emotions)

Because... (explain why the situation makes you feel this way)

What I would like is... (give a clear and direct description of the outcome you'd prefer)

or

What are we going to do about this? (enlist the teenager in coming up with a solution)

Case study – Callie's story

Callie came to a parenting evening at her teenage son's school and described the way they had constant quarrels over his untidiness. She said: 'He doesn't see it's a problem or appreciate how it makes me feel. I just think he's so lazy – I can't get him to do a thing round the house.' She didn't think that this four-part strategy would make any difference, mainly because she felt he knew how angry his untidiness made her feel, and just didn't care. One of the exercises during the evening was to think carefully about needs and feelings. What Callie eventually realized was that it wasn't anger she felt towards her son, but rejection. After practising with other parents, she went home and said: 'Paul, when you left that dirty cup and plate on the kitchen table it made me feel really depressed and rejected, because it feels as if you have no respect for me or care about how I feel. What I'd like you to do is to clean up after yourself rather than just leave it for me.' She came back to the next session, saying she was stunned. She'd taken a deep breath and said the 'When... I feel... Because... What I would like...' as prepared. And her son had said: 'Oh. Sorry, Mum. I didn't realize you felt like that. Okay.' And he went and swept away the crumbs, washed up his cup and plate, and put them away.

The key issue with this strategy is that it is an appeal, not an attack. Rather than making a general assault on what you think the other person 'always does', or labelling them as lazy or trouble, you tell them how you feel about one specific situation. And instead of judging them or criticizing them, you invite them to join you in solving it.

UNDERSTANDING AND ACCEPTING FEELINGS

Understanding and accepting feelings and needs doesn't mean that we always have to try to meet them. After all, you can't satisfy your teenager's need to fit in with their peer group – that's their struggle, not yours. You can, and should, satisfy their need to be accepted, acknowledged and loved by you. Many of their needs are things they have to seek to fulfil themselves. However, you can make a tremendous difference simply by understanding, recognizing and acknowledging that they have such needs, and by encouraging them to name and voice them. Your role is then to support them in working out what they want to do. The best tactic is to offer a listening ear and a shoulder to cry on, and ask 'What can I do to help you?' Avoid taking over by jumping in with unsolicited advice, much less taking any action for them. Often, the very act of recognizing there are underlying needs, and acknowledging the feelings behind the behaviour, affects the behaviour.

Case study – Sonia's story

Jenny and her daughter Sonia have been having arguments. Sonia explains: 'My mum and me, we had a really bad time of it last term. I was shouting at her – a lot. One day, she came back and turned round to me and said 'I can see you're really angry. Want to tell me about it?' and I just screamed at her that of course I was angry, wouldn't anyone be angry with an interfering old bag as a mother? And you know what she did? She smiled and said – again – 'I can see you're angry. I'm here if you want to talk,' and walked out. I just sat there. See, mostly before we'd end up screaming at each other. And it made me think about why I was angry. And it wasn't really about her – it was about my friend who was my bessie mate one minute and frenemy the next. But I can't shout at her 'cos then it just gets awful. So when my mum comes back, I tell her. And instead of laughing at me like she has done, she listens. And she's really nice about it. She doesn't tell me what to do like I thought she would, or tell me it was my fault, she just listens. She asks me what I want to be different and we talk around that a bit. So I try that on my friend, and we've been getting on better too.'

TALKING THINGS THROUGH

By talking issues through with your teenager, by sharing your feelings with them and listening to theirs, you may find their behaviour alters. After all, if the main aim behind their behaviour is to make a point and they've voiced it and you've heard it, there's less need for the behaviour. But the behaviour may still go on. Except, once you can recognize that there are needs underneath it, and have some idea what they and the feelings are, you may find the behaviour itself is less annoying. You can understand that it's not personal – it's not a deliberate wind-up aimed at you, and that makes a difference.

Insight

Bad behaviour isn't personal. It isn't done to wind you up, however much it seems or feels that way. It's a reaction to what is going on for them and around them. Helping teenagers recognize this can help you both.

Essential points to consider

▶ *Understanding and accepting the underlying feelings and needs beneath behaviour doesn't mean that you shouldn't challenge the behaviour – but do this in a constructive way that doesn't bring about a defensive or angry reaction in your teenager.*

▶ *Nor does understanding needs mean that you have to meet them. Just trying to understand what's going on for your child/teenager and acknowledging their needs will help – then you can support them to work out what to do, rather than taking over.*

▶ *Your attitude is likely to change when you understand their needs, even if the unacceptable behaviour doesn't stop – you will see it is not purely intended to wind you up.*

GETTING OUR OWN NEEDS MET

It isn't only teenagers who are experiencing change, from child to adolescent. Parents are also going through profound alterations, becoming the parents of teenagers rather than the parents of children, with a whole new set of skills to learn and practise. Just as teenagers will act out the confusion and contradictions of the process, becoming moody or tetchy, so parents can find themselves hitting out too. Watching your child pull away from you can trigger feelings of jealousy, rivalry and loss and fears of being made redundant. You also need to understand and acknowledge your own feelings and consequent behaviour about your child growing up, to yourself and to them. If you are to help them with their process, you also need to ask for support and help in managing yours.

To do this, you may need to get your own needs met. When concentrating on your teenager and how they behave, you may be ignoring the fact that you too could be feeling angry, left out and rejected. You may be showing this through shouting, being depressed and not listening to them. Understanding how your children are feeling, making links between your own and their emotions, not only helps both of you manage the situation; it also helps you to feel closer to them. Just as it helps you to feel closer to a friend or partner when you share feelings, so it helps you to feel close to your teenager when you can talk to each other about how you are feeling.

Dealing with conflict

A good mantra for dealing with conflict is 'ACT, not react'. Conflict between teens and parents tends to come about because we all react – we respond to behaviour, triggered by feelings without understanding those feelings or seeing the underlying needs. Someone may shout or slam a door and the next thing you know, you've all reacted and been caught in a downwards spiral of argument and tears.

If instead, you'd taken control of the feelings and ACTed rather than reacted, you might have been talking rather than quarrelling. What is meant by ACTing?

ACT is short for:

- ▶ *Adult*
- ▶ *Child*
- ▶ *Tools*.

Adult is to remind you to ask yourself about what is going on for you – what are you feeling, what are your needs?

Child is to remind you to ask what is going on for your teenager – what are they feeling, what are their needs?

Tools is to remind you to look at what you could say or do to help all of you get what you want and need from the situation. In the following chapters we'll be looking at some tools, exercises, strategies and tips that can help both you and your teenager get what you want.

As a parent, one of the best legacies you can offer your child is to show them how to express their feelings, understand their needs and take action to meet them. Looking at and unpacking your own feelings and needs gives you more choices as to how to behave. Telling teenagers, or children, to do as you say – not copy what you do – is a waste of time. Your children model themselves on you, so the first step if you want to support them is to practise what you preach, first and last.

Insight
▶ *ACT, don't react. Write it out and stick it up on the fridge door!*

Essential points to consider
▶ *Understanding how they are feeling helps us to feel closer to our teenagers.*
▶ *ACT, don't react.*
▶ *Understanding needs is a key tool in resolving frustrating situations. The question to ask is not 'How can I change my child's/teenager's behaviour', but 'What is the need behind the behaviour?' This will help you take action together to meet the need that is causing the behaviour.*
▶ *Dive under the behaviour to see and understand the needs. 'Listen to the tune not the words' – feelings are a signal and can help us work out the need.*
▶ *It is the behaviour, not your child/teenager that is the problem; they are expressing their feelings and needs through their behaviour.*
▶ *As a parent you can model to your child/teenager how to express your feelings and needs and take action to meet your needs. This will help them become more aware of their own needs, how to express them and give them more choice in how they behave.*

HOW TO USE AN 'I' STATEMENT

One vital technique to use when building communication is an
'I' statement. 'I' statements are all about being able to say what
'I want' and what 'I need'. They help the person speaking, and
the person being spoken to, to be clear about what is really
going on.

When you use an 'I' statement, you can:

- ▶ *be aware of your own feelings about what you want*
- ▶ *stand up and be counted about your feelings and needs*
- ▶ *help other people understand what you are saying*
- ▶ *be clear, honest and direct*
- ▶ *make your point without blaming, criticizing or judging
  other people.*

'YOU' STATEMENTS

When we're upset we sometimes blame the other person for what
has happened. 'Look what you made me do' or 'You make me
so angry!' Alternatively, we try to avoid taking responsibility for
angry or critical remarks by saying they belong to someone else:
'Everyone thinks it's your fault.'

These are 'You' statements and they seldom give the other person
a chance to understand what we're upset about, how we feel or
why, or give them an opportunity to make any changes. 'You'
statements may be a way of not being overwhelmed by anger or
despair. Instead of 'owning' feelings, we hold them at arm's length:
'One feels like that, doesn't one?' 'That's how you do it, don't
you?' But instead of helping, they make the other person defensive
and increase hostility and conflict.

WHAT AN 'I' STATEMENT DOES

Using an 'I' statement respects the other person and their point of
view. It helps you say what you feel and want, but avoids making the

other person feel like the problem. This makes it far easier for both of you to come up with a solution, take responsibility and act positively.

It can take some time to get into the habit of using 'I' statements. Most of us have had a lifetime of being told it's selfish or big-headed to say 'I'. But the more you use them, the more you'll find they work and help you and the other person feel good about the exchange.

An 'I' statement:

▶ *describes the behaviour you are finding difficult*
▶ *explains the effect it has on you*
▶ *tells the other person how you feel about it*
▶ *invites them to join you in finding a solution.*

For example: 'When I come home and find you haven't done your chores, I feel really upset and angry. I feel as if you're taking me for granted and not listening to me. I'd like you to do the chores we've agreed, when we've agreed. If you're having a problem with that, let's talk about it.'

Insight

Saying 'I' is neither selfish nor arrogant. It's an important way of making your needs known.

CHANGING BOUNDARIES

Adolescence is a stressful time for teenagers as well as the adults around them. Teenagers are going through a lot of change and trying to take control of their lives and this can lead to rude, rebellious, awkward behaviour. As a parent, you are often struggling to keep up. Boundaries need to change as children grow older and you can – indeed, should and must – let them do much more than they could as children. You may be making decisions about what you feel they can and can't do, and both parents and teenagers have to deal with issues – such as sex and drugs – that you haven't faced before. Through all of this, your role as a parent changes as you become less of a nurturer and carer and more of a guide and supporter. It helps to realize that far from being uniquely awful or rebellious or disobedient, your teenager is probably perfectly normal. Nearly all adolescent–parent difficulties come from the normal process of growing up. All teenagers have ups and downs of mood, go through periods of boredom or apathy, show extremes of energy or enthusiasm, or become temporarily withdrawn and uncommunicative. It can be maddening, but seldom means there's cause for alarm – it's 'situation normal'.

COPING STRATEGIES

Here are some coping strategies to help you through the frustrating times:

▶ *Remember your own teenage years.*
▶ *Talk to other parents of teenagers.*
▶ *Share time and experiences with you teenager.*
▶ *Ask for help.*
▶ *Do things for yourselves.*

Remember your own teenage years

Didn't you act in the same or similar way to your teenager, and didn't your parents say the same things that you're now saying? Remembering what it felt like and what happened when you were a teenager can put your disagreements with your adolescent into perspective. You'll realize that what is going on between you now can't be as abnormal as you might fear, since you, and probably all of your friends, had the same experiences. Casting your mind back can also help put yourself in their shoes.

From an adult point of view you may know all the things they long for or demand are short-lived; in their shoes, you can remember and recognize how important it feels from their side.

Talk to other parents of teenagers

You'll soon see you're not the only ones experiencing some turbulence. You're not unique in coming under these pressures, nor unique in finding them hard to cope with. Neither is your teenager unique in their demands and their anxieties. Not only is it reassuring, it also helps if you're under pressure from your teen to do things 'all my friends are doing'. You can find out if they really are allowed all the freedoms your teen says they are, and you and other parents can share strategies and support each other.

> ## Insight
>
> If we're struggling with teenagers, it's easy to get into one of two modes. Either we stay quiet about what's happening with friends or relatives because we fear our teens are uniquely awful and to blame, or it's all our fault for being such bad parents. Or, we complain bitterly about them and get into a mutual 'blamefest' about them, bolstering a mutual belief it's all the teenagers' fault. What actually helps is sharing the fact we're having a stressful time and realizing that it's neither our fault nor theirs but just a natural developmental stage. Then, we can share methods of coping.

Share time and experiences with your teenager
It can sometimes feel as if all you do with your teenager is work through the day-to-day grind, and fight. Make opportunities to enjoy doing something with them, or simply chat with them, so that your relationship is about more than shouting and conflict.

Ask for help if you need it
Because parents are the carers in a family, it's very easy to get into the mind-set that says you have to manage on your own. For a start, being the parent of a teenager means handing over some of the responsibility to them and giving yourself some breaks. But any parent needs to know that they can't carry it all on their own shoulders all the time. Parents tend to feel it might be a weakness or a sign of failure to ask for help. I'd say it's a sign of strength to know your limitations, and to have the sense and the confidence to ask for support when you need it. Given all the pressures parents work under, it's normal to need support sometimes.

Look after yourself
It's also okay to do things for yourself sometimes – to relax and charge your batteries. It will help you to feel better about yourself

and your teenager, to feel better about life and more able to cope. Looking after yourself helps you take better care of your teenager.

Essential points to consider

▶ *Children are dogs, teenagers are cats. In the adolescent years, you need to become a different kind of pet owner.*

▶ *There are always reasons for your teenager's behaviour. Try to look behind their actions to see what their real needs are.*

▶ *Understanding their feelings does not mean you always have to meet them, but the very act of acknowledging them can affect your teenager's behaviour.*

▶ *Acknowledging and accepting your own needs is just as important as dealing with those of your teenager.*

Dealing with anger

Both focused and free-floating anger can be a problem with teenagers. They are struggling to make some sense of the changes in their bodies and in their feelings at this time and sometimes moodiness, sexual attraction or the desire to be in some sort of control can all mix to make them furious. Just as with any other strong emotion, anger is a natural feeling to have and is neither right nor wrong. But how we use our anger – or allow it to use us – and how it manifests itself can make it hurtful, scary and entirely destructive. Anger in itself can have an important function. Just as pain tells you not to lean on a hot stove, so anger tells you that what is happening is not acceptable and that something needs to change. Feeling angry can be:

▶ *an early warning signal that important needs aren't being met*

▶ *a push towards making some changes*

▶ *a way of showing other people how we feel and what we need to happen.*

Both adults and teenagers may often find themselves feeling angry, and find it difficult to deal with the strong emotions. Feeling angry and not expressing it:

▶ *makes us feel powerless and helpless*
▶ *means our needs don't get met*
▶ *makes us ill – depression, headaches, stomach ache, back ache*
▶ *leaks out as resentment, souring and damaging relationships*
▶ *causes anger to build up and explode in 'dirty' anger.*

IS SOME ANGER MORE DESTRUCTIVE THAN OTHERS?

Dirty anger is a helpful concept to understand. Anger is normal and is something you'd expect to feel in certain situations and can be helpful. Dirty anger is when anger spills out in uncontrolled and hurtful actions or words, harming both the person who is angry and everyone around them. Dirty anger is:

▶ *blaming, insulting, hitting or bad mouthing*
▶ *'kicking the cat' – dumping bad feelings where they don't belong*
▶ *raking over past grievances.*

Dirty anger does our teenagers and us no good at all. It leaves the person showing it ashamed and guilty and doesn't get the result they want. Letting yourself or your teenager get away with dirty anger harms your relationship with them and damages their self-esteem.

DEALING WITH MELTDOWN

Sometimes, teenagers seem to push you too far and the arguments and conflict start to resemble childhood tantrums. When young people are in the grip of strong feelings they are not able to think straight or listen to reason. The young person gets emotionally flooded. What they may need is to get the feelings out safely and to calm down enough to sort out the problem.

Imagine your teenager as a vessel – a cup, a glass or a pot. Normally, they're half-full with thoughts and half-full with feelings. Both balance each other out so they can think and feel and keep a steady balance between the two. When your teenager becomes upset, their feelings rise up and flood them. The glass is now three-quarters full or more of feelings, and their rational thoughts are drowned out. In that state, they can't think for themselves or listen to you. In the face of a meltdown:

▶ *don't take it personally*
▶ *listen carefully*
▶ *help your child work out what's behind their feelings*
▶ *set limits on the behaviour, while helping them find ways to solve the problem*
▶ *wait until the storm is over, then acknowledge the painful and strong feelings they have been experiencing.*

Don't take it personally
Your teenager may direct their anger at you, and they may indeed want you to listen and do something. But much of the time they are feeling upset about issues that have little to do with you, or that are only compounded by interaction with you. For example, the row might really have started by an argument they're having with a school friend, and then becomes all about 'you and your interfering'. Listen and take responsibility for things they might want differently from you, but don't get upset or angry back at them.

Insight
Strong feelings are infectious. One of the things you can do for your teenager is to recognize when their anger or confusion might be pulling you into feeling the same. The best way to deal with their anger is to stand back from it and not let it become yours.

Listen carefully
Make your start-point a desire to understand rather than a need to win the argument or make them behave. Listen to the tune, not the words, so instead of hearing 'I hate you! You're not the boss of me! Why don't you leave me alone!' you hear 'I'm really upset! I'm trying to manage on my own and it feels like you don't trust me!

I wish you'd help me in ways that I find useful!' By diving under the words to ferret out the real meaning, you can help them work out what they really are feeling, and what it is they need. And remember, just the act of listening to them helps to lower the emotional temperature and bring them back into a thinking/feeling balance where they can work out what they need to do. It can also help to name what you think your child might be feeling, for example, in the face of apparent screaming anger, to say, 'You sound really frustrated' or 'It sounds as if you're feeling scared.'

Help your child work out what's behind their feelings

By naming the emotion – we'll deal with that in detail in the next chapter – you can help your teenager work out for themselves what it is they want or need. The anger or upset, taken out on you, the slammed door or the kicked cat, may stem from their need for inclusion: 'Sounds like your friends are ganging up on you and leaving you out at the moment. You'd really like to be able to join in.'

Set limits on the behaviour

Understanding your teenager's feelings and needs and why they act the way they do is not the same as condoning or accepting some behaviour. Having calmed them down by listening and restored the thinking/feeling balance, you can then set limits on their behaviour while helping them find ways to solve the problem. So you might say, 'I'd like you to find a way of dealing with this without shouting at me, slamming doors or kicking the cat. What do you think would help you?'

Wait until the storm is over

When calm is restored, you need to acknowledge the painful and strong feelings your teen has been experiencing. Help them work out how they were feeling, what they needed, what they can do to express such feelings in the future and get what they need without hurting themselves and others. Say: 'I can fully understand how awful you were feeling and I'm sad about it. You have every right to feel so upset. What can we do to make sure next time we manage this in a different way so you can talk to me and you don't hurt yourself or anyone else?'

Sometimes simply recognizing and accepting their feelings and needs is enough. Other times, you may need to help your teenager work out what they are going to do. Moving on may mean having to accept there is nothing that can be done to change a situation, but you can always change how you act or feel about it. First, you may need to let the initial flush of emotions die down. What often blocks any advance is the anger that is flying around.

WHAT IF ARGUMENTS SEEM OUT OF CONTROL?

Sometimes teenage behaviour may indicate some real disturbance or unhappiness. Signs could include:

- *uncharacteristic outbursts of aggression*
- *becoming withdrawn and showing no interest in their normal activities*
- *crying more than usual and/or being persistently sad*
- *not seeing friends and becoming increasingly isolated*
- *not eating properly or sleeping well*
- *finding it difficult to talk or explain their feelings to you*
- *self-destructive behaviour such as heavy drinking, self-harm, taking drugs beyond levels of teenage experimentation.*

Uncharacteristic outbursts of aggression
All teenagers can have moments when they 'lose it' – so can we. But you know your teenager, even if they do seem to have changed so much. If you feel their temper is more unpredictable and explosive and their response more violent than you'd expect, it might be time to look for help.

Insight
While you shouldn't blame teenagers for feeling their strong emotions, it doesn't help them if you protect them from the consequences of their actions. If slammed doors or rampaging
(Contd)

results in damage, expect them to clear up and make reparation once they have had the chance to calm down, and don't replace items of theirs they have destroyed free of charge.

Becoming withdrawn and showing no interest in their normal activities

All teenagers can change their habits, putting aside train sets and dolls for an obsession with people they fancy. They might stop being sociable and hole up in their rooms, writing poetry or haunting social networking sites. But, again, you know your teenager. If you listen, consider and think about it, you'll know if withdrawing from the family is also withdrawal from life.

Crying more than usual and/or being persistently sad

Hormonal upsets can trigger moodiness and crying jags, and teenagers' preoccupation with the injustices of the world can make them sad. But permanent gloom is a sign of more than teenage blues and needs help.

Not seeing friends and becoming increasingly isolated

Teenagers might change friends, and may also shift their main contacts from face to face to online. But a teenager who has no real world friends, or avoids the ones they did have, is one who should ring alarm bells with you, and needs extra help.

Not eating properly or sleeping well

Teenagers may go through dietary panics and change what they will accept from you in an effort to slim down. They may also become creatures of the night, preferring to stay up late even if having to get up early. But you should be able to discern if your teenager is eating enough and sleeping enough – their health will suffer if they are not, and it may be part of a pattern of depression. Trust your instincts, and if you feel worried, talk it through with them.

Finding it difficult to talk or explain their feelings to you

All teenagers can go through periods of not wanting to talk to their parents and of struggling with emotions they find hard to put into words. But it is a matter of degree. Again, you may need to trust yourself if you feel your teenager is having a hard time managing their own feelings.

Self-destructive behaviour
The teenage years are the time when young people tend to experiment with alcohol, drugs, sex and other behaviour that verges on the self-destructive, such as getting into arguments and joyriding. But experiments are one thing, taking risks in order to harm themselves is another. Trust yourself and if you feel your child's behaviour is beyond normal experimentation, it's time to look for help.

EXTREME REACTIONS

If you do feel your teenager is reacting beyond the usual teenage angst, the first move would be to consider what may be at the root of their problems. Common situations that may trigger uncharacteristic behaviour could be:

▶ *bullying or peer pressure*
▶ *difficulties with school work and high expectations*
▶ *learning difficulties such as undiagnosed dyslexia*
▶ *girlfriend/boyfriend problems*
▶ *worries over their appearance*
▶ *parents not getting on/family changes*
▶ *death or illness in the family or among friends.*

You may need to seek help and support for yourself before you can be of help to your teenager, and the best place to start looking for support for all of you would be your own family doctor, your teenager's school or specialist advice services – you'll find more suggestions in the Taking it further section.

YOUR TURN

In this chapter, we looked at 'I' statements and their importance. Look at this list of 'You' statements and turn them into 'I' statements.

'You' statement	'I' statement
You're so lazy!	
Why do you always have to leave such a mess?	
You shouldn't be so rude to your father.	
Why can't you talk to me?	
You spend too much time on that mobile phone!	
You can't be trusted to do as I ask.	
You can't go out looking like that!	
Now look what you made me do!	
You make me so angry!	
You're a waste of time!	

Review the chapter to see if you're on the right track.

THINGS TO REMEMBER

▶ *Young people need what they have always needed from their parents: love, support, encouragement, nurture, acceptance and attention.*

▶ *Behaviour is a signal of our feelings; feelings are signals of our needs. If we're feeling happy, it's likely our needs are being met; if we're feeling upset or angry, it's likely that important needs are not being met.*

▶ *Everyone has feelings and needs; they are not right or wrong, they simply are.*

▶ *Noticing your own and your teenager's feelings gives you important information about what you and they need to do differently and helps you take useful action, rather than getting stuck in reacting and blaming.*

▶ *Teenage behaviour can be viewed as troublesome, annoying and disruptive. Recognizing the feelings and needs under the behaviour can help you to separate the person from the behaviour.*

▶ *It helps you help your teenager if you think about things from their point of view.*

▶ *You should support your teenager in solving their own problems, only butting in when asked.*

▶ *'Do as I do, not as I say': you need to be a positive role model for your teenager and not operate double standards, behaving one way yourself and expecting them to behave differently.*

▶ *Look after yourself as well as looking after your teenager. Looking after yourself will mean you will take even better care of them.*

▶ *Remember, it is their behaviour, not your teenager, which is the problem. They express their needs and feelings through behaviour and looking for and acknowledging these needs and feelings can help you to find out what your teenager is really trying to tell you.*

4

....

Communication

In this chapter you will learn:
* *how to keep communicating with your teenager*
* *how to be sharing and open*
* *how to treat your teenager as an equal*
* *how everyday chats can lead to important talks*
* *how to get out of unhelpful patterns*
* *how to avoid an 'interfere-iority complex'.*

The importance of communicating

The key to building a positive relationship and sorting out difficulties with your teenager is to keep the channels of communication open. We tend to consider the importance of big talks about significant topics with adolescents, but the ability to connect when it really matters is often based on the ability to connect when it *doesn't*. The way you relate to them in day-to-day life will make it easier – or harder – to sort out the key issues.

We can get locked into unhelpful ways of communicating – bickering, nagging, criticizing – that once we're in, we find hard to avoid. Your teenager may still need your guidance and the boundaries that you draw and hold, but you may have to get tactical to get this across. How you assert your authority may need to be different when dealing with an authority-averse teen rather than an automatically respectful child. Your teenager still needs to know you are interested but watchful, that you care and are on their side, even if you don't always agree with them. You need to have the skill and the emotional resilience to go on offering help, even in the face of indifference and opposition.

HOW TO 'SKILL UP'

You can reduce the amount of indifference and opposition, if you skill up. Teenagers often behave in ways that make it difficult for us to give them what they need most – love and acceptance. You can't change your teenager, but you can change what you do – and when you behave differently, it often results in the other person matching you and altering their position themselves.

Imagine yourself and another person standing at opposite ends of a see-saw. You want to be closer to that person, so your solution is that they move towards you. You could ask, order, or beg the other person to move – but what if they're not listening or in a mood with you? That may be the situation you face with your teenager. There's another option. You move. Step forward, and the other person has to move too, to keep their balance and to stop themselves falling off. You may think, since you're not balancing on a bit of wood, this effect won't work in ordinary life, but you'd be surprised. Change your position, and you will usually find other people change theirs too, to match.

WHAT SHOULD YOU DO TO KEEP COMMUNICATION OPEN?

If you want to keep lines of communication open with your teenager, what should you be doing? It can help if you:

▶ *look for opportunities to talk off-message*
▶ *use 'I' messages*
▶ *use open questions*
▶ *share something of yourself*
▶ *treat the young person as an equal*
▶ *practise what you preach*

- *listen without judgement or criticism*
- *appreciate them for their positive qualities*
- *give unconditional love but hold strong boundaries over behaviour*
- *give frequent 'strokes'*
- *include the young person in family activities but give the choice to opt out*
- *understand and take action only when asked for help.*

LOOK FOR OPPORTUNITIES TO TALK OFF-MESSAGE

Often, as a parent, you're so aware of what you see as the important issues you'd like to discuss with your teenager – unsuitable friends, doing homework on time, playing loud music, wearing unsuitable clothes – that you forget to simply pass the time with them. If your teenager knows every exchange is going to be hijacked by you trying to squeeze in a lecture on something, they're going to avoid have those face-to-faces. Some surveys show that the majority of exchanges between parents and their children entirely involve complaints and rebukes. Some teenagers even say the only time their parents talk to them is to tell them off. But if they're used to you chatting about fun stuff, inconsequential stuff, their stuff, they'll stop and tune in and be relaxed with you. Then, when you do want to discuss something important or ask them to do something differently, they're likely to listen.

Insight

If you've got out of the habit of just chatting with your teenager, make a conscious effort to do it again. Use an opener such as 'Tell me about your day' to show you're interested and don't have an ulterior motive for the question.

USE 'I' MESSAGES

Remember the tool we looked at in Chapter 3? If there is an issue you're concerned about, it simply isn't effective to broach it with a 'You' message: 'You left the kitchen in a mess last night!'; 'You didn't feed the cat!'; 'You just wind me up every day!' Instead, try an 'I' message: 'I was upset this morning when I came down to find you hadn't cleared up after yourself last night because I had to do it before I could make breakfast. Next time you make a late night snack, please clear up after yourself. You could do it at the time or make sure you come down before me to do it in the morning. Thanks!'

OPEN AND CLOSED QUESTIONS

Using open questions is another vital tool in making communication easier. A closed question is one that stops communication rather than starting it. There are two types. One is the question that can – and sometimes only – be answered with a yes or a no, such as: 'Are you going out?'; 'Do you have homework?'; 'Did you have a good time at school today?' There are some questions that seem to ask a bit more, but can still be seen as closed questions because they ask for short and uninvolved answers, such as: 'Where are you going?' (Answer – 'Out!'); 'What are you doing this weekend?' (Answer – 'Nothing!').

The second type of closed question is the one that leaves the person 'questioned' nowhere to go. In effect, it isn't a question but a statement pretending to be one, such as: 'What sort of a time do you call this?'; 'You're not going out dressed like that, are you?'; 'Call that a room? It's a pigsty!'; 'Why don't you ever do the washing-up?'; 'Is that the way you talk to your parents?'

Why closed questions don't work
There are two problems with closed questions. One is that they can stop the conversation dead. The person being asked the question can just respond to the immediate query by saying yes, no or not a lot, and need go no further. Try it with your partner or another adult. You'll find it takes quite some effort to elaborate further than just answering the immediate query.

But even more important, they tend to push the person being asked into only giving you a short answer. The reason for this is that a closed question suggests or even tells the person what you want to hear. 'Did you have a good time at school today?' implies that you expect them to have enjoyed school and goes some way towards saying that if they answer 'No' you might come down heavily on them to explain what they're doing wrong.

And most important of all, when we use closed questions as a way of making a criticism – about their appearance, behaviour, attitude – it's quite clear the question isn't to be answered; it's to be swallowed. And it's usually a quick step to an argument.

Using openers
Try an opener instead. An opener carries with it a different message, one that says, 'Tell me more, I'm interested and listening.' Some examples of openers would be:

- ▶ *'Tell me about your day.'*
- ▶ *'You seem fed up/in good spirits. Tell me about it.'*
- ▶ *'You look as if you had a good/tiring/disappointing time last night.'*
- ▶ *'That T-shirt/hairstyle/music track is striking. Tell me why you like it.'*

Insight
The latest trend in music, clothes or adornment can seem hideous or laughable. But wasn't that what our parents thought about our tastes when we were the same age?

SHARE SOMETHING OF YOURSELF

If you want your teenager to feel relaxed and happy about sharing their concerns and feelings with you, one way to set the tone is by being open yourself. This doesn't mean burdening your child with worries that would frighten them or be inappropriate for them to know in depth. Young children look to parents to be in control and all-knowing. As they develop into adolescents, if you keep up a facade of never having problems yourself, three barriers may emerge between you and your teenagers. One possibility is that they simply begin to feel totally incompetent. They have all these anxieties which no one else seems to share and it's not enough for them to think, 'Once I become an adult, just like my parents

I'll be okay.' Instead what they may think is, 'Nobody else is as stupid as I am and I'm never going to get there.' The second barrier may evolve because, even though they may have an inkling that your invulnerability may be a front, they still may feel you don't share and therefore can't appreciate exactly how they are feeling. When a teenager shouts 'You don't understand', they are often speaking from the heart and really feel you can't understand what they are going through. The third barrier comes about when they know perfectly well that you are struggling with as many anxieties as they are, but won't admit it. In that case, your child may be unwilling to open up to you because they see you as insincere, hypocritical and in denial. If you have those problems and can't even face up to them yourself, what help would you be to them if they came to you for advice?

TREAT THE YOUNG PERSON AS AN EQUAL

You may still feel that your teenager does not have the experience, knowledge or ability to cope on their own, or to stand eye-to-eye with you. But one day soon, they will. Sometime soon you're going to have to offer them the respect you'd give a peer, and the sooner you begin to treat them as capable, competent, thinking beings, the sooner they will act like it. Treating a teenager as an equal does not make them cheeky or arrogant or out of control. On the contrary, it gives them every incentive to live up to your trust. Part of this is accepting that you and they may have different views, beliefs and opinions. This isn't easy. All through their childhood you may have assumed they were a chip off the old block – a mini-you, who accepted what you told them and followed in your footsteps. Your teenager may well end up with very similar ideas to yours, but while they are an adolescent, trying everything out, they may well diverge. And they may stay that way. Get used to it and embrace it. You have friends who disagree with you on all sorts of things – you still like and respect them. You can do so with your own teen, too.

PRACTISE WHAT YOU PREACH

Although in the midst of discovering who they are – what will be the defining characteristics of their personality and what they are going to believe in – teenagers have particularly good bullshit detectors. They hate hypocrisy and double standards. One way to lose your teenager's trust or belief is to tell them to do one thing while flagrantly breaking the rules yourself. Lectures on alcohol and drugs may fall on deaf ears if you drink and partake, even if you think it's different. They may reject your advice on the grounds that you do it too. They may also decide that since you ignore your own strictures on one issue, they can ignore what you say on others too. Young people will always do as you do, not do as you say. As the parent of a teenager you need to be able to debate, defend and stand by what you'd like them to do. Modelling good behaviour to them will always be more effective than preaching it.

LISTEN WITHOUT JUDGEMENT OR CRITICISM

It's not easy listening to our children without having the urge to jump in, comment and fix. What most parents have is an 'interfere-iority' complex.

The interfere-iority complex
We feel that we have to guide, instruct, inform, to do our job properly. You'd probably never dream of spying on friends, colleagues or relatives – or if you did, you'd feel a bit shamefaced, knowing that interfering in someone else's life in this way is unethical. But many parents think that reading our teenagers' diaries, listening in to phone calls, checking their texts or voicemail or email, speaking to teachers or other involved people behind their backs and without their permission are perfectly defensible. After all, we reason, it's 'for their own good'. We feel it's part of our role as a parent to make them feel better, to solve their problems, to know what they should be doing. So when we feel that our young people have a dilemma, or are doing something we're not happy about, or are simply telling us about their life, their day, their friends, we rush in with our comments and judgements and our fix, providing what we think they want or need, regardless of even strong messages to the contrary. Needless to say, the response we meet is often hostile or impatient, and can result in our teens being even less willing to open up to us.

You should always be a parent, not a friend, to your teenager – that's what they want and need from you. But you don't always have to be in parental mode.

Seeing parenting as a job where you are in charge gives you a vested interest in feeling you can solve any difficulties experienced by your young adult. You tend to think the inexperience of young people is the same as their not being competent or capable. Standing by and letting them find their own solutions may leave you feeling anxious and angry and incompetent. It is a source of pride that you know best and make decisions for them. This means you get upset and angry when they complain or resist your help or direction. What you need to do is give them the same support that you would a friend – simply listen without passing comment, without making judgements or offering criticism. You keep quiet because you know: 1) it may be inappropriate to offer advice, it's not what your friend asked for and if they wanted it, they'd ask; 2) it wouldn't be effective to do so – your friend would be upset and not only ignore your advice – it may even strain the friendship. Sometimes you need to give your teenager exactly the respect and behaviour you'd give a friend. Judging, blaming, criticizing and labelling can destroy self-esteem and cause distance between you and your teenager; they increase conflict, making teenagers unwilling to cooperate. All their energy goes into defending themselves, meaning they have none left to make any changes.

APPRECIATE YOUR TEENAGER FOR THEIR POSITIVE QUALITIES

We can all find things we dislike about our teenagers: they leave their rooms in a mess; they treat the house like a hotel; and they spend too much time on the phone or computer chatting to friends. But if that's all you see, you may find it hard to get on. What helps is to make the positive effort to see what you like about them: their enthusiasm and liveliness; their kindness and concern; their sense of humour. Look for the positives and remind yourself of these every time you're tempted to be angry or upset with them over something you feel they've done or not done.

GIVE UNCONDITIONAL LOVE BUT HOLD STRONG BOUNDARIES OVER BEHAVIOUR

Your teenager needs to know that you love them, no matter what. That is not the same as condoning, accepting and allowing all their behaviour. When you find yourself in conflict with your teen it helps to remember that it's the behaviour, not the teenager, you may not like, and the behaviour, not the teenager, you may want to address. Much of the time, the escapades they get up to are normal for their age and development. But there are obviously times when you want to pull them up.

The key to being effective is not to make it personal. The best approach is to be specific, to avoid labels and to make your requests clear. Say: 'You left your coat on the floor. I don't appreciate having to tidy up after you. Next time, coats in the cupboard, please.' That works far more effectively than, 'You're so messy! What am I going to do with you? I'm not your servant, you know!'

With the second approach, the teenager is told what they are – messy. No way for them to change; they're labelled and judged. Why try to do anything to please you when it's clear you've made up your mind about who, and what, they are? A label – lazy, messy, stupid – is a description of a person and it's something that sticks; 'You're lazy' – no point in doing anything about it because that's what you ARE. And by not mentioning what it is that has upset you, the teenager may not even understand what they've done wrong. What follows is probably a shouting match and no resolution.

With the first approach, the teenager is told exactly what upset you and why, and is given a clear request of what to do to remedy the situation. What probably follows is an apology, a quick response and a smile and a kiss. Much better all round.

GIVE FREQUENT STROKES

We all need to be rewarded, to be praised and thanked and appreciated. Sometimes we forget how much we need to value others, and to be valued by them. Often, we forget how easy it is to give pleasure and how a little can mean a lot. Counsellors call the sort of action that gives a lift to morale 'a stroke'. Strokes can be spoken – telling someone you love them, thanking them for helping you or saying that you value them. Or they can be shown by contact – hugging or kissing someone or giving them a back rub. Or they can be acted out – making them a cup of coffee, giving them a small present or doing a chore you know they'd like done. Sit down and think about the strokes you think your teenager would like to receive, or that you'd like to give. Think also about the strokes you'd like to receive. Check out the ones you could give – try them out or ask your teenager if they'd like them. Also, tell them what *you'd* appreciate. Keep the communication going by agreeing to give each other at least one stroke a day.

INCLUDE THE YOUNG PERSON IN FAMILY ACTIVITIES BUT GIVE THEM THE CHOICE TO OPT OUT

The teenage years are really the time when young people begin to have their own social life that they manage themselves; that includes friends and contacts they have made – and that often excludes you. It's the time when family activities may become deeply embarrassing – they don't want to seem a 'Billy No Mates', reduced to socializing or going out with family. Even if embarrassment isn't a factor, they may not want to miss out on anything their friends are doing and so won't want to waste valuable time with you. But teenagers can surprise you and if you assume they want nothing more to do with family events and leave them out, they may be hurt and feel rejected. It may be reassuring to want them to go on sharing time with you, but you need to get this into perspective. This is the period of their lives when they learn, practise and perfect the skills of making and keeping friends. If not now, perhaps never; so they need to be given the choice to stay with you or go with them. If given free choice, you may well find they include themselves in family activities more than you'd expect. If you pressurize, the result may be conflict and arguments; they may make a stand by cutting off communication and staying away just to make a point, rather than because that would have been their original preference.

Case study – Naomi's story

Naomi says: 'I've been taking my three nephews to the pantomime every year for about ten years – ever since the youngest was old enough. This year the eldest is 18 and I did wonder if he was getting bit old – whether he'd feel affronted or embarrassed to be seen at a kid's show. I know last year he was adamant I shouldn't push him forward as I do the younger ones (to their delight I must add!) to go on stage. So I asked, and was so charmed when he said, "Oh yeah! Wouldn't be Christmas without a panto with you, Auntie!" I'm so glad!'

UNDERSTAND AND TAKE ACTION ONLY WHEN ASKED FOR HELP

Communication with young people is tremendously boosted when they feel you understand them and what they are going through, and it rises to a new level when they trust you to butt out when necessary. There are times when they may want you to intervene and there will obviously be times when they want you to give advice and support. But in both cases, the relationship will be better and the invitation to help more likely if they know you will wait for the request, not jump in or assume it's your right and your place to do so.

Encouraging your teenager to communicate

Young people are far more likely to want to communicate with you if certain conditions are maintained. If your teenager has self-confidence and self-esteem and thinks highly of themselves, they are far more likely to have a positive attitude towards being in contact with you, and everyone else. You can oil the wheels of communication with them if you encourage them to have:

▶ *contact with other adults*
▶ *close friendships*
▶ *heroes and heroines*
▶ *opportunities for self-expression.*

CONTACT WITH OTHER ADULTS

When teenagers are regularly in touch with adults other than their parents, such as family friends, parents of friends, older siblings, aunts and uncles, grandparents, teachers and youth workers, it has several positive effects on their ability and willingness to communicate with you. Such exchanges reinforce their belief that adults have their best interests at heart and will listen to and respect them. Adults who have faith in them affirm their positive qualities, help them feel good about themselves and encourage them to go on listening and learning. Also, they see that most adults – even those with different styles of parenting – share common concerns and attitudes, so that if you've set a standard in something, the chances are the other adults will back you up; this is helpful and reassuring for your teenager. While they may want to think that other adults will say that bedtimes are unnecessary, and that chocolate is a main food group, in reality, it's comforting for them to find that Mum and Dad sometimes do know best.

Insight

'Chosen adults' – adults they choose to look up to and listen to – are an important aspect of teenager's lives. It's easy to feel jealous when a teenager seems to put more value on something a relative or friend says to them than what you say. It's not a rejection of you, but an addition for them.

CLOSE FRIENDSHIPS

Close friendships may sometimes seem like a drawback rather than an advantage – after all, isn't half the problem that your teenager would rather talk with their friends than you? The reason why close friendships are so important, and such a boon, is that it means they are talking to someone. If they didn't have friends, the odds are that they wouldn't be talking to you instead, but worrying on their own. They're practising getting on and sharing. They're seeing themselves as people capable of making relationships and of communicating. When they've had the opportunity to say, 'I don't need you! I can do it on my own, with people I choose!' they'll come back, to apply the skills they're trying out – on you. Friends give them the arena in which to learn, and the mirror that reflects back an image of who they are. The lessons they learn with friends may be tougher and more honest than the ones they'd get from you, because family is always there, but friends have to be earned – and that's why they need them.

HEROES AND HEROINES

All teenagers go through periods of being attracted to, if not obsessed with, heroes and heroines. They can be pop idols, actors – and recently even gaming characters based on real people – or totally invented. Being told for the 27th time the minute details of some pop star or footballer that you really don't care about can seem tedious – but it's important to be interested and encouraging. Heroes and heroines, whatever their actual worth, set goals for young people. You can challenge their actual achievements by discussing what it is your teenager finds appealing or admirable, but simply dismissing their hero or heroine tells your teenager that in dissing their champion, you dismiss their choices. Having ambitions, any ambitions, is a good beginning. If you're communicating, you can help your teenager begin to assess what it is they admire, what it is they might like to copy and what goals they may want to set themselves modelled on their hero.

OPPORTUNITIES FOR SELF-EXPRESSION

Communication can often be improved if you can encourage your teen to explore their feelings and thoughts by listening to or playing music, by reading, painting or drawing, creating animations or films, acting – in fact, any form of self-expression. It's something they may take for granted while young, but once children become teenagers they often become embarrassed about performing in public or even in private. Showing them a lead by doing it yourself can give you something to talk about.

> **Essential points to consider**
> ▶ *The key to building a positive relationship and sorting out difficulties with a teenager is to keep the channels of communication open. The patterns of relating established in day-to-day life will make it easier or harder to sort out the big issues.*
> ▶ *Establishing a 'chatting' relationship will help on both sides; teenagers need to know we are interested, that we care and that we are on their side, even if we don't always agree with them.*

The tone of voice we fall into when addressing our teenager can have a dramatic effect on how well we communicate. If you're having difficulties, it's worth thinking about the tone you adopt. Is it:

▶ *chatty*
▶ *nagging*
▶ *interrogating*
▶ *sarcastic*
▶ *teasing?*

If we can chat, and then talk seriously when appropriate, we'll be communicating. All the others put a severe strain on our ability to listen and hear them, to respect and care for them.

▶ *Nagging is not the same as assertively insisting they do something they need to do. We'll look at techniques you can use to put your point across and your foot down later.*

*But often, you can get into a cycle of repeating in such a way that
your teenager simply 'turns off' and no longer hears anything
but, 'Yada, yada, yada'. You may feel what you are doing is
asking them to comply, and you have to repeat yourself only
because they won't do as you ask. What they hear is persistent
fault finding and complaints, along with your demands.*

▶ *Interrogating is not the same as asking questions. When you
ask questions, you have a genuine desire to hear and learn, to
share and enjoy. When you interrogate, you're on a mission to
gather evidence against your teenager.*

▶ *Being sarcastic is not the same as being funny. Sarcasm is
sneering or cutting – it's a taunt, not a joke and teenagers
know it. Some families may manage to use it with affection
but that's because it's allowed both ways. Teenagers tend to
get all too much of it, and feel hurt. Even if you don't mind
sarcasm being used against you, you still need to be aware if
anyone you use it against finds it upsetting, and stop.*

▶ *Teasing is like sarcasm; it can be lots of fun and very amusing
to the person doing it, less so for the person on the receiving
end. Occasional sarcasm and occasional teasing are fine as
long as: you take as much as you give; it's done with genuine
affection; it stops if the other person cries foul; and you check
if the other person is happy with it. If the majority of your
interaction with your teen lies in either sarcasm or teasing...
you're not communicating.*

Insight

How you say something is as, if not more, important than
what you say.

Bridging the communication gap

Bridging the communication gap can be hard. It's very difficult to
have a conversation when you feel it's one-way – you're trying to
talk over music from a couple of earplugs, or blaring out through
speakers turned to maximum, or talk through a bedroom door.
However well you're doing, sometimes your teenager may not be

in the mood to talk. Try to insist, or lose connection, and you can get locked into the unhelpful ways of communicating we've just looked at. These are hard to get out of – it's rather like being on a roundabout or carousel. Round and round you go, bickering and snapping and no matter how many times you promise it's going to be different, you find yourself saying the same old things with the same old result. So how do you stop it? Remember, you can't change your teenager – you can only change what you say and do. You can stop the carousel if you:

▶ *stop pushing*
▶ *jump off*
▶ *use your weight as a break.*

STOP PUSHING

Much of the time, a carousel of unhelpful communication can begin by you getting upset by something your teenager did or didn't do, or said. You react, they react and off you go. Try holding the mantra of ACT in your mind; don't react, ACT. Deliberately break the cycle by ignoring any behaviour that irritates you. Take a deep breath, sit down and think through:

▶ *A: What am I feeling; what is going on for me; what do I need?*
▶ *C: What is my teenager feeling; what is going on for them; what do they need?*
▶ *T: What are the tools I can use? In this case it will be to refuse to get wound up.*

JUMP OFF

Jump off the carousel by making an effort to change the way you talk; catch yourself if you begin to nag, interrogate, use sarcasm or teasing, and change it to chatting. Be around when your teenager is likely to be home and initiate conversations about things you know they like, even if they don't interest you. Balance it up by talking about things that concern you and try to draw your teenager in – neither of you have to share an interest to be able to share the other person's pleasure in it. When they do talk, pay attention but don't ask too many questions – just enough to encourage them and let them know you are listening. Make interaction between you positive – make a point of noticing and appreciating the things you like about them. You could also listen or make contact without talking – a quiet gesture such as a touch on the arm says 'I'm here' and will remind your teenager that you care. Above all, initiate any conversations you want to have about sensitive subjects when you are calm, rather than waiting for your teenager to speak and then reacting angrily. Keep at it – don't expect an immediate response. It can take time for your teenager to realize that you have stopped pushing and jumped off, and for the carousel to stop.

USE YOUR WEIGHT AS A BRAKE

Once you've jumped off and are no longer on the carousel, going round and round, your teenager might still react as if it's going. Relax at this stage and you might be dragged back onto it. So keep going. Ignore behaviour that irritates you and watch your tone – there will be more on listening and talking in the next chapter. If you believe in yourself and what you are trying to do, you can help both of you to get off the carousel.

I've been using playground metaphors to describe how to visualize what you're doing, and how to change it – see-saws, roundabouts or carousels. You can also think about this process as a dance. Even if you dance on a dance floor without touching your partner, both of you still mirror each other's moves. If you change your steps, the dance cannot carry on the way it was. The other person may ignore you at first, but gradually they will seek to match you. Changing your steps will initiate a new dance, one that suits you both.

Insight
Think of those dance steps when talking with your teenager. Try getting in step with them, mirroring their stance, for instance. It's surprising how effective it can be to get on the same wavelength with the person you are talking to, simply by standing or sitting in the same way.

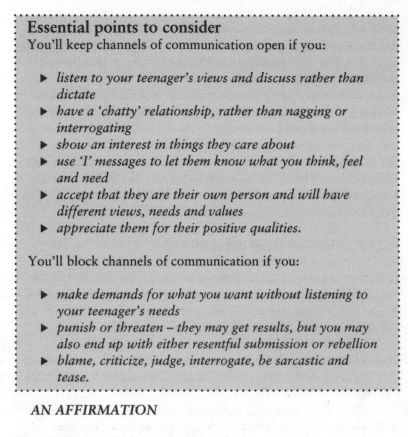

Essential points to consider

You'll keep channels of communication open if you:

- ▶ *listen to your teenager's views and discuss rather than dictate*
- ▶ *have a 'chatty' relationship, rather than nagging or interrogating*
- ▶ *show an interest in things they care about*
- ▶ *use 'I' messages to let them know what you think, feel and need*
- ▶ *accept that they are their own person and will have different views, needs and values*
- ▶ *appreciate them for their positive qualities.*

You'll block channels of communication if you:

- ▶ *make demands for what you want without listening to your teenager's needs*
- ▶ *punish or threaten – they may get results, but you may also end up with either resentful submission or rebellion*
- ▶ *blame, criticize, judge, interrogate, be sarcastic and tease.*

AN AFFIRMATION

When you're really fed up with your teenager, try this exercise to turn the situation around. You can do this on your own or with your partner.

First, sit down with a sheet of paper and pen or pencil – or a computer screen – and jot down all of the things that upset you. At this point, don't think them over; just get them out into the open. When you run out of steam, start looking at the things you've said. Go through them and change every one from being about the person to being about their behaviour, and be specific. For example, instead of saying, 'Joe's so lazy' say, 'I was upset because yesterday his room was in a mess even though I'd asked him twice to tidy up.' A formula that could help would be 'I feel/ felt upset when...' You may find that this helps you eliminate some issues – if you can't back them up with a specific, perhaps you're making an unfair assumption. It may help you to consider what is going on behind the behaviour – which in itself may defuse the situation.

By seeing it's the behaviour and not the person you're upset about, you can then begin to make some plans as to how you can change the situation. What has and hasn't worked? What could work? What would you like to sit down and discuss with your teenager?

But before you do, complete the next part of the exercise. Take your pen and paper or screen and write down everything you like about your teenager. Scribble it all down, again without consideration. After you've identified everything you can think of, go through your thoughts and again, concentrate on behaviour and specifics. A formula that could help would be, 'I like it when...'

Look at the two lists. What in the second contradicts the first? How can you use the behaviour you like in the second list to right any aspects in the first list?

You can discuss with your child what has come up from the first list and agree changes that will benefit you both. But before that, write out the second list and give it to them, saying 'I thought you'd like to see this – it's a list of all the things I appreciate about you.' Don't qualify, don't undermine what you've discovered; give it as a gift. We can get into the habit of criticizing, and out of the habit of praising. Simple, unalloyed, unconditional praise is very powerful. Praise is far more an effective tool than criticism in that children will repeat behaviour that gives them attention. Praise them when they do something you like and they will repeat it. Criticize them, and instead of avoiding the behaviour you don't like, they may repeat it because it gets them noticed.

READING MINDS AND MAKING ASSUMPTIONS

'I know just how you feel!' is something we often say to reassure or placate someone we're talking to. And it can be right – we may be able to empathize and put ourselves in their shoes. But sometimes, we make assumptions about another person's thoughts, feelings and needs, and that can lead to arguments and differences, especially when it's a teenager we're dealing with. The reality is that you can't read minds. A situation that would have you feeling one thing can find your teenager on an entirely different track. There's nothing wrong with this; you can both still be on the same wavelength and you can help and support them, if you check out what is going on. If you want to communicate with your adolescent, it's really important not to think you know what is going on inside their head. Instead of assuming, because you're their parent and close to them, that you have the inside track – check it out. Always ask: 'Am I right in thinking...'; 'Have I got it right here... you think/want...?'; 'Just let me get this clear, you're saying...?'

The rules of good communication

Communication is an art and a skill. Some of it comes naturally – that's the art. But being a good communicator and being able to have easy, productive and enjoyable conversations is also a skill that requires abilities and proficiencies that we need to learn and practise. In the next chapter, we'll look at these in detail, but in brief:

- *In any conversation, there are two roles – the listener and the speaker. For communication to be flowing, you need to swap over the role of listener and that of speaker constantly – for you to speak and then listen, listen and then speak.*
- *To have a good conversation, it needs to be the right time – not when either participant is doing something else, or is angry or upset. Ask: 'Is this a good time?'*
- *Your body language tells the other person if you're listening to them; use it to engage with them and signal engagement.*
- *Being upfront and direct helps; if you've got a problem, tell the other person 'I need your help to get this sorted.'*
- *Being clear and 'checking out' is vital.*
- *Use reflective and active listening, not interrupting. Leaving physical and verbal space for the other person are all essential. Learn this skill in the next chapter!*

CONSIDER THE TYPE OF CONVERSATION YOU WANT TO HAVE BEFORE GOING AHEAD

There are all sorts of conversations we can have, and sometimes we confuse them. If you want to communicate with your teenager, it's important to recognize what you really want to say, and choose your moment. If you want to have a conversation that offloads – that tells them how fed up you are about something – doing it when they are tired or fed up, or already in a mood, will only lead to conflict. If you just want a chat, wanting to do so while they are in the middle of homework that has to be done will only annoy. Consider the purposes of the following types of conversations.

To unload
We all have moments when we want to offload irritation, confusion or downright anger. It may be something that your teenager has done or not done, or it may be about something or someone entirely different, and you just need to be able to dump on a convenient and understanding audience. It's an entirely justifiable conversation… but best had when people are already calm and collected, and have a reasonable period of time to have the whole conversation and then unwind. Choose your moment.

To organize something

Sometimes, we just need to check out an arrangement – to organize or clarify what is happening. It can take a few minutes and it is something that can interrupt other issues, or be done as people are about to leave or have just arrived home, if done cleanly and clearly. Make it clear you will only take a short time, and keep to that boundary.

To sort out your own thinking

Sometimes, you need to bounce ideas off someone else, to have them help you sort something in your own mind. You might need to make it clear this is about your ideas and feelings and not about them, and while you listen to their ideas and responses, to refrain from bringing them into the equation. Again, this is the sort of conversation that needs to be allocated time.

> **Insight**
> Learn to identify what sort of conversation you want and resist hijacking one for another.

To bond

Bonding conversations can be short and sweet or long and involved. They can need time and space, to kick back with a cup of coffee and a slice of cake to allow quality time to talk and listen and enjoy each other's company. Or they can be significant exchanges while doing the washing-up or driving. Communication that bonds can be the chance for your teen to open up and tell you significant things about themselves and their lives. The important aspect of it is that you need to seize the opportunity when it arises. If you're always too busy or have 'important' things to do when your teenager approaches you, the moment may not repeat. Too many missed opportunities and the window closes.

Just to chat

Chat can be long or short, trivial or have hidden nuggets of important information. Just chatting with your teenager is as much fun as chatting with your friends – and has as much hidden importance.

You may recognize how much a bonding talk brings you together, but chat and gossip does the same thing.

HOW TO PUT A NAME TO FEELINGS

When you are trying to communicate with your teenager, it helps to be able to put a name to both your feelings and theirs. All of us have feelings. At times, we feel happy, sad, angry, rejected, confused and much more. However, many of us have picked up from our parents and other influences the idea that some feelings are 'bad' – not things we should be feeling. Feeling angry is often seen to be unacceptable; so is being jealous. When we have these feelings we feel guilty: 'I shouldn't be feeling this. I must be a bad person to feel like this.' Sometimes, we blame others: 'You make me feel angry – it's all your fault – you're the bad person!'

In reality, all feelings are natural and having them is normal. Feelings are just feelings – you can't help them and there's no shame in having them. What you can help is what you do about them. Taking out anger on someone in an unhelpful way doesn't make you feel better, or deal with the feeling, either. However, often you can't deal with the emotion you are feeling because you don't actually know what it really is. Teenagers, particularly, can find it hard to put into words what they are actually experiencing. Using the following technique can help you and anyone else to isolate, understand and put a name to these feelings.

Get a pack of Post-it notes or slips of paper and write out the words listed on the next page, and any other words you can think of, to describe feelings. Stick them on a wall or spread them out on a table. Then mull them over, talk them through to pinpoint the word that best describes what you are feeling. You or the other person may be angry. Or, you might be feeling abandoned or worried or embarrassed. Once you know what it is, you can discuss why these feelings are there and what you can do about it. Simply acknowledging the real emotion – and realizing you don't have to feel guilty for having it – can help and often makes the feeling diminish or lose its power.

abandoned
alarmed
angry
anxious
bored
bothered
calm
cared for
cheerful
cheesed off
cold
confused
content
cross
dejected
depressed
disgusted
down in the dumps
dumped
edgy
embarrassed
envious
fed up
forgotten
frightened
fuming
glad
gloomy
hacked off
happy
humiliated
ignored
in despair
in high spirits
jealous
jittery
jumpy

left out
loved
loving
low
miserable
neglected
nervous
nervy
on edge
out of sorts
p***ed off
panicky
peaceful
pleased
quiet
rejected
relieved
resentful
sad
scared
sensitive
shamed
shown up
sick and tired
snappy
stressed
tense
thrilled
troubled
uneasy
unwanted
upset
uptight
warm
worried

YOUR TURN

Review the communication tools we looked at in this chapter. In addition to 'I' statements, we explored:

▶ *looking for opportunities to talk 'off message'*

▶ *using open questions*

▶ *sharing something of yourself*

▶ *treating the young person as an equal*

▶ *practising what you preach*

▶ *listening without judgement or criticism*

▶ *appreciating them for their positive qualities*

▶ *giving unconditional love but holding strong boundaries over behaviour*

▶ *giving frequent strokes*

▶ *including the young person in family activities but giving them the choice to opt out*

▶ *understanding and taking action only when asked for help.*

Write out the complete list, stick it somewhere you can see and make a conscious effort to go through them one by one over the next week. When you get to the end, go back and do it again until all of them become a daily habit.

THINGS TO REMEMBER

▶ *Listen to your teenager without judgement or criticism and treat them as an equal.*

▶ *Notice their positive qualities and tell them what they are.*

▶ *Encourage them to join in family activities (without pressurizing).*

▶ *Encourage contact with other wise adults, for example a family friend, older sibling, aunt, uncle or grandparent.*

▶ *Encourage and accept their self-expression, such as listening to/playing music, drama, art, and physical outlets.*

▶ *Let them know about other people's needs and how to get along together.*

▶ *Young people often behave in ways which make it most difficult for us to give them what they most need. It's often helpful to remember the needs underlying their behaviour and that it is the behaviour we are sometimes unhappy with, not the adolescent themselves.*

▶ *Practise what you preach. Your teenager hates hypocrisy and double standards. Modelling good behaviour to them will always be more effective than preaching it.*

5

Listening and talking, negotiating and compromising

In this chapter you will learn:
- *how to listen sensitively*
- *how to use active and reflective listening skills*
- *how to use the 'open' question*
- *how to negotiate and have a constructive argument*
- *how to come to an agreement*
- *how to respond*
- *how to pick your battles.*

Listening is an important skill in any relationship, in any family, no matter what age your children. But it becomes the key to heading off or sorting out all sorts and levels of misunderstanding and conflict when children become teenagers.

To truly communicate with someone else, and especially young people, you first have to listen. This may sound obvious, but how many times have you had a conversation with another person and realized that they weren't really listening to you? How often do you talk to someone, and know that they're simply waiting for a gap in your words to jump in with their pre-prepared speech? And how often have you talked with someone and not known whether they were listening or interested, because their attention appeared to be elsewhere? It's more than a little off-putting to open your heart while your confidant's eyes are fixed on the distant horizon.

The ability to listen sensitively is a skill we have to learn; it is not an art we're born with. Nobody can read minds – not even our own offspring's, however much we'd like to think we know what is going on in their skulls. If you want to understand what they think and feel, why they do certain things and how to get on the same wavelength, you have to enlist their point of view. So if you want to make it clear that you are paying attention, you need to know how.

Putting up barriers

It's actually very easy – depressingly easy – to stop someone from opening up to you. As a parent, you want to be available and sympathetic, but how often do you interrupt, impose your own ideas, finish sentences, switch off, talk too much or contradict the other person when you're trying to communicate? You may feel, while doing all these things, that you're involved with the dialogue and these interventions show how much you are engaging with your teenager. From their point of view, we may be doing nothing of the sort. The dialogues between John and his daughter Nicci in Chapter 2 are an illustration of this misunderstanding.

In all these scenarios, the way John responded caused barriers, preventing Nicci from confiding in him or getting what she wanted and needed from the conversation. Each time, however much he might have wanted to be sympathetic and helpful, by interrupting, imposing his ideas, finishing sentences, switching off, talking too much or contradicting, he stopped Nicci dead in her tracks. Think about the people you might know or have seen on television or heard on radio who you would say are good listeners. What is it that they do to make you feel comfortable and able to confide in them, and get what you need from the exchange? There is a skill to listening in a way that opens people up instead of shutting them down. Two highly effective skills are active listening and reflective listening.

Communication is always two-way. To get your point of view across you first have to establish that you will also listen.

Active listening

Active listening is when you show in many non-verbal ways that you are paying attention to what the other person is saying. You don't interrupt, ask questions, or make comments; you make eye contact, nod and make the sort of 'Uh-huh', 'Um' and 'Ah?' sounds that say, 'Yes, go on, I'm listening to you.'

Try active listening with your teenager by using this exercise. The rules are that each of you should take a turn being the listener and the speaker. Use a kitchen timer or alarm clock. Toss for who goes first. The speaker gets two minutes to talk, on any subject they choose. Their only task is to keep talking. The listener's task is to hear and encourage the other person to talk – but without saying a single word.

You may like to try this a few times. After the first attempt, share impressions of the process. How did it feel to listen and not ask questions? How did it feel to be listened to, knowing you wouldn't be interrupted? The problem with chipping in with your own ideas is that it often doesn't help, as much as stop your teenager coming to an understanding and a solution. Often, your questions aren't really there to help the other person but to show that you know better, and simply saying, 'I understand' frequently begs the retort 'No you don't!' But making it clear you are listening and taking in what the other person is saying can be reassuring and empowering. Being heard gives the speaker a chance to hear themselves too. Instead of wasting energy on making you pay attention, or bringing the subject back to what they wanted to discuss, or arguing with advice that is inappropriate, they can bounce their own ideas off you and see their own way to a resolution. It often feels very awkward and odd at first, on both sides. You'll get used to it, and be amazed at exactly how effective it is as a tool. Once you've tried active listening, go one stage further and add reflective listening to your skills.

Reflective listening

Same rules – each of you should take a turn at being the listener and the speaker. Use a kitchen timer or alarm clock to time a two-minute period. The speaker gets two minutes to talk on any subject they choose. Their only task is to keep talking. The listener's task is to mirror back to the speaker what they have said. For example, this time, instead of saying 'Uh-huh' or 'Um' to what they say, repeat it. You can use their words or your own words. Reflective listening isn't just parroting, it's rephrasing and checking, which means you don't have to get it entirely right first time, every time – the speaker will correct you and it still works. The point is that you are making the attempt to listen and hear what they are saying, not putting your words into their mouth. It will sound a lot stranger to the person doing the reflective listening than to the speaker. Useful phrases to use in front of your mirrored speech may be: 'It sounds as if you're saying…'; 'I imagine you're feeling…'; 'It seems to me that what you're saying is…'; 'What I hear you saying is…'

You may like to try this a few times. After the first attempt, review how it felt. How did it feel to be focusing on the other person's words in order to be able to repeat them back accurately? How did it feel to have the other person repeating your words back at you? Having your own words coming back at you not only gives the speaker the chance to hear what they've said and clarify it, but makes them fully reassured that they have been understood. It often feels very awkward and odd at first, on both sides. You'll get used to it, and be amazed at exactly how effective it is as a tool.

USING LISTENING SKILLS

See how John got on with Nicci when he tried using these skills.

John: Had a good day, dear?

Nicci: Well, not really, Dad. Mrs Brown got on my case and told me off for not doing the science project the way she'd said we should.

John: Uh-huh?

Nicci: Yes. She said we had to do it in groups and I wanted to do it with Debbie and Beth.

John: Ummm?

Nicci: Well, Debbie was away all last week and Beth and me, we thought she was coming back so we did it together, 'cos we thought she'd be back in time to catch up.

John: You thought Debbie would be back in time for the three of you to finish the project together.

Nicci: Yes, but she's got flu so she isn't even going to be back this week. But Mrs Brown just ripped us off for doing it in a pair, she said it needed at least three of us and why hadn't we joined up with someone else. That wasn't fair, was it?

John: I can see you feel upset about this.

Nicci: Well, I suppose we should have told her last week that we were waiting for Debbie.

John: Uh-huh.

Nicci: It was a bit silly not to let her know, wasn't it?

John: You think it was silly not to let her know.

Nicci: Well, maybe the best thing would be to talk to her tomorrow and explain and say we're sorry for not having told her sooner.

John: So you're going to talk with Mrs Brown tomorrow.

Nicci: Yup. Thanks for helping, Dad.

Insight

Parents often find it hard to hang back and not jump in with a fix for every ill their teenager suffers. We're used to doing it all for them.

We can see from this successful scenario that listening, using a skilled approach can:

▶ *help make your relationship with your teenager closer and sort out problems*
▶ *build their self-esteem – and yours*
▶ *increase understanding and reduce frustration.*

The qualities of active listening include:

▶ *an inner attitude of acceptance, trust, care and a desire to understand, not sort out*
▶ *giving attention and being in the present*
▶ *an awareness of non-verbal communication*
▶ *using open questions*
▶ *checking out*
▶ *accepting and acknowledging feelings*
▶ *identifying needs*
▶ *asking questions which help a person move on by identifying how their needs can be met.*

Let's take a closer look at the qualities of active listening outlined above.

An inner attitude of acceptance, trust, care and a desire to understand, not sort out
If we are in conflict with our teenagers, an atmosphere can sometimes build up where we don't trust them or sometimes even care for them, and where we no longer accept what they tell us. We may not take the time to understand how they feel or why they say or do what they do and the only help we feel able to offer is instructions or demands on fixing the situation the way we see fit. When you not only listen to your teenager but really *hear* what they say, you'll accept, trust and care about them. But it can work the other way too. Even if relations between you are strained, if you make the effort to change your mindset and begin to accept and trust, you'll then find you can listen to them, and they to you.

Giving attention and being in the present

Our high tech, information culture works against both these skills; so often, communication with one person goes on at the same time as thinking about other people, thinking about things you should be doing, texting, mailing, messaging someone else and being plugged in to music while watching a screen. To listen effectively, both of you need to give each other attention, in the here and now. In a busy life, it takes effort to remind yourselves how important that is: 'Right! I'm turning off my mobile and the TV so I can pay attention to you. You too?'

Awareness of non-verbal communication

Your tone of voice, the way you make eye contact and lean towards someone shows them you are paying them full attention and listening as much as your words. If you want to listen effectively, and be heard, be as conscious of how you come across in your body language, not just what you say.

Using open questions

As we've already seen, open questions are an important tool in listening. An open question invites your teenager to talk to you along their own lines, not your agenda. For example, you might ask, 'How was school today? Were the tests all right? How was maths?' and an answer might only tell you about school work. But if you ask, 'Tell me about your day?' you may then learn news far more momentous to your teenager: a quarrel with a friend, a new bond with an ex-enemy, a rumour about some after-school activity on offer soon. Open questions allow your teen to tell you what is important to them, and without restrictions.

Checking out

Checking out means briefly feeding back the gist of what has been said to show you've understood. Sometimes you get it right, sometimes you get it wrong – in which case the other person can correct you. Not checking out means you soldier on, possibly having lost the plot, which doesn't help. It's a vital part of listening and talking.

Accepting and acknowledging feelings

Sometimes, what our teenagers say is painful or uncomfortable
to us. But if you want to build a level of trust, you need to listen
and accept what you hear. Arguments or lack of understanding
so often come about between young people and their parents
because we don't accept what they are saying, for example:

'I hate you!'	'You don't mean that.'
'I've had an awful day!'	'I'm sure it's not as bad as all that, dear.'
'I'm hungry!'	'You can't be, we've just eaten.'
'I'm fed up. I wish I was dead.	'You're exaggerating!'
'It's not fair!'	'You're just tired.'
'Nobody ever listens to me!'	'Calm down – stop shouting.'
'Nothing ever goes right for me!'	'Don't be so intense – you take things so seriously.'

DENYING FEELINGS

When you deny a feeling, it doesn't go away, but the person
expressing that emotion is left with a triple load. They still have
the uncomfortable emotion, because even though they've tried to
offload on to you and thus deal with it, you've shoved it back into
their arms. They also have the additional emotional burden of
anger, hurt or bafflement (or all three) with you for not hearing.
Worst of all, they must grapple with confusion and distrust of their
own feelings. They've clearly announced their emotional state to
you, and you've said it doesn't exist.

Have that happen enough times in your life and you do start to
doubt your own responses.

We don't necessarily do this because we disbelieve what our
teenagers say. We genuinely feel that if we can argue away the
feelings, deny their very existence, we can banish them. Alas, it

doesn't work like that. Sometimes, we see their response as a comment on and criticism of ourselves. If our children feel bad, we assume we are failing them and we rush to make it better, as if accepting their unhappiness will intensify the distress and denying it will make it vanish into thin air.

ACKNOWLEDGING EMOTIONS
In fact, accepting, acknowledging and allowing bad feelings is the first step in learning to handle them and to let go of them. Good listening is about allowing the other person an opinion, not surrendering your own. You can listen to what your teenager says, and accept that this is how they might be feeling or seeing a situation, without having to agree with their point of view or condoning what they think. In fact, sometimes being a 'Yes person' and agreeing with everything they say prevents them from progressing. If you side with them when they protest the teacher has been unfair or their best friend was horrible, you prevent your teen from working through their emotions to accept that they might have contributed to the difficulty and need to compromise themselves. But by acknowledging their emotions and accepting that they exist, you tell them they are acceptable and valued by you. Everyone's entitled to be angry sometimes, and entitled to have conflicting feelings, too.

For example:

'I hate you!'	'I can hear you feel that you hate me at the moment.'
'I've had an awful day!'	'You feel you've had a bad time today.'
'I'm hungry!'	'You still feel hungry, even though we've just eaten.'
'I'm fed up. I wish I was dead!'	'You're really feeling bad.'
'It's not fair!'	'You're feeling very hard done by.'
'Nobody ever listens to me!'	'I can hear you're feeling unappreciated.'
'Nothing ever goes right for me!'	'You are feeling as if things aren't going right for you.'

We spend so much time and effort denying angry and negative feelings and trying to pretend to ourselves and everyone else that we don't feel like that. How many times have you said 'I'm fine, nothing's wrong!' when you might really have liked to scream 'I feel terrible!' and been given a hug. Teenagers have strong and genuine emotions – they feel, and you may be scared that their emotions can overwhelm them and you and get out of control. But reflecting on and allowing feelings doesn't prolong them, enlarge them or make them real where otherwise they would not emerge. What it does is allow them to be discharged. Even temper tantrums are actually very healthy – a good shout, moan or sob can get it all out of the system.

Part of the wish to deny feelings is the fear that we can't do anything to help them, and the helplessness that this engenders. You may be surprised to find that, sometimes, just acknowledging an emotion diminishes it, for example:

'I've had an awful day!'
'You feel you've had a bad time today.'
'I got caught in the rain and missed my bus and then I found I'd left my bus pass at home and I had to pay full fare.'
'You feel pretty fed up.'
'Yeah, well. Thanks, Dad! What's for supper?'

Listening to your teenager doesn't mean giving in to them. By accepting what they feel, you can also then go on to say you can't do anything about it unless they tell you what they're angry about. Sometimes, listening to and accepting the emotion also leads to your accepting a compromise on what you all do.

Insight
Denying emotions doesn't make them go away. Accepting them doesn't make them any more real than they already are.

Identifying needs
Accepting and acknowledging emotions is the first step to identifying the need underneath. Once we can listen to our

teenagers, we can take the next step of pinpointing with them exactly what is going on, for example:

> 'I had an awful day!'
> 'You feel you've had a bad time today.'
> 'Yeah, I had a dust-up with Sam.'
> 'You're really upset by that.'
> 'She said I'd let her down but I didn't mean to. I was late 'cos I was talking to Gita.'
> 'Sounds like you want to please everyone and have them like you – Sam and Gita too.'

Moving-on questions

Sometimes what people want and need is only for you to listen and hear them – to use active or reflective listening so they know that you sympathize and understand, and are supportive of them. Sometimes, however, what is needed is a push to help your teenager not only identify their needs but to move on and work out how they can be met. You may need to use 'moving-on questions' to advance them. A moving-on question might be: 'What would you like to happen?'; 'What would happen if...?'; 'What would it be like if...?' You may also need to challenge a lack of self-confidence, such as 'I can't do that', 'No one likes me', 'It's too difficult', or insistence that nothing can be done by asking: 'What stops you?'; 'How do you know that?'; 'How would it be if you could...?'; 'Who told you that?'

Negotiating and having a constructive argument

We can often find ourselves on the brink of an argument when our teenager comes to us with a request, or more likely, a demand. We may be tempted to put our foot down and give a quick ruling on what we think they should do. That's the time to go into negotiating mode. You may think, as an adult and a parent, you shouldn't be negotiating as it shows weakness and parents should always be in charge. If so, consider this; when it comes to living with teenagers, negotiation is always more effective than one person giving orders. So how can you negotiate?

The key rules for negotiating are:

- *talk when everyone is calm*
- *gather information*
- *listen to your child's views as well as letting them know what you need and why*
- *be clear about what is (and is not) negotiable*
- *pick your battles*
- *make an agreement*
- *build in reminders for agreements*
- *review boundaries regularly*
- *have lots of fun together.*

TALK WHEN EVERYONE IS CALM

Picking a neutral space and a time when everyone is relaxed is the best approach. Talking an issue through over a family meal or a cup of coffee can give all of you time to have your say and listen to the other side without feeling rushed or pressured. This also gives you the opportunity to consider the request before discussing it, by deferring it until you've made the coffee or all sat down for the meal. For example, if your son says, 'There's a party on Saturday – I'm going' or your daughter says, 'I'm not doing my homework tonight and that's that!' you ACT, don't react. Open the door to negotiation by acknowledging what has been said in a neutral way: 'There's a party and you want to go/You don't like doing homework on a Friday night. Let's talk it over at supper tonight/get a cup of coffee, sit down and discuss it.' Stay non-committal and take the time you need to think about how you feel.

GATHER INFORMATION

Once everyone is sitting down say, 'You'd like to go to the party/ You don't like doing homework at the beginning of the weekend.

I'd like to hear more and talk about it.' Ask for more information and listen. You may want to know: where the party is to be held; who's going to be there; whether parties like this have had trouble; whether it's a free-for-all or if there will be someone on the door to screen party-goers; whether there will be alcohol and what sort; what time they expect to come home and how. You may want to acknowledge they're feeling tired and jaded but need to know: when your teenager plans to do their homework; how they propose planning and preparing; whether they think they will allow enough time doing it later in the weekend. Take time to think about how you feel about the situation and what information you need to make your decision. If your teenager is pushing you for an answer, say that you can give them a 'No' quickly, but if they want your agreement to something, you need time to talk it through.

Insight

A useful statement to have prepared is 'If you want an answer now, it's no. If we can talk about it and you give me more time to consider, it may be yes.'

LISTEN TO YOUR CHILD'S VIEWS AS WELL AS LETTING THEM KNOW WHAT YOU NEED AND WHY

In a discussion, to reach a settlement that everyone is happy with, it's important that both sides feel they have been heard, even if they don't get exactly or all that they want. Swap between listening and acknowledging your teenager's feelings and needs, and stating your own. When making your feelings known, use 'I' messages to put your point across. Instead of saying 'No!' or 'I'm not sure you can be trusted' say, 'I feel worried about that because I need to know you'll be safe/you'll still do what is required.' Be prepared to hear your teenager's feelings and needs underneath their words. The heartfelt cry, 'I hate you – you spoil everything!' really means: 'All my friends will be there, I'll feel left out if I don't go/I'm just not in a fit state after school to do my homework, I need a break!' Make it clear that their feelings and needs are important to you and be aware that if anyone becomes 'emotionally flooded', you may need to call a time out and come back to the discussion later.

BE CLEAR ABOUT WHAT IS (AND IS NOT) NEGOTIABLE

You might like to make it clear from the start what issues you can and will budge on – and those that you won't and can't. You might relax the boundaries if your teenager can overcome some of your objections, for example, guaranteeing a non-drinking safe driver or proving that an older brother/bouncer will be on the door of a party. Going to a party where there may be a genuine risk of violence could be something non-negotiable. Driving home in an overcrowded car or being driven by someone who drinks and drives – or drives recklessly – may be another. So is avoiding homework with excuses. Make it clear that you may be prepared to review other issues, either as your teenager gets older, or if they can show due cause.

PICK YOUR BATTLES

There are certain issues you will want to debate – parties, sexual behaviour, alcohol and drugs and driving unsafely. There are many issues teenagers and parents endlessly bicker over – music, clothes, and friends. When you negotiate, focus on the issues that really matter. If you back off over the small things and don't try to over-control, you can stand firm when you need to. Negotiating takes time and can feel messy while you are in the middle of it. You may find yourself thinking 'I can't be bothered with this.' But negotiating is actually quicker than a whole saga of shouting, storming off, sulking, and door slamming. Laying down the law may be quicker still – but you will probably have to put up with a resentful, miserable atmosphere. Or the result could be that they sneak behind your back, laying themselves open to even more risk by doing the things you don't want them to do, unconsidered.

MAKE AN AGREEMENT

Once you've gathered in all the information you need, heard the feelings and opinions of your teenager and been satisfied they have heard yours too, come to an agreement. Sometimes a conflict is about needs and beliefs. For example, you and your teenager may never agree on the belief that every teenager has a right to party as often as possible, or that homework is a waste of time. What you can do is discuss and agree to differ on your opposing beliefs, then negotiate agreements around behaviour so that important needs of yours – safety, preparation for their future – can be met while they also get something, such as agreement to go to a party or defer homework to an agreed time.

Check out that the agreement meets your needs and your teenager's needs and that the outcome is acceptable to you both. Check out that you both have the same understanding of what has been agreed. One way of checking this out is to say 'Yes' to a contract. State clearly – or even write down – exactly what you and your teenager have said will be done. Work out a fair exchange and one that you can both agree on. Make a precise record of the decision, including:

▶ *what you've both agreed to do*
▶ *how you agree to do it*
▶ *when you agree to do it by*
▶ *for how long you have agreed to do this.*

Build in reminders for agreements
Anyone can forget the details of an agreement. They can be about one-time specifics like parties or more general issues such as bedtimes, when homework is done or household chores. If you think agreed behaviour is slipping, remind your teenager without blaming them – having a written agreement makes this easier.

Insight
Stick contracts and agreements on a notice board in a family room. That way, you can all see and refer to them.

Review agreements regularly
Review such arrangements regularly. If the terms of the agreement are not being met, discuss why and whether the contract needs to be redrawn or whether something needs to be adjusted. Young

people need to test boundaries from time to time – be prepared to stand firm unless it's time to review the agreement.

HAVE LOTS OF FUN TOGETHER

Teenagers cooperate more if they enjoy being a family, rather than feeling that family life is just about rules. If you want to encourage them to cooperate, the first step is to make most gatherings around the table an enjoyable experience where the family laughs and jokes, swaps stories about their day, and shares opinions in a positive, caring atmosphere. Then, when you do need to resolve an issue, the practice gained in sharing the fun times helps you to focus on feelings and needs, and swap between listening and expressing yourself, on the route to a resolution.

NEGOTIATING WITH TEENAGERS

Taking the time to negotiate with your teenager:

▶ *takes the win/lose out of the situation – everyone gains*
▶ *increases trust and their willingness to cooperate; when they know you'll listen to them, they'll listen to you, and when you do have to say no, they'll accept it was for a good reason and that you will agree something they want another day*
▶ *increases mutual understanding and reduces frustration; taking your time and showing respect lowers the temperature and helps them to ask questions and listen in a calm atmosphere*
▶ *sets up a format for dealing with disagreements and conflict; once you have tried it and it has worked, you all know the rules for subsequent discussions and agreements.*

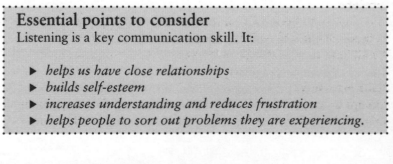

Essential points to consider
Listening is a key communication skill. It:

▶ *helps us have close relationships*
▶ *builds self-esteem*
▶ *increases understanding and reduces frustration*
▶ *helps people to sort out problems they are experiencing.*

Responding in a way that helps

If you're listening and talking, it means you can respond in a way that helps rather than hinders your teenager solve their own problems. There are quite a few responses you may have had thrown at you when young, and it's worth considering them to see if, rather than following the pattern that you found unhelpful, you might learn a more supportive and effective way of dealing with problems.

You may have learned to respond by:

▶ *dismissing*
▶ *labelling*
▶ *being inattentive*
▶ *deflecting*
▶ *directing*
▶ *denying emotions*
▶ *trivializing views*.

Your teenager may come to you and say, 'All my friends are going to be at the shopping mall on Saturday and I've got to go with you to Grandma's. I'm going to miss out. It's not fair.' Let's look at some unhelpful responses to this problem.

Dismissing
You may feel it would take the sting away to say, 'Oh, that's no big deal. It happens to everyone. Nothing special's going to happen and they may not have such a good time.'

Labelling
You may try to buck up your teenager by making them feel that their complaint makes them unacceptable: 'Don't be such a baby. We all have to miss things sometimes – it's part of growing up.'

Being inattentive
Perhaps they approach you at a bad time and you've got your mind on something else: 'What? I've got my hands full. You'll be fine.'

Deflecting

Maybe you'll decide the best tactic is to change the subject: 'Oh never mind. Hey – the programme you like is on – go watch it.'

Directing

You may try to manage the situation by telling your teen exactly what you think they should do, or not do: 'Now, I suggest you tell all your friends you'll be away. I can ring them for you if you like. That way they'll know what's happening and I'm sure they'd hold back on anything exciting for when you get back...'

Denying emotions or opinions

Faced by a distraught teenager, many parents feel the best thing is to wish the pain away, by insisting it isn't there: 'You don't feel upset, do you? Of course not. It'll be fine.'

Having views trivialized

You may downplay the issue, hoping that if you can paint it in a less significant light, the situation will reduce in importance to your adolescent: 'What a silly thing to be worried about. There are far more essential things in life to fuss over.'

Insight

There are always solutions to be found. The trick is to help your teenager become part of the solution rather than the entire problem.

How should you respond?

So how should you respond? Constantly teaching your teen by saying, 'Do this. Do it this way' is actually as forbidding and disempowering as constantly telling them, 'No' and 'Don't'. It's certainly less effective than encouraging them to learn how to do it their own way. Telling them what not to do deprives them of self-esteem and self-confidence. Telling them what to do deprives them of trust; you don't trust them to work it out themselves and you stop them learning how.

Dismissing, labelling, being inattentive, deflecting, denying emotions and trivializing views all fail to help. Being enthusiastic about your teenager and what they do and praising them is far more effective than criticizing or directing them. Addressing issues and describing what you are hearing works. You have an AIM – and the aim is to help:

Acknowledge feelings: 'You really wanted to meet your friends. You're upset you have to come on a family event instead.'

Identify needs: 'Sounds like it's important to you not to be left out.'

Move on: 'What can we do to find a solution?'

You might agree that your teenager can sit this family visit out but go another time. You might help them to agree that the family visit is important and simply having their protest heard was enough to let off steam and come around. You might agree to go and return a bit earlier so they can manage both. Whatever you both decide, listening and talking will help you respond in a way that is better for you both.

GIVE IT IN FANTASY

Sometimes, simply being able to recognize how strongly your teenager wants this particular thing can help. You may even want to grant their wishes, but in fantasy not reality, to let them know how much you see their point of view, for example:

'I'm fed up. I wish I was dead!'
'You're really feeling bad.'
'Life is awful!'
'You sound as if things are pretty hopeless.'
'Oh, Dad. I'm never going to get a boyfriend I like.'
'I wish I could wave a magic wand and make the perfect man appear for you.'
'That's silly!'
'Maybe, but I wish I could, because I would if I could.'
'I know you would. Thanks, Dad.'

THE BROKEN RECORD

There will be times when you have to draw and keep to a boundary in the face of protest and even hostility. As a parent you may have to be unpopular occasionally because you are the adult; you do make the decisions and you can know best. A useful technique for putting your foot down, when it's justified, is the 'broken record'.

Even when you do listen, talk and use all the necessary strategies to negotiate and seek consensus, you may not get the 'right' response. Young people, after all, are not robots and won't run with the intended programme just because you seem to push the correct buttons. They have their own thoughts and agendas, and may need some time to see in what ways they too may benefit from your new style of parenting. If you're coming up against arguments for arguments sake, or if they are just dragging their heels, don't allow yourself to be diverted or drawn into arguments, just be insistent. The keys to the broken record are:

▶ *say something that shows you've heard and recognize what your teenager is saying to you and sympathize: 'I can see... you say... I realize... that may be how it feels to you...'*
▶ *be clear and specific about what you want done*
▶ *do not lose your temper*
▶ *stand your ground.*

Here is an example of a successful broken record exchange:

Mary: Si, you agreed to tidy this room up by the time I got home and it's not been done. Please do it while I make tea.
Si: Oh, Mum. I'm busy now.
Mary: I can see you have things you want to do, but I'd like you to tidy the room now.
Si: I'll do it after tea.
Mary: You say you'll do it after tea, but I'd like you to do it now please.
Si: You're always nagging me!
Mary: I can see how you might feel I'm getting at you. But please, I want you to tidy the room now.

Si:	God, you're just doing this parenting thing at me again and I hate it!
Mary:	That may be how it feels to you, but I'd like you to tidy this room please.
Si:	Mum, I've had a really hard day. Can't I just have a few minutes peace and then I'll do it?
Mary:	I realize you've had a rough day. Please tidy this room up now.
Si:	Okay. Okay. I'm doing it.
Mary:	Thank you. I appreciate that.

Keep your temper – but persist.

Be polite, don't raise your voice or lose your temper. Persist, repeating the request and go on far longer than you might think would be comfortable. If you keep it calm and don't rise to any bait or argument, you will be surprised how many times you can simply repeat a message. If you're not getting anywhere, after as many attempts as you feel able to repeat, try one final time:

> *'I've asked you ten times and I'd like to ask you once more to please tidy this room now.'*

If you then feel you are getting nowhere or are losing your cool, break off saying:

> *'Okay, we'll leave this for ten minutes and then we'll discuss it again.'*

Go away and congratulate yourself for not having lost your temper and for having left the door open for further talk. After ten minutes, go back. You may find your teenager has started doing what you requested – if so, thank them without further comment. If not, resume and continue. If you do this without reproaches, complaint or threats and without getting hooked into arguing, it isn't nagging. It's making yourself clear. Your teen will get the message that you're serious, won't be deflected, drawn or incited to violence (verbal or otherwise) and that you will persist. Sooner or later, they are likely to cooperate.

HOW TO LET THEM SEE IT FROM YOUR POINT OF VIEW

We talk about looking up to or looking down on people. It's
common for people to make comparisons and judge others on
things such as looks, intellect, financial position or career. How we
react to authority may depend on where we think we fit into the
order of things. But looking up and down can also be physical –
we all assume that children, whom adults look down on, are to be
looked after and guided. The balance of power in a family changes
as our teenagers grow taller, become more emotionally mature and
more able to argue rationally. Teenagers, who are finding their
place in life, testing and pushing boundaries in order to determine
their own sense of authority, will push those boundaries as hard as
possible. An interesting exercise is to ask people to stand up and
arrange themselves in a line in order of height. Ask each person
how they feel about their position in line. Ask if it affects how they
see themselves in terms of their standing in the family and how that
might have changed in the last few years.

TURNING THINGS UPSIDE DOWN

When you have had that conversation, it can be useful to offer
your young people a day or a weekend in which positions in the
house are turned upside down. If you want to know how your
teenager feels about the relationships in your house, and to offer
them a chance to be in your shoes, have a day where they play your
roles and you play theirs. If you think they would take advantage
of this to point score or work off grudges, what does that say
about the way you treat them? If you think that it would be risky
and dangerous, negotiate some mutually agreed rules beforehand.
Obviously taking the car and/or emptying the drinks cabinet would
be ill-advised on their part, but if they are going to act like an
adult – which is the point of the exercise – they wouldn't behave

irresponsibly, would they? The aim of the exercise is for them to experience what it may be like to have to organize the family, thinking ahead and making sure there is food in the house and that it gets to the table at the right time, that everyone does their chores and fulfils their responsibilities. It is also for you to see what it's like to be at the receiving end of instructions and having to ask permission to see you friends, turn on the television or use the house phone. Ideas-storm together exactly what you feel you have to do over a weekend and hand over responsibility for that.

Then, having tried this, the following weekend role-play being with each other as adult to adult. Treat your teenager the same way as you would treat your partner or visitors, consciously dealing with your teenager as if they were the same age as you, and see how this affects your behaviour, and theirs.

YOUR TURN

If you want to put your foot down successfully with your teenager over the issues that matter, it helps to pick your battles and only insist when it's really important.

Of these subjects, which would you want to stand firm on (but negotiate how you're both going to agree on that) talk over with them (because there is some wiggle room) or let go (because it really doesn't matter in the long run)?

	Stand firm	Negotiate	Let go
Untidiness in their own room			
Untidiness in family rooms			
Doing chores			
TVs, laptops and mobiles in their rooms			
Having a tattoo or piercing			
What time they come home at night			
Watching adult content films or games			
Their clothes			
Doing homework as soon as they get home			
Their friends			
Drinking at parties			
Drinking and driving			
What music they listen to			
Playing music loudly			

Talk over with another adult, and then your teenager, what you have written and why. After discussion, are there any changes you would make?

THINGS TO REMEMBER

▶ *To truly communicate with your teenager, you first have to listen.*

▶ *Using active and reflective listening skills can help you to get your young person to open up to you.*

▶ *Responding in a way that helps may mean having to rethink the ways you have responded previously.*

▶ *Pick your battles – don't give the same weight to the trivial and the serious. If you can let go on the small things, you are more likely to be able to stand firm on those issues that really matter.*

▶ *Teenagers cooperate more if they enjoy being a family, rather than feeling family life is just about rules.*

▶ *Aim to develop an inner attitude of acceptance, trust and care, and a desire to understand, not sort out. Most of all, try to have fun together.*

6

Whose problem is this?

In this chapter you will learn:
- *how to separate your problems from theirs*
- *how to* not *fix it*
- *how to give your teenager responsibility*
- *what helps and what hinders.*

One of the skills you'll need as the parent of a teenager is to know your limits – to know what is yours to manage and what is theirs. When dealing with a teenager it's important to be able to separate their problems from your own. Just as teenagers are struggling to set their own boundaries, establish their own independence and separate from their parents, so parents in a way have to do the same. You need to help them, and help yourself, by knowing where you and your sphere of influence ends – and theirs begins.

As a parent you often have a tendency to want to sort out your teenager's problems. After all, when they were babies it's what you had to do – recognize when they were hungry, cold, tired, needing a cuddle – and satisfy that need. As a child, you did the same – protected them, nurtured them, cared for them. Now they are a teenager, you may try to do as you have always done because you think that is the best thing you can do – protect, nurture and fix anything that hurts or worries them. It may seem the best thing to do, but it is not always the most helpful thing to do. When I was a child my mother would sometimes say, 'I'm cold! Go and put on a sweater!' It was a joke, but it contained a kernel of truth – sometimes parents can't separate their own comfort and their teenager's. In seeking to do your best you may stray into making inappropriate demands to try and satisfy the wrong one. When you are feeling protective about something that is upsetting them, or frustrated or angry about something your teenager is or isn't doing, it usually helps to get clear in your own mind why it is a problem for you.

What is 'problem ownership', and how can it help us?

Problem ownership is about locating whose needs are not being met in a particular situation. It's important because it's only when you can work out who 'owns' the problem that you can find a solution for it. Think for a moment about the apparently silly scenario of a child being told to put on a sweater because the parent is cold. The child puts on the sweater – and probably feels uncomfortably hot and then gets cranky and behaves badly, because in fact they had felt perfectly comfy without it and did not need it. Meanwhile, the parent goes on feeling cold because it's they who needed the extra layer, and they get bad tempered. Sooner or later, a row results. It's only when the parent can say, 'Seeing my child run around in this weather makes *me* feel cold, but *they* seem fine. I'll go and put something warm on', that we achieve a proper result.

We've looked at ways of understanding feelings and needs in Chapter 3. We can use these strategies to work out what the most helpful thing is for us to do in the many different situations that arise with our teenagers. When there's a problem, the most effective first step is to establish 'Whose problem is this?' The way you can work this out is by asking, 'Who's upset here? Whose needs are not being met or need meeting first – mine or my teenager's?' The person whose needs aren't being met 'owns' the problem. The person who 'owns' the problem is the one who needs to do something to change the situation.

Insight

It's neither unusual nor abnormal for parents to have some difficulty knowing and acknowledging where their child ends and they begin – to feel their pain and want to fix it, or to confuse your needs with theirs. Remember the sweater – is it you or they who needs to wrap up warm?

Remember ACT:
- ▶ Adult *is to remind you to ask yourself about what is going on for you – what are you feeling, what are your needs?*
- ▶ Child *is to remind you to ask what is going on for your teenager – what are they feeling, what are their needs?*
- ▶ Tools *is to remind you to look at what you could say or do to help all of you get what you want and need from the situation.*

So when something is happening that you find upsetting and you want to be different, stop and think about what's going on for you and your teenager before you speak. It's not about whether what they are doing is 'wrong' or bad behaviour. It will be about behaviour which is stopping one of you getting your needs met.

IS THIS YOUR PROBLEM, OR MINE?

Sometimes our children's behaviour causes us a problem. For example, you come home and your teenager is playing a game on the computer console or TV, with the sound turned up as loud as possible. The phone rings and when you answer, you can't hear what is being said.

The reality is that it's not your teenager's problem – the sound perfectly meets their needs. It is your problem, because you need it to be quieter, so you can hear. So responsibility for that problem lies with you. When you own the problem, you need to let other people know what is going on for you and what you would like to happen, if the situation is to find a happy resolution. Instead of shouting at your teenager and dumping it in their lap, 'Turn that annoying row down! What's the matter with you? Have you no consideration?' making them feel as if it's their problem, try expressing your own problem using a clear direct statement: 'Hey boys. I can't hear what's being said. Can you please turn the sound down while I'm on the phone?'

At other times it may be your teenager that has the problem, such as panicking on a school day morning because they can't find their shoes, haven't done their homework or are running late because they overslept, as this case study highlights.

Case study – Misha's story

Misha brought a problem to her parenting group that was bothering her. 'For the third time this week my youngest left his lunch at home. It's driving me crazy because he must have done this at least a dozen times this term – if it's not lunch it's his gym kit or something. Luckily, I work only a street away but it means I have to rush around and go in early to be able to it fit in dropping it off. How can I make him remember?' Other participants came up with various ideas – leaving notes, checking him before he leaves, until the obvious question was asked: whose problem is this? 'Well,' said Misha, 'I know you're going to say his, but I worry if he hasn't got his lunch or if he gets in trouble for not having his kit.' 'Okay,' said one mother, 'but if it's your problem then you can't complain. If you want it solved then you have to state squarely where it belongs. If you go on making it your problem he has no reason to change his behaviour, has he?' Misha was obviously startled by this, and asked, 'So what should I do?' The group all laughed, and one dad said, 'Let him stew! It's his problem so let him solve it. Tell him you won't be bringing any more left-behind kit to school from Monday so if he leaves it, it stays left. He'll learn.' A week later, Misha reported she'd told her son he was on his own, and when he called on day three to say he'd left his lunch, she said, 'Tough.' She said she'd felt awful all day but was amazed to have her son tell her that evening, 'You should have done that ages ago, Mum. I sorted it. It's my fault, anyway.' Three weeks later, she reported no more incidents had come up since then.

Solving their own problems

If it's your child's needs that aren't being met, it's helpful if you are clear in your own mind that they 'own' the problem. It's important to let them solve their own problems – to come to an understanding of what the feelings and the needs are, and to work out what they may do to solve the situation – if indeed, they can.

One of the lessons you sometimes have to learn yourself, and pass on to your child, is that some problems don't have a neat or comfortable solution. All you can do is to accept it – which is a solution in itself. You can't, for instance, make a non-residential father return, or a girl or boy they're attracted to return their feelings if they don't feel the same. All you can do is acknowledge the pain and help them get over it.

Being clear that they 'own' the problem doesn't mean you just leave them to it. It means that you give them support to sort it out for themselves, with help if necessary – help that they decide upon and ask for. Encouraging them to own their problems furthers your teenager in growing emotionally and becoming more responsible. Leaving responsibility with your teenager encourages them to learn how to handle upsets and develops their ability to take responsibility for themselves. The most helpful thing you can do is support them and help them work out what they can do to sort situations out, not rush in to fix it for them.

Insight

Helping your teenager out when they have a problem can mean that problems persist. After all, if they are always rescued they have no incentive to make changes. Give love and support, but let them fix their own stuff.

WHY YOU ALWAYS FEEL THE NEED TO HELP

Parents often have a tendency to want to sort out their teenager's problems, for several reasons. You tell yourself it is because they may make a hash of it – they need your help. For example, you might jump forward to take a full glass of water out of a young child's hands to stop them spilling it as they bring it from sink to table. Left entirely on their own, they may struggle. Carrying it for them means there are no spillages. But if you do that, what happens? A young child will not learn at that point to carry a glass carefully, making sure it doesn't spill. When they have to finally do it on their own, they may be more careless and clumsy than if they had had the chance to practise. As a result, they are likely to feel incompetent and incapable – not only about that exercise but many other things – because what they have learned is not that they can make mistakes but that they are clumsy, inept and stupid and you'll do it for them because you're so much better. Learning and making mistakes, while having their struggle respected and efforts acknowledged and encouraged, builds self-esteem and confidence. Having this learning process taken out of their hands, even if it then gets done 'properly', destroys self-worth. The question to ask sometimes may be, 'What happens if I let them try? Is it so bad?' If a child spills water, you just say, 'Oops! It's harder than you think, isn't it? Never mind, you'll get it. Go fetch a cloth to clear up!' Of course, there are some scenarios where the 'try it for yourself and learn' rule can be painful and dangerous – finding out that it's not a good idea to shove a fork into an electric socket, for example. But with these exceptions, taking on board the principle – which is that children and teenagers learn best and gain confidence from making their own mistakes, being told 'Go ahead, give it your best. You did that just right!' or 'Never mind, you'll do better next time' – is worth it.

Insight

'Respect the struggle' is a good motto for the parent of a teenager. Acknowledge it's hard but that you trust them to work it out for themselves. Offer to coach them and help them think through their options and ideas – but leave the decisions and the application to them. Given that sort of respect and support, they'll manage far better than you might expect.

MANAGING ON THEIR OWN

Even with your support, encouraging your teenager to manage on their own can prove difficult. Some problems can't be solved. Some take time and patience. Some require changes you or your teenager may not be prepared to make. But this is what real life is all about and the sooner they begin learning they have to make hard choices and work at compromises and negotiation, the better for them. It simply isn't giving them a good start on the road to adulthood and self-determination to make them dependent on others to sort out their problems, or for them to get the idea that they can't manage on their own.

It's better for you too. In the long run it can become a burden for a parent to be responsible for everything. It's tiring, it's distracting and it can lead to resentment and conflict: 'Do I have to do *everything* around here?' It can also lead to confusion. How many times have you gone head-to-head with your teenager when, if you thought about it in retrospect, you'd realize the two of you were talking different languages? For example, you may have felt it was their problem and tried to get them to do something about it; they felt no compunction to change – it wasn't about something that bothered them. Or perhaps they dumped a predicament in your lap and became increasingly demanding and distressed because you weren't 'coming up with the goods' because it wasn't a matter you could do anything about.

WHY YOU PERSIST IN DOING IT FOR THEM

But here's the other reason why you may find it hard to support your teenager's self-determination. For all it avoids you being overworked and an aggrieved martyr, when you support your teenager in doing it for themselves, you hasten the day when they will no longer need you. Dealing with their own problems makes you redundant. It's hard to be contributing to your child separating from, and eventually leaving, you.

YOUR PROBLEM OR THEIRS?

Consider these scenarios:

▶ *Haji comes home upset because her best friend ignored her at school.*
▶ *Jason is angry because his girlfriend stood him up.*
▶ *Ange is frustrated because her new MP3 player, given to her for her birthday, is broken.*

Whose problems are these? It can be painful to hear that your teenager is feeling sad – feeling left out, losing a boy or girlfriend, having something they value go wrong. It can remind you of times in your own life when something similar happened. You may be keen to fix the situation they are suffering now: 'Because I know what it's like and I don't want you to suffer as I did.'

That's exactly the time to draw a clear boundary and decide whether it's your problem or theirs. It may feel hard but it's often important to resist getting sucked in. You don't help your child if you take it personally. That often comes from a secret and forlorn hope that you can rewrite the past. If you can help them, you almost feel it might mean you wouldn't have experienced that same loss in your own past. Your desire to fix the problem can be a way of easing your own pain – past or present. You need to be able to manage your own feelings in order to respond helpfully to your child – to bite a lip and stand back and let them manage their own discomfort. You can let them know you care by listening and being there, which can't necessarily take the pain away, but can help them cope and find their own resources.

In all these scenarios, it was the teenager who had the problem. Your problem might have been in wanting to do something – anything! – about it. But the best strategy would be to AIM to help:

▶ *Acknowledge feelings: 'You sound sad/angry/fed up.'*
▶ *Identify needs: 'You wanted her to like you/it was something you'd wanted for a long time.'*
▶ *Move on: 'What would you like to say to her/do now?'*

Now consider these scenarios:

▶ *Eddy is late for work because his daughters weren't on time for the school run.*
▶ *Tania is annoyed when her son Pete leaves a towel on the bathroom floor.*
▶ *Lee is worried when his daughter doesn't arrive home at the agreed time.*

Whose problems are these? You may be annoyed about something your teenager has done but if you want the situation to change you need to identify where the responsibility really lies. If you're the one who amends your behaviour because of something they do and then get upset, maybe the solution is to stop compensating. If you're late because they are late, analyse the situation, and lay out the new rules: 'Tomorrow I leave on time, whatever state you're in. If you're not ready you'll just have to make your own way to school. What could you do to make sure that doesn't happen? Is there anything I can do to help?' You might agree to give them a five-minute warning, and help them prepare their school bags the night before. You might need to acknowledge that it is your problem: 'Pete, I get upset when towels are left on the floor, not on the rail. I'd like you to hang up your towel in future please so I don't get angry.' Or 'I get worried when you don't get home at the time you said. If it happens again I'd like you to ring and tell me you're running late please. If you've got a problem with getting home, tell me and let's see if we can sort it.'

> **Insight**
> Always keep promises, always carry out sanctions. If your
> teenager can trust you to say what you mean and mean what
> you say, your relationship will thrive.

You could apply the skill of problem-solving to this, which we will look at in the next chapter. But once you've talked it over, if you've said you'll do something (or not do something), such as leave on time, throw wet towels onto a bed if they aren't hung up to dry, or refuse permission for your teenager to go out until they can respect your anxieties, keep your resolve and do it. Being clear about where the responsibility lies – it's your anxieties or irritation that is at stake here – and you can work far more effectively towards agreeing a solution.

Sometimes it will be a shared problem, in which case you will need to listen and negotiate.

In a situation where both people have the problem because both have unmet needs, you need to decide whose needs need to be met first or share the problem: 'How can we sort this out together?'

> **Essential points to consider**
> ▶ *Know your limits – what is yours to manage and what is your teenager's?*
> ▶ *Only when you work out who 'owns' the problem can you find a solution for it.*
> ▶ *It is all-important to help a teenager to deal with their own problems, to work out what they can do to solve the situation.*
> ▶ *Don't persist in trying to do everything for them. It is a natural process for them to develop their own independence and you should help, not hinder, them to achieve this.*

What helps, what hinders?

A useful exercise is to think of a time you talked to someone when you had a problem or were upset. If they were not at all helpful, what did they say and do? What was their attitude? What did they say and do to make it difficult? Sit down, think carefully and make a note of the elements that might have contributed: their tone of voice, their body language, their behaviour.

Then think of another time you talked to someone when you had a problem or were upset. What did they say and do that was really helpful? What was their attitude? Again, think carefully and make a note of the elements that might have contributed: their tone of voice, their body language, their behaviour. When you can pinpoint both unhelpful and helpful behaviour you can often eliminate the bits that get in the way and increase your use of the aspects that help when talking with your teenager.

Case study – Mick's story

Mick came for help after a particularly bruising series of arguments with his son, Ryan. 'He'd been having a tough time at school and every time he came home I'd be on his case, asking him what

(Contd)

had happened and whether his marks were improving, and if not, why not. He said he was having a problem with one teacher and I just said it was his fault and was telling him how to sort it. I can look back and cringe now because all it ever ended in was shouting matches – the whole family was suffering. It was my wife who said we had to find another way, this wasn't working. So we had a couple of parenting sessions and I have to say it all made sense. When I stopped feeling "Don't you tell me how to raise my children!" I tried listening, and reflecting back. I remembered this guy I used to know when I was at school, who really helped me, and I tried to listen to Ryan in the sort of way I remembered this guy had. He respected me, and he'd just sit and nod and let me get on with it. And I put myself in Ryan's shoes. When I did that, one of the things that struck me was that maybe he was right – he did have a problem with this teacher. The teacher was very good, but I asked around and heard from some other people that he can take against the kids who are smart with him. When I stood back, Ryan and I were able to work out a few things he could do, with me cutting him some slack, and him trying a bit harder. I changed – I stopped nagging. Ryan changed, inasmuch as he started doing more work and planning his time better. I could help him with that, once he didn't see it as me telling him what to do.'

This case study illustrates the following useful points:

▶ *When your teenager has a problem you can respond most helpfully by supporting them rather than sorting it out for them. The way you can do this is by listening.*
▶ *When you listen you give your child a chance to express the feelings and gradually come back into a balanced state where they can start to think through the problem or let go of the feelings and move on.*
▶ *When a child is upset, they can't think straight or begin to sort out what they want to do – they are overwhelmed or 'emotionally flooded'.*

▶ *It is useful to think of a time you've talked to someone when you had a problem or were upset and what they said and did was not at all helpful. What was their attitude? What did they say and do?*

▶ *It also helps to then think of a time you've talked to someone when you had a problem or were upset and what they said and did that was really helpful. What was their attitude? What did they say and do?*

YOUR TURN

It's important to know whose problem it is when you're dealing with teenagers. If it's your stuff, you need to deal with it. If it's theirs, they do – perhaps with support from you. But it only leads to arguments if you're on their case for something that is actually your problem, or trying to fix something that is theirs.

In these scenarios – whose problem is it?

	Teenager's problem	Parent's problem
Jane is furious with her son Tom because he talked for ages about going youth hostelling with one friend and now he says he's going camping with another set of friends.		
Sandi has lost her mobile phone and is badgering her mum to buy her a new one.		
Lee has broken up with his first girlfriend and is miserable.		
Neil has forgotten his lunch for the third time this week and asks his mum to drop it off at school.		
Patty has announced she has to have her sweater for school today – it's dirty, at the bottom of her bag.		
Paul doesn't want to do German for A level and his dad wants to talk to Paul's teacher to insist he does.		

Talk these through with another adult and then your teenager. Did you and your teenager differ at first about whose problem it was? Did you agree eventually?

THINGS TO REMEMBER

▶ *The skill to try to develop is to know your limits – to know what is yours to manage and what is your teenager's.*

▶ *Only when you have worked out who 'owns' the problem can you find a proper solution.*

▶ *Having your teenager 'own' their own problems does not mean just leaving them to it. It means giving them support to sort it out for themselves – with help if they ask for it.*

▶ *Think back to your own teenage years and recall what was good or bad in the way your parents and other adults dealt with your problems; what helped and what hindered you?*

▶ *Your teenager dealing with their own problems makes you redundant. It's hard to contribute to your child separating from and eventually leaving you – but that's the natural journey to independence you must help them to take.*

7

Points of conflict

In this chapter you will learn:
- *what the major issues are and how to deal with them*
- *what is often behind the arguments*
- *how you and your teenager can have different beliefs*
- *how to understand your needs and their needs*
- *how to use the six-point plan to resolve difficulties and conflict.*

Parents and teenagers will argue. You'll snipe, bicker and quarrel, and it will be about major issues such as drinking and driving and getting qualifications or a job, and minor issues such as tidying their rooms. Common issues that teenagers and parents conflict over include:

- ▶ *friends and when to see them*
- ▶ *their appearance*
- ▶ *tidiness and chores*
- ▶ *use of technology such as the internet and mobiles*
- ▶ *money*
- ▶ *food and eating*
- ▶ *sex, drugs and rock and roll*
- ▶ *family change and loss*
- ▶ *homework and school attendance.*

What is behind the conflict?

A lot of the time, what we're arguing about is not actually the reason we're in conflict. A row over whether your teenager comes in on time and eats the food you make them can be about your feelings of rejection and loss. Once upon a time, they wanted to share dinner times with you and ate the food you lovingly prepared. Now, their friends are more important to them than you and by turning up their nose at your meal, you feel as if they are throwing your love back in your face.

We're going to be looking at some of the common issues, but it needs to be said that it doesn't matter what the problem or issue is, the strategies for getting it sorted are the same. Whether it's about sex, drugs and rock and roll, money, eating or body piercings, you need to employ the same techniques and strategies, some of which we've already discussed. You'll need to keep in mind active and reflective listening techniques, using 'I' messages and open questions. You'll want to treat your teenager with respect, to practise what you preach and to jump off that roundabout of circular arguments. You'll accept and acknowledge their feelings and look for the needs underlying their behaviour. You'll AIM and ACT, and just occasionally hold that boundary firm and use the broken record.

Pick your battles

It's important to pick and choose the situations over which you want to disagree. You'll 'win' more often if the battle is about something you have good reason to want to insist upon. In other words, something which you might reasonably ask them to agree upon, or compromise over. The more fights you have over trivia or your personal taste as opposed to theirs – or their beliefs as opposed to yours – the more often you will get tied up in destructive and futile arguments. If you reserve 'no' for the few occasions when you feel strongly, your teenager is more likely to respect your point of view and come around with good grace.

When you and your teen aren't getting on, every little annoyance can blow up into a grand stand-up row. The trick is to save disputes for the important things – and to make those fights constructive discussions rather than conflicts. Try this exercise to work out your priorities. Sit down and write out:

▶ *the things you really don't want happening*
▶ *the things that just get on your nerves*
▶ *the things you actually like about your teenager.*

You can see these three categories as the three colours of a traffic light:

▶ **red** *is the stop sign: something you really need your teenager to change or not do*
▶ **yellow** *is a warning: something that puts you on edge that they should be aware of*
▶ **green** *is go: something you really like and they might think about doing more, as a way of getting the balance right.*

Complete the categories and talk over what you've written with your teenager. Why do these come to mind? Can you think about earlier times when these things have pleased or annoyed you? What does it remind you of when your teen does them? Sometimes what annoys or hurts us in the 'here and now' is more about an echo from the past than about what your teenager is actually doing. If you can locate the real source of your distress you may find the present behaviour worries you less.

Think of the relationships in a family as a piggy bank. Each time you have a row – and make an entry in the red or yellow category – you take a coin out. If you're forever taking out, pretty soon the bank is empty and you have nothing left. But every time you put a coin in – by making an entry in the green column – you fill up the bank. Having disputes does less harm to family harmony if you keep filling the bank as well as taking away.

Insight
Find ways of filling up the bank – sharing time together, seeing the positive aspects of your teenager and praising and thanking them.

Belief and value-based conflict

Some conflicts are about beliefs or values. That's not just about significant issues such as religion or whether family are more important than friends, but whether or not we believe it's important to look neat and whether it's necessary to tidy your room. You now have a battery of strategies to use to help you discuss and negotiate with your teenager.

You can ACT:

▶ Adult *is to remind you to ask yourself about what is going on for you – what are you feeling, what are your needs?*
▶ Child *is to remind you to ask what is going on for your teenager – what are they feeling, what are their needs?*
▶ Tools *is to remind you to look at what you could say or do to help all of you get what you want and need from the situation.*

You can AIM:

▶ *Acknowledge feelings: 'You sound fed up.'*
▶ *Identify needs: 'I want you to tidy your room and you disagree.'*
▶ *Move on: 'What are we going do about it?'*

You can only negotiate with the goal of each person getting their important needs met. You cannot negotiate to change your teenager's beliefs. You may want to, and try to influence them, but beliefs are something people build for themselves and hold to for their own reasons. Going head-to-head over a belief can be futile and frustrating, and often that's what leads to circular and dead-end arguments. Being clear about whether a conflict is about needs or beliefs can help you avoid those arguments that go nowhere and cause resentment and distance between you and your teenager. We are all likely to have different things that we are able to let go of and those we feel are beyond debate: one person may feel using drugs is a total no-no; another may feel that it is actually less important than the need to get academic qualifications. The bottom line is that if we are not prepared to negotiate at all, we are likely to be in constant conflict.

CONFLICTING BELIEFS

Conflicts of beliefs can cause the most difficult arguments because the contenders may not be anywhere near the same wavelength. If you don't share the same beliefs that are behind your request, your teenager may not be able to understand why a particular behaviour is a problem. You're hassling them to get up in the morning and go to school; they think school is a waste of time – look at the number of people who do very nicely without school qualifications. You're getting on their case about tidying their room; they honestly can't see what's wrong with it – they can find the bed under the sea of clothes and CDs, so what's the difficulty? You're warning them about sex and pregnancy; they think you're so out of date. In becoming independent and developing their own beliefs they are likely to reject your views, so you're bound to clash on such issues.

Accepting that your teenager may have different beliefs from yours can take some of the heat and blame out of the situation. That doesn't mean you have to change your own beliefs or see them as in any way belittled. It doesn't mean that you have to put up with behaviour that is a real problem for you. What it means is that you agree to disagree over the beliefs behind the conflict, yet aim to negotiate changes in the behaviour if it is stopping either of you getting important needs met.

At a separate time, once the situation has calmed down into a dialogue, you can discuss beliefs with your teenager and hear each other's point of view. This will help you to understand them, will demonstrate to them that beliefs are to be taken seriously and that you respect their right to hold independent opinions. By only setting out to make changes on the important things and letting go of the less important ones, your teenager is more likely to take notice of what you are saying. You can hold firm boundaries over behaviour that you find unacceptable and have them respect that more if you also respect their differing views.

The fact is that there is no right or wrong and no 'one size fits all' way to resolve most dilemmas. The most effective way to do so is to consider the issues and in each case ask yourself: 'What are my needs as a parent here for myself and for my teenager? And what are my teenager's needs?' Answer those truthfully and you will be able to see a way to negotiate, compromise and hold your important boundaries.

Friends

Teenagers and parents often clash over the issues of friends. It may be about the friends themselves – whether they are 'a bad lot' and you suspect they are leading your adolescent astray. It may be about the time they get home from being with them, the things they get up to together: having parties, hanging around getting into trouble, doing risky things. There might also be issues about friends taking the place of family: whether your teenager wants to spend weekends or special festivals and holiday periods with you or with friends, or whether you let them duck out of duty visits and family events or ask them to come along, regardless of whether they want to or not. What if they want to do their own thing? When should you let them?

With the issues of gang culture and knife crime – which are now so much on people's minds and in the press – anxiety about your teenager's friends and out-of-home activities can take on an extra edge. How can you raise issues such as these in a way that does not antagonize or anger your teen, but keeps them safe?

Insight

Whatever your relationship with your teenager, you may find their choice of friend worries or antagonizes you. That's natural and more about your feelings of loss and jealousy than about the people themselves. But if your teenager seems to be gravitating towards people you hate, ask yourself how much you show your love, respect and appreciation of your child. Feeling loved and accepted by their parents lessens the need to get up their nose with a choice of friends.

What are your needs?

You need to feel that your teenager is safe. You don't want to think that your teenager is hanging around with friends who have different values, different backgrounds, and who give a bad example. The problem with this is that sometimes we discover that every other teenager in the group has a parent with the same anxiety. The truth is that sometimes there are no bad examples and no evil ringleaders. Sometimes, young people are simply doing what comes naturally to young people: hanging out, chatting and chilling, perhaps doing a little experimenting with stuff to smoke and drink, but nothing really harmful. Sometimes, it can get out of hand, not because of anyone's bad intent, but because group dynamics often lead people to do things they'd never do on their own. You need to know they are out of harm's way, but you also need to know that they recognize your anxieties and that your peace of mind matters to them.

The strategy for dealing with this is to talk with your teenager about your anxieties. Remember: 'When you... I feel... because... what I'd like is...' For example:

'When you go off with your friends and I hear you've been seen in the park drinking cider, I feel really anxious and upset because I'm worried you may hurt yourself, or upset other people, or even act irresponsibly or antisocially when drunk. What I'd like is for us to find something else you could do, or all of you could do, that doesn't involve such behaviour.'

Parties

Sooner or later, your teenager will want to throw or attend parties, go off doing something you don't like, or spend a weekend or a holiday away from you. How are you going to deal with this? Say 'No', because your need for reassurance is the most important thing to you? Say 'Yes' because you feel helpless or want a quiet life? Or use the techniques of discussion – gathering information, listening to views, being clear what you will and won't negotiate over and making an agreement – to help you come to a resolution. If knife crime or gangs are your worry, don't forget that the consensus seems to be that teenagers who do get involved have poor role models – particularly male role models for boys – and both little to occupy their time and poor expectations and horizons. Your challenge then, is to make sure they have quality time with either parents or strong replacements, and that their ambitions and expectations of themselves and their future are set realistically, but high.

What are your needs for your teenager?

When they're late for the umpteenth time and getting right up your nose, you may be tempted to say, 'Suspended animation until they are 20.' But the truth is that you want your teenager to have friends that stand by them, that they value and with whom they have fun. But you also feel they need to be home on time, to retain your trust and the good relationship you'd like with them and to be able to go to bed on time and have enough sleep. You want them to have the self-confidence and self-worth that comes when they have a supportive social network. You want them to have freedom, independence, peer acceptance and fun.

What are your teenager's needs?

To help them achieve everything you want of them, and to help us achieve everything you need for yourself, you have to understand your teenager's needs. They need friends. They need to be part of a group, to belong and be accepted and to blend in. They need friends they can trust, who give like for like and stay loyal. They need to be different from their parents and from adults – to have clothes and language and music and activities that they can ring fence off from parents, adults and other teenage groups and be able to say, 'This is me, this is ours, I belong, you don't.' Teenagers tend to want to feel different and separate from everything outside their chosen group, and exactly alike to everyone inside. Everything they wear, do, listen to and believe is part of the entrance ticket to their own group and a banner that says to outsiders, 'Keep out! You don't belong'. Try to understand their language by all means – don't

ever use it. Try to appreciate their clothes – don't wear them.
Try to be sympathetic to their friendships – after all, if the child
you love finds this particular person like-minded, they must have
something going for them – but don't criticize or carp. And if
the friendship collapses, don't say, 'I told you so, I never did like
them', for two reasons. One is that they may be best mates again in
a few days time. The other is that when you criticize their friends,
you criticize your teenager's ability to make choices, decisions and
judgements.

To keep their friends, to keep membership of that exclusive group,
they need to align with the group philosophy and be at group
meetings. If you need to keep them safe and within boundaries,
the most effective way of doing so is to understand their needs and
find ways of putting your needs and theirs together. For example:
'You want to go out and stay out late so you'll be with your friends.
I want to know you're safe, and I want you to be in before 10
because it's a school night and you need your sleep. How are we
going to manage this?'

Insight

Being part of a group they have chosen is a vital aspect of
being a teenager. We also choose our 'tribe' and wear a
uniform to express that choice, but in far less obvious ways.

Appearance

What they look like is really important to your teenager and a great
source of worry and anguish for you as their parent. You might be
concerned that your friends and neighbours think you don't look
after your kids if they go out in what appears to you to be dirty or
scruffy clothes. You may feel their hair or make-up makes them
look slutty or outrageous, or that body piercings make them look
cheap or aggressive. You may also be concerned that their clothing
suggests a sexual readiness that either you don't feel they should
be – or believe they don't realize they are – signalling.

What are your needs?
You need to feel like a good parent – one who sends their children out into the world in washed and ironed clothes in good condition, with themselves equally clean and presentable. You need to have your teenager dressed appropriately, not looking like an adult in their twenties on their way to a nightclub, or even like a working girl or rent boy on their way to work. You don't want them in what appears to you like a Halloween costume, all in black with white make-up (both sexes), or with their bellies hanging out between low-slung jeans and a skimpy top, or with jeans hanging down so you can see their underwear, in case people are shocked or antagonistic to them – or look down on you for allowing it. You think future employers will balk at studs or the holes they make in their eyebrows, tongues and lips, and you want to keep your teenager's body intact.

What are your needs for your teenager?
You do need your teenager to feel good about themselves, to wear clothes they feel comfortable and attractive in. Mostly, you'd like them to be warm. You'd like them to feel they can express themselves through their appearance. You just wish what they express could be a bit tidier.

What are your teenager's needs?
Your teenager doesn't want to look like you. He or she needs to make the strongest possible statement in how they dress and what they put on and dangle from their body that they are separate to you, and 'at one' with their friends. Every generation has to reinvent what shocks their parents and divides them from the last generation, and what connects them to their peers. Some fashions return, some continue and some are new, but they all do the same thing – divide and unite. It's always a carefully crafted look, however grungy or casual it seems. And it's never, in essence, any different from what you wore when you were their age. If you do have concerns, an opening gambit could be: 'Wow! That's some look. It seems fun but can you just sit down a moment and talk me through it. Are you sure you won't get any hassle if you dress like that? What if someone took it the wrong way? Ease my mind and let's talk through what you'd say and do.'

Tidiness

Parents of teenagers often agree that household chores and
tidiness are areas they and their teenage children clash over a lot.
It sometimes feels as if a wave of clothes and belongings not only
swamps their own rooms but overflows and sweeps through the
house, drowning you, the cat and everything else. Arguments
can become heated and often circular because neither of you is
recognizing each other's needs here.

What are your needs?
You might long for order and control. On one level, that can mean
a simple desire to have your home seem tidy, with bits and pieces in
the right place where you can find them. Under the surface, this need
may be intensified by the fear that you are losing control of your
family and yourself. It feels as if yesterday you had lovely, loving,
biddable children who looked up to you and would do what they
were told. Today, you have slouching, grunting monsters that seem
to only care about themselves and ignore everything you say. Your
home is being taken over by them and refashioned into something
alien, as they have been remade into something you don't recognize
and feel is not yours. When you insist on going into their rooms and
trying to make them tidy up, perhaps at the root of this is a desire to
still have some influence over them. If you can knock their room into
shape, maybe you can recreate them as the children you remember.

What are your needs for your teenager?
You may need to feel they still belong in the family and have a
stake in it, and that they should be sensitive to the needs and
feelings of you and other members of the family. You may also see
whether and how they do chores round the home as an indicator
of how much they still feel they belong to the family, and how
prepared they may be for their future. After all, if they seem to
simply come home to use it like a hotel, to eat, sleep and be given
clean clothes while contributing nothing, you may fear for their
ability to look after themselves later on. It's not just that they
won't know how to work the washing machine and iron; it's that

they may not understand that these things have to be done to run a home and a life.

Insight

Being shouted at for not doing what you want can seem an easy price to pay – it's over sooner or later and you go on doing whatever you were doing because the shouting has wiped clean the slate. Your teenager has no incentive to do better if you collude with their not helping out in this way.

What are your teenager's needs?

One adolescent need may be for a quiet life. Your teenager may have so much else going on in their mind at this stage in their life that they really don't realize what effect they are having on you, and what they are taking for granted. If food, clean clothes and toothpaste continue to appear and all they have to offer in return is to listen to the occasional rant in the background, they may see no reason to change. But the main need they have, which has to be recognized and harnessed if you are to find a solution, is for a stake in life. The change from order to chaos in their room shows the maelstrom in their mind as they fight to find their own personality, tastes, opinions – in short, themselves. It can be confused and hectic in there, and the room mirrors this. Also, it's a very undemanding way of saying 'You are no longer the boss of me!' You want it tidy, so it won't be. It's a slightly less harmful way of showing rebellion, after all, than throwing bombs. But what they also want to do is claim some territory of their own, other than their own rooms. That tide of clothes and belongings, as well as unwashed cups and plates, proclaims one thing, 'I was here!' It also says, 'And this is mine!' Cats rub their faces on the things they claim, dogs pee on it. Be grateful all teenagers do is leave a T-shirt or discarded computer game there.

So, what can you do? You can recognize their need for ownership and territory in several ways. One is declaring their room off-limits to you. They can do what they want in it, as long as it doesn't become a health hazard. If cups and plates disappear and you don't have enough, they'll be eating out of the pan until they bring them down and wash them up. If they don't have clean clothes for school or work, that's their look-out. With control, comes responsibility. The other tactic is to formalize the undertaking of chores by everyone.

Chores

Nobody likes doing chores. Children will forget them, but teenagers will complain about them, fight over whose turn it is and generally make it so difficult that in many families, adults give up and do it themselves – it seems less hassle and a way of guaranteeing the work gets done, and properly, with the least conflict. Sometimes you let them get away with it rather than allow people to think you're a bad parent for not being able to manage. But doing chores is a vital part of your teenager's life and preparation for their future. Given that your teenager demands adult privileges, household chores are a perfect way of demonstrating that with power comes responsibility. However much they may complain or object, whatever arguments they put up against it, it would be of benefit to you all if you insisted chores are done. Explain that:

▶ *one aspect of being an adult that they need to learn is that if they want the fun, they also have to do the work. Everyone who lives in your house pulls their weight and does their chores*
▶ *since this is their home too, they have to do their share*
▶ *growing up brings privileges and duties: the privilege is having a say; the duty is mucking in and doing their bit*
▶ *of course, that does mean you have to hand out both privileges as well as duties, which is why family discussions are so important.*

HOW TO DRAW UP A CHORE CHART

How should you draw up a chore chart? For it to be something that everyone 'buys into' and agrees, it's best to make it a cooperative effort. But it does help for one person in the family to take responsibility for managing it and making it run. That doesn't have to be one of the adults; you can delegate this to your teenager, as a way of further enlisting their cooperation and sense of ownership. To forestall arguments you could rotate this, asking each young person to take responsibility for a week or a month at a time. Have a family discussion to agree the following:

▶ *What are the routine chores that need doing? These could be washing-up or feeding and walking family pets, filling the dishwasher, loading the washing machine, laying tables, vacuuming the living room, and so on.*

▶ *Decide which chores have to be done, come what may. Different families have different ideas of what's important – come to your own agreement.*

▶ *Decide which chores are quick and easy, and which are long and hard.*

▶ *Draw up a list of chores, and assign them. You might like to give everyone a mix of easy, medium and hard chores for each time period. Or you might opt for each person having easy, medium or hard weeks. You'll find some children like, and even fight for, some chores or hate others, and not all agree on which. You might opt for everyone having their set chores from then on, or rotating so everyone gets a go at all of them, with some allowance for age, height and weight. Whatever measure and scheme you decide, share out chores equally. That's the essence of being in a family; everyone pulls their weight and does their part.*

▶ *You might also want to agree on what might be 'extra' chores, such as washing cars or mowing lawns, and negotiate whether these can be done as paid-for jobs. Some families may want to tie chores into pocket money – you get it if you complete your chores, or the amount you get is dependent on chores. You may want to consider whether this introduces an element of, 'Shall I, shan't I?' into the equation. Children wouldn't be very amused if Mum or Dad felt it was optional and depended on how they felt that day as to whether they got their evening meal or not. In the same light, whether or not you do your chores should be approached as similarly non-negotiable. Everyone does chores. End of story.*

Agree what you're going to do, and then draw up a written agreement or contract setting it out. Ask everyone to sign the contract; 'We, the undersigned, agree...' Review the contract regularly and if it's not working, go back to the table to discuss why and what you'd like to do to make it work.

Insight

Add the chores you do – shopping and cooking, going to work, paying bills – to the chart. They can't share in bill paying or going to work, but it can help you make the point and then delegate some of what might be considered 'your' work – shopping and cooking a meal every now and again, for instance.

Using technology

Perhaps the one significant difference between today's parents and their teenage children is the possibilities offered by technology. We had televisions and videos and access to the family phone. They now have mobiles and laptops with access to the internet. But the internet does not just give them the way into information; it's an entry to social networks and chat rooms. It also opens the way to online gaming, of all sorts, and pornography. And, of course, traffic is two-way. You can get out to the world... and the world can get in to you.

What are your needs?
Parents may need to stay in their comfort zone. If you haven't had the opportunity to become proficient in what new technology can offer, you may find it scary. One of the big issues for parents

to face with teenage children is feeling incompetent and inadequate. Technology usage is bound to make you feel that, because your teenager will probably be better at using new gadgets than you. When they get their hands on a mobile, an iPod, a laptop, they will quickly learn all the tricks to get the best out of it, mainly because they have no fears. You may be scared of breaking it, of pressing the wrong button and doing something you can't recall and of looking foolish. Since, on the whole, they don't pay for it, they start off with a fearless attitude that you find hard to copy. Because you don't want to look silly, you often shy off trying; so your teen gets far ahead of you and into what feels like a no-go zone. Because one of your main needs is to know your teenager is safe, you then may conclude the best attitude is to be protective and restrictive, often overly so.

What are your needs for your teenager?
You want your teenager to be safe. You've heard that it's easy to access inappropriate material on the internet, and that paedophiles use networking sites to target teenagers, so in your eyes, the internet may seem a dangerous and unpleasant place that you'd rather your child used sparingly or not at all. You may be alarmed at stories of young people using their parents' credit cards on the internet to run up large bills. You may also be concerned that your teenager spends so much time on the internet that it amounts to an addiction and prevents them getting on with more important things – school work, family life and face-to-face interaction with real life friends. Of course, you may also be worried your child could be the target of cyber bullying – bullying that arrives on their mobile phones or through social networking sites or specially set-up websites.

But you also want your teenager to have the best and grow up capable and proficient, and using technology with confidence is an important part of modern life. Using the internet can be such a positive activity, helping with school work, giving them confidence and enjoyment. So you often struggle with the balance between safety and appropriately free access.

What are your teenager's needs?

Most teenagers would probably feel that if you took their mobiles, iPods and computers away you might as well lock them in a trunk and throw it in the sea. Teenagers need connectivity. They need to practise and perfect their social skills – to chat, to get to know, to fall out with and make up with their friends. They use texts on mobiles, email and social networking sites on the internet in the same way as we used to use the family phone – to keep in touch, to chat and share when away from school, where, after all, they are often with friends but unable to talk as they are in class. But they can do it with far less disruption to your routines, since they're not hogging the family phone, and it is probably cheaper.

Those are 'soft skills' – they also need to practise and perfect the hard skills that come from manipulating technology and software. Teenagers playing games on their computers or gaming modules are not only having fun – they are also learning about hand/eye coordination, fast reflexes, assessment and judgement. Much of what they do on the computers as children can be used later in the workplace and it raises their self-confidence and self-esteem to feel competent and capable in this arena. They need to be doing the same things as their friends, so teens with little access to the internet can feel left out.

Insight

The internet is no more – nor less – a dangerous place than your local playground. It's how you use it that makes it safe or not.

RULES FOR SAFE INTERNET AND MOBILE USE

Anything and everything can be dangerous if used without care. The fact is that the benefits and joys of the internet and other technology far outweigh the drawbacks. Our parents didn't have the reassurance that mobile phones bring – to ring a teenager to find out where they are, to be rung and asked for a lift rather than have them walk home in unsafe surroundings. What we need to do is minimize the dangers, so we can enjoy the benefits.

To make it easier for you to be confident in letting your teenager have access to modern technology, make some common-sense rules with them. Talk through the issues with your teenager and explain these family rules to your child:

▶ *If they're going out, their mobile must be charged up and on. Refusing to answer brings sanctions – being grounded until they can be trusted.*

▶ *If they need a lift home, they call and ask. Never take risks.*

▶ *At home, there are times when all mobiles should be off and landlines left to the answering service. Mealtimes should be family time.*

▶ *If communicating with anyone they don't already know in the real world, they must not tell them anything that could allow them to get in contact offline. They must keep their home address, school name, or telephone number to themselves. Use an online name that doesn't reveal their real name, age or where they come from. Be careful to whom they reveal their age.*

▶ *Be choosy about handing out their mobile number. Only give it to their friends and ask them not to pass it on without their say so.*

▶ *Never say 'Yes' to a face-to-face meeting with another user without a parent knowing and agreeing. If a meeting is arranged, it has to be in a public place and with an adult present.*

▶ *Don't get into 'flame wars' – angry and abusive exchanges. Never respond to messages or chat that are dirty, hostile, threatening, or make them feel uncomfortable. Tell an adult if they see any messages like that.*

▶ *Don't forget that in cyberspace, no one can see you. That 12-year-old girl or boy who likes the same things as them, could be, in reality, a 40-year-old man out to exploit them.*

▶ *Remember that everything they read online may not be true. If it's 'too good to be true', it probably is. Be very careful about any offers that involve them coming to a meeting or having someone visit the house.*

- *Computer use is a family activity. If you want to get to know their online friends, it's for the same reasons you'd like to know their other friends – to keep them safe and happy.*

MAKE A CONTRACT ON TECHNOLOGY USE

You might like to write out this contract, talk it through with your teenager and ask that both of you sign it.

- *I will keep my mobile charged up and on whenever I am out. I will always answer when a parent calls or texts, or call or text back as soon as I get a message. If I need a lift home, I will call and ask – I will never take risks.*
- *I will not give out personal information such as my address, telephone number, my parents' work address or telephone number, or the name and location of my school without my parents' permission.*
- *I will tell my parents right away if I come across any information that makes me feel uncomfortable.*
- *I won't say 'Yes' to a face-to-face meeting with someone I know online, without first checking with my parents. If my parents agree to the meeting, it will be in a public place and a parent will come along.*
- *I will never send my picture or anything else without first checking with my parents.*
- *I will not respond to any messages that are mean or in any way make me feel uncomfortable. It is not my fault if I get a message like that. If I do I will tell my parents right away so that they can contact the service provider. I won't use my computer or mobile phone to send nasty messages to anyone else.*
- *I will talk with my parents so that we can set up rules for going online. We will decide upon the time of day that I can be online, the length of time I can be online and sites I can visit. I will not access other areas or break these rules without their permission.*
- *I will not give out my internet password to anyone (even my best friends). My parents will need a very good reason and we will discuss this if they ask for it.*

- *I will check with my parents before downloading anything or installing software or doing anything that could possibly cause any damage to our computer or give access to a virus or worm.*
- *I will not clear history to hide what sites I have visited after being on the internet and will be prepared to discuss with my parents the sites I have been to.*
- *I will help my parents understand how to have fun and learn things online and teach them about the internet, computers and other technology.*

YOUR RESPONSIBILITY

As a parent, you have a responsibility to keep pace with your children in these areas. To make sure you have some knowledge and confidence with the technology your children are using, you should:

- *Get to know your mobile phone and computer. Learn how to text and access the internet and familiarize yourself with the services your child uses. If you don't know how to use a chat room, get your child to show you. Join social or parenting networks so you can see how it works.*
- *Report anything in chat rooms or in messages that is inappropriately sexual or threatening by forwarding a copy of the message to the service provider and asking for their assistance. Keep a copy on your computer. If your teenager is the subject of mobile text bullying, keep the messages and take it up with the school, or the police.*
- *Don't fall for internet scams and hoaxes. Visit www.snopes.com regularly to see the latest and catch up on the old ones. If you want your child to keep safe, you need to learn how to do so as well.*
- *Make computer use a family activity. Keep computers in public areas – kitchens, living rooms, landings or hallways – and not in bedrooms, so young people know that while you should and do respect their privacy, you can and will at any time wander by and see what they are doing. This also prevents them staying up to all hours messaging or gaming.*

Insight

It can seem a shortcut out of arguments to let your kids have
their own televisions and computers in their rooms. In fact,
it causes far more family problems than it resolves.

Money and 'The Bank of Mum and Dad'

Money is always a point of conflict between teenagers and parents.
Not only how much they may want, but their attitude towards it –
somehow money appears and you could conjure up endless amounts,
if it wasn't for your inherent meanness. Should teenagers have
pocket money to spend as they want while you shell out cash when
it is needed, or should they have an allowances and responsibility for
certain purchases? Should they be paid in exchange for chores and
work and if so, how much? Money tends to be a huge issue in this
designer-obsessed culture. You can find yourself spending enormous
amounts on the 'new big thing': an article of clothing, a piece of
technology or even a leisure pastime. And next week or month,
peer pressure brings your child back to ask you for the next new big
thing. Fashion means their appearance may change – and thus the
need for a new wardrobe – at least once a season and sometimes
more. But the rate of technological development also now means
that all those little gadgets they love change shape, colour and/or
function and new ones appear, almost by the month.

What are your needs?
You may need to keep some sort of handle on what is being
spent in your household, for all sorts of reasons. One is simple
economics. You need to know more is not going out than is
coming in. But you may also need to be on top of it to feel that
you're still in charge of this household – a feeling you may be
rapidly losing. Parents sometimes battle with two conflicting
emotions about money and their teenagers. One is the desire to
give them as much, if not far more, than you had – to perhaps
make up for any deficiencies you felt you suffered. The opposite
emotion is of sneaking jealousy – the small, dark voice that cries
'I didn't have it, why should you?!' Parents may need to recognize

these warring feelings and bring them in line with what is realistic and achievable. It's not helpful for anyone in the family to give teenagers free rein because you want to rewrite some injustices in your past, if by doing so you strain the family budget.

What are your needs for your teenager?
You need your teenager to become self-reliant and to be able to manage money now and in the future. You'd also often like for them to make some contribution to the family coffers, either by earning some of the money they want or need from an outside source, so taking the burden off you, or to see giving value around the house to be fair return for their allowance. You need your teenager to understand the value of money, that it has to be earned and that you have to work hard for the things you all enjoy. You need them to know that sooner rather than later, they will have to take over responsibility for earning their living. But you also want your teenager to be concentrating on the important issues at this time in their lives – working for qualifications for the future – rather than on making money now.

What are your teenager's needs?
Teenagers see money in several ways. It's a means to an end, a way of getting all the goodies they'd love to have. They also see it as a status symbol – that having money of their own to spend is a way of showing their maturity. Your teenager needs to feel in charge of their cash. They also often want to be able to contribute, to take some of the weight off your shoulders and to say 'thank you'. They often want to work, so that they can have a real say on what they do with their own money and can feel grown-up about earning it. They also see it as a proof of love – the more you love them the more you'll give them. This is an issue that needs discussing and challenging, and would be part of a discussion on family budgets.

CHANGING FROM POCKET MONEY TO AN ALLOWANCE

The sooner you shift from your teenager having pocket money – which is simply free cash to spend as they like – to an allowance, which carries with it certain responsibilities, the better. As apprentice adults, young people rise to responsibility and they need to learn how to handle cash now while they have your guidance and a safety net, rather than putting it off until they are on their own and can court disaster. Young people need to see that money can be divided into three sections:

- *money to be spent now on pleasing yourself*
- *money that has to pay regular bills*
- *money that should be saved for future needs – unforeseen bills, holidays, presents for other people, and so on.*

Teenagers tend to be big on the first section, especially since that's the way they began with pocket money. Some children learn from example to put money away, saving up for Christmas and birthday presents for family and friends, or for an item they want and know they have to buy for themselves. But the second section is the one they may find hard to visualize, because that's what parents do for them. It may then be the financial aspect they fail on, when they go independent for the first time. As a parent, you can help your teenager get control over their future as well as present finances, by setting up a system that gives them an income and also requires them to handle it. You can help them by explaining your own budget – where money comes from, how you spend it. Nothing quite knocks on the head the fantasy that Mum and Dad could give them everything they wanted if only you weren't so mean, as showing them bills and explaining how many hours you need to work to pay them.

TEENAGE JOBS

In some families, you may be happy to have your teenager do a paid job of some sort either in holidays or at weekends. You'll want to regulate this, to make sure they are safe and happy with the work, that it gives them responsibility and a sense of achievement but that it does not interfere with their school life.

You may then wish to sit down with your teenager and agree what they and you expect them to have to buy or do with the money they have (be it their allowance or their earnings) and how much you will give them and when. You may also want to discuss with them where to keep their money: in a bank account or building society, a credit or savings account. Allowances can be paid monthly or quarterly and you can give them in cash or pay them into a bank account. You might want to start by handing over to them the responsibility for out-of-school travel and entertainment – an agreed amount to cover going to see their friends or visiting cinemas, for buying games, DVDs, books or music. You may want to give them an agreed amount for their mobile phone tariff, but insist they always keep minutes back for emergencies. You may want to give them responsibility for all or some non-school clothes. You may want to start small and as they demonstrate good practise, increase the money and the areas they can be in charge of.

And most important of all, you will have to stand firm if they blow it. They may need a safety net in some cases, but the principle should be that they won't learn if you bail them out. So if your adolescent spends an entire entertainment budget for a month on a concert and then can't go to the cinema with friends – tough. Earn it or miss out. If they spend the whole clothing allowance on a new pair of boots, and then need a new pair of jeans – tough. Make do with an old pair. If you made similar spending choices, you'd face the same consequence, so it's a learning experience. Tough for you to maintain, but vital for them to learn.

Insight

It's a balance; you don't want to scare them and put too much of a burden on them by giving them some insights into the family budget, but neither should you leave them in blissful but damaging ignorance.

Food

Existing on a diet that almost entirely consists of 'unhealthy' food such as chips, crisps, fizzy drinks and chocolate, is normal teenager behaviour. But so, too, is becoming obsessed with diets and healthy food, and reading out the contents of packets as you cook or they eat. It's all part of asserting independence and making individual choices. But it can be confusing as they insist they'll only eat food that encourages weight gain while seemingly obsessing about their body shape.

What are your needs?
Food can be a battle ground for parents and teenagers. We want to nourish and nurture them, and making and offering food is often the way we show love and care. For this reason, having food refused can be intensely painful and annoying, leading often to furious rows around the dinner table and meal times. You need to be aware of the way food, like money, often stands in for love and appreciation. People ask for it or refuse it, offer it or control it as a way of signifying emotions as much as a way of handing out nourishment. What you may need is to feel you are still both caring for, and to a certain extent in control of, your child when you feed them. That may clash with their needs. You may also need to feel that the food you give them is the best. If you have grown up with unhealthy patterns of eating, this may mean you eat too much fat, too much sugar – and indeed, *too much*. But your need to care for your child can make it easy to become defensive, either when teenagers, the media, the school or a doctor suggest you might do well to change.

What are your needs for your teenager?
You may need to know that your teenager is staying healthy and that eating well is part of this. It's reassuring to know that as they grow older they are likely to eat a more balanced diet. For now, they have their own reasons for making food an issue. You may want your teenager to change their diet and come into conflict if you try to institute healthier eating at a time when they do not want to. Or, you may find yourself in conflict if you feel they should be eating more and they do not.

What are your teenager's needs?
Food is love, but it sometimes also feels like dependency. Teenagers love their parents' meals and a kitchen with 24/7 chocolate biscuits,

juice and potato chips. At the same time, they are beginning to resent the way it ties them down to needing you, and to their having to eat what you set out and when. This is why they may become picky and choosy, asking for things you don't have and turning up their nose at things you do, and why they may be late, or early, for dinner. They need to break away and be separate and while family mealtimes are a pleasure, a shelter and an inspiration, they may have moments of resisting the pull.

Teenagers also need to assert their links with their peer group, which is why 'breaking bread' with them – sharing burgers, fizzy drinks, packets of potato snacks and chocolate – becomes so important at this age. They may not need the food – they had breakfast with you and will have dinner – but they want the chance to share that round-the-table ritual with friends.

Insight

A teenage preoccupation with food and diets may be a good excuse for the family to revisit and revise what you all eat, so you can put together a healthier lifestyle for you all.

WHEN EATING HABITS INDICATE A PROBLEM

Sometimes, of course, food can satisfy your teenager's desperate need to assert control over their body or give themselves comfort or distraction in less than helpful ways. Anxiety about school, friends or their body image, problems with stress, anger or depression can all lead to an eating disorder. Teenagers with self-destructive eating habits such as bingeing, constant snacking or excessive dieting, can be struggling to manage an underlying problem. All of these may seem like problems to you, but to your teenager they may feel like a solution – their way of coping with a need, for order or control or sanctuary.

It helps not to let food or weight become a big issue or battle, to give information and opportunities for healthy eating, without nagging or criticizing. Above all, you need to avoid labelling teenagers as fat, skinny, overweight, podgy. You need to use your listening and communicating skills to find opportunities to listen to your teenager and check in with them regularly, in a supportive rather than intrusive way. Teenagers need to be appreciated for the things you like about them and what they do: issues around food and eating can be a sign of low self-esteem.

Teenagers may also, in time of an awareness of healthy eating, want to challenge the diet you feed them. Their teenage years may be the perfect opportunity for the whole family to revise and revisit what you do eat, for the better. Using your communication skills, you may want to sit down with them and draw up a new plan for the future.

If you suspect your teenager has an eating disorder, such as bulimia (bingeing followed by vomiting or laxatives) or anorexia (avoiding or refusing food), seek professional help quickly. The earlier these conditions are treated, the greater the chance of stopping them.

Sex

Sex is the hot potato – the issue in the UK and US that we're most nervous about raising with our teenagers or have them raise with us. All the evidence suggests that if parents talk to their children about sex, young people are more likely to delay having sex, and to use contraception when they do. More important perhaps, it helps them to see sex in perspective – as a natural part of life that should give pleasure when appropriate rather than anxiety or embarrassment.

What are your needs?
Parents, perfectly naturally, feel the onset of a teenager's interest in sex as the final separation. With sexual interest comes romantic attachment, which means the parent ceases to be first in their hearts. As your teenager becomes a sexual being, you move up a rung – they become sexually active and it feels as if you become sexually redundant – the old person who's now sexually past it! It's not uncommon for a parent to feel intense loss around this time.

You may express it as sadness at the loss of their childhood, but equally it might be the loss of your own youth and sense of self as having the right to passion. You need to reclaim your own territory, to avoid it becoming annexed by your teenager's development. The territory can still be yours, even if your teenager is taking their own steps towards sexual maturity. You may also want the exclusive right to discuss sex with your child, rather than delegate it to their school, to be assured that the messages coming across are ones you uphold. With power, comes responsibility. Young people deserve the right to be able to have their questions answered and if you are going to do it yourself, you must do it. Parents often shy away from talking about sex because they feel they don't know enough and don't want to seem incompetent. You may need to brush up on the facts yourself, from books or places such as the Family Lives/Parentline Plus site (see Taking it further).

What are your needs for your teenager?
In this arena, perhaps above all else, parents need to feel their teenagers are safe. You don't want them being emotionally hurt. You don't want them being physically harmed. You don't want them doing anything irrevocable that will alter their future for the worse – becoming a parent too soon or acquiring a sexual infection such as HIV/AIDS or herpes. You'd like them to enjoy love and happiness, but not too soon and with the right person.

What are your teenager's needs?
Because we shy off talking about sex in the UK and US, except to laugh and snigger about it, your teenager may be feeling confused about the whole process. In countries such as Holland and Sweden, several generations have grown up with good quality relationship and personal education in school. The result has been that parents and teenagers find it easy to talk about both the emotions involved and the physical changes and urges. In both the US and the UK, sex education is patchy and generally very poor. Young people learn too little too late and tend only to cover reproduction in science lessons. The issues that teenagers really want to discuss – What am I feeling? How do relationships work? How do I negotiate what I might want or not want to do? – are ignored.

Teenagers need more than one-off or merely mechanistic lectures in how pregnancy occurs. They may be worried about whether their body is 'normal' in shape, size and reaction, anxious about whether they should have done it by now, wondering if they might be gay, lesbian or straight, experiencing pressure to engage in sexual activity before they feel ready. They may have unrealistic ideas about what having a relationship or being a parent might do for them, and need to be able to discuss these issues. They need to be able to learn facts and also hear a range of attitudes and opinions in order to make up their own minds. Many teenagers are under pressure from their peers and influenced by a sexualized society. Yet many find entering adulthood quite frightening and young people themselves say that the people they most want to talk to them about sex are their parents.

Insight

Sex is not something you talk *to* your teenagers about. To help them learn the facts, manage the feelings and make the best choices for themselves you have to discuss it *with* them.

DON'T MAKE ASSUMPTIONS ABOUT YOUR TEENAGER'S SEXUAL ACTIVITY

You don't want to jump the gun! Sexual awareness is a very different matter to sexual activity and your teenager may ask questions long before they actually want to put what they've learned into action. Talking about sex does not encourage or condone sexual behaviour. Parents can feel powerless to influence their adolescent's sexual activity, but the truth is that those parents who do open the lines of communication find that it not only becomes easier to talk openly about sexual relationships but can also give easy-to-understand messages, such as: waiting until older and ready before embarking upon sexual activity; the importance of relationships and caring for a partner; contraception and the importance of safe sex. But don't assume that because your teenager talks about it freely, knows a lot more than you did and seems sexualized and relaxed about it all, that they are sexually active. Make no assumptions.

One way to get your teenager to consider the consequences of their actions is to ask 'What if...' questions, such as: 'What if someone wants to kiss you and you don't?'; 'What if you'd like to go out with someone – what would you do?'; 'What if your boy/girlfriend wants sex with you and you don't?' Discussion with your teenager is often best triggered by something you are both watching on TV or is on the news.

It helps for you to have discussed with your partner and have clear in your mind some of the classic dilemmas you might encounter, such as: What do you say if your teenager wants to have a boy or girlfriend stay the night?; How do you react if you discover your 15-year-old teenager is having sex, and either using or not using contraception? What do you do if you realize your teenager is gay?

WHERE DO YOU STAND?

The point is that you have to decide where you stand on these kinds of issues. You may have strong views that say 'No' to premarital sex under your roof, that they shouldn't be doing it at all before the age of 15, that contraception should be a no-no at any age, and that homosexuality is not something you want to accept. You are entitled to your opinion, of course but what you may need to consider is the effect of standing by your beliefs. Does it change your teenager's behaviour? Does it drive them away from you and into risky and unprotected territory? Between two and six teenagers out of 30 will probably grow up to be lesbian or gay. They are likely to be feeling isolated, anxious about growing up different from most of their peers and frightened of prejudice. They need to be able to talk to parents, to be accepted and to have access to information about safe sex for when they become sexually active. And as for sex under your roof – of course you can say what goes in your own home. Will it mean they sneak from bedroom to bedroom in the night, and is that preferable to you moving your boundary? Will they resort to having their sexual explorations in more uncomfortable and less safe surroundings? These are all the issues you need to explore, and discuss within your family to arrive at a decision that you feel comfortable about, but that your teenager can manage too. Listen, communicate, AIM and ACT and come to your own conclusion.

Insight
You have the right to your own feelings and beliefs. But so too does your teenager. Discussion and communication helps all of you do your best for each other.

Drugs and alcohol

There isn't a single human culture that does not use some substance or some behaviour that is mind altering. Some cultures chew plant products; some smoke them and some brew liquors from a variety of fruit and vegetables or vegetation. Others will chant, dance and sing to achieve a blissed-out state. When you look at your teenager's use or risk-taking in this area, you need to put it in context, not just of our particular society's behaviour, but also of your own. How might you be modelling or contributing to the situation?

What are your needs?
As with so many issues, you need to feel your teenager is safe. You also need to feel that whatever happens to them, you tried to protect them and keep them from harm. So it may make you feel very uncomfortable to recognize how much alcohol and drug use may be about the unconscious messages you collude with or contribute to, or about issues they are struggling with that you may not have been able to solve.

What are your needs for your teenager?
We'd all like our teenagers to avoid illegal drugs altogether, and use only those substances that are common and allowed in our society with care and only when the right age. You need them to be safe, happy and healthy, and so often drug use seems entirely unsafe, miserable and unhealthy. You need for your teenager to come to you with problems that might make them want to take drugs or for help in resisting peer pressure to experiment.

What are your teenager's needs?
Teenagers need to decide for themselves. They often have a
very cynical view of adult attitudes to drugs and alcohol, pointing
out that as a society we do seem to consume an awful lot of
alcohol and tobacco, and what's the difference between those
and the substances they may prefer? Teenagers need unbiased
information in order to make informed decisions. If they do try
something, they need you to react without anger and blame. Any
conflict over the issue and teenagers are likely to continue – if for
no other reason than to annoy or worry you – but just not talk
about it. They need you to establish a dialogue where you can
communicate your concerns and listen to theirs. They need an
honest dialogue; if you are a smoker and/or drink alcohol, your
teenager will challenge your grounds for objecting and they need
you not to be defensive, but to consider their argument.

GETTING DRUGS INTO PERSPECTIVE

Drugs are widely available to young people today. We live in a
drug-using society where it is acceptable in many youth cultures
to use all sorts of products as well as, or instead of, the ones some
adults take, such as alcohol or tobacco. Not all young people use
drugs, and even if they do, most use is experimental, short-term and
non-problematic. This is not to say that drugs are not a serious
social problem, nor that individual drug users can't develop
problems, but it is necessary to get the issue into perspective. As
your teenager will no doubt tell you, fatalities and illness caused
by alcohol and tobacco far, far outweigh those caused by ecstasy
or marijuana. Both of the latter can be extremely harmful and
dangerous, but so too can nicotine and alcohol. Drugs have
different effects and we can't lump them together. Not all drug
use leads to dependence; drugs such as heroin, crack cocaine, and
nicotine have higher 'dependence potential' than others.

To help your adolescent avoid beginning to use, you need to raise
their self-esteem and self-confidence and to have honest dialogues
with them about the risk and your anxiety, and why they may
accept the offer of something to smoke, swallow or chew. If your
teenager does come to you and admits, or you realize that, they

are using, the first rule is not to panic. If you find drugs or drug-taking paraphernalia in their rooms, it may belong to a friend and not them. Give your teenager a chance to sit down and talk it over with you, with the aim of finding a resolution, not of having an argument. If you're scared or angry, say it in words first rather than shout, and let the heat die down before talking. If you want to help your teenager stop or reduce their drug use, you need to understand the reasons why they are taking it. It may be they're keeping up with friends. It may be because they see whatever they are using as less damaging – and cooler – than your drug of choice. It may be because they like the effects after a long week at school or work, just as you might be glad of a drink on a Friday night. It may be because they have problems they are trying to deal with.

Whatever the reason, use communication skills to discuss their particular goal, and if drug use is the best way to fulfil this goal. You may need to research the substance to find the risks and benefits. You may need to research the legal situation too – many young people may find it a sobering thought to look at what a conviction for drink driving or carrying and using cannabis might entail, and how it might affect their future. And if the real reason they are using it is to boost self-esteem or deal with unhappiness, those are the issues you both need to address. Go for the cause rather than the symptom and once the cause is dealt with effectively, the symptom is likely to go away.

Insight

All human societies and the majority of human beings use a drug of some sort. The issue for you as a parent is to communicate with your teenager so that if and when they do use something, whether legal or illegal, they do so with informed choice and in safety.

Rock and roll

After sex and drugs, rock and roll has to follow. But there is a serious point, as music can be a flash point in some homes with teenagers. Loud music can drive parents up the wall and it can often be one of those little habits they have that leads to conflict.

What are your needs?
You may want peace and quiet. You may like music other than theirs and find it invasive and unpleasant to have to hear their musical tastes leaking out of the bedroom door. It's another territorial thing – just as with clothes and belongings scattered around the house, you may feel overwhelmed by their musical footprint and want them to retreat.

What are your needs for your teenager?
You do want them to have something for themselves and to get pleasure from it. Especially during the teenage years when your teenager can seem so moody and so put upon by the miseries of the world, it's often good to see them enjoying something. But does it have to be rap, at 100 decibels?

What are your teenager's needs?
Music is one of those issues that can often divide parents and teenagers – although less so now. A lot of music on the market is fairly cross-generational and enjoyed by everyone in the family. This can be to many a teenager's horror – one thing that teenagers need to feel is that what they like is unique and theirs, all theirs. It's another tribal thing; this is mine, not yours – this proves my membership of a group to which you do not belong.

Music can be negotiated: when it's played, at what volume and for how long. But you can also think laterally; iPods with headphones mean they can hear and you can't. Bliss! Check, however, the volume your child is playing their music; prolonged exposure to sounds over 90 decibels can lead to hearing loss.

Divorce and relationship breakdown

Sadly, today one in three marriages end in separation or divorce and this may be an issue you need to tackle with your teenager.

How do you handle this and maintain your teenager's life and wellbeing?

What are your needs?
During an intensely difficult and painful period, a parent's need for protection and comfort may overwhelm their ability to care for their children. Their anger may need an outlet and be directed not only towards the other parent but their children too. A parent may also need to feel that their children still love, support and forgive them – often in competition with the other parent. Managing co-parenting apart may feel difficult with continuing anger or feelings of loss, rejection and resentment and one parent may feel the need to sever all connection with their ex-partner.

What are your needs for your teenager?
Separated parents need to feel that their children are unaffected by their new arrangements, and that they will grow up untouched by the change in family circumstances. They may need their teenager to pick sides and to show loyalty to them, not the other parent, and want to see that as a way of settling the situation. If seeing the non-resident parent throws up anger and conflict, choosing sides and refusing contact is seen as making it better.

What are your teenager's needs?
Teenagers need both parents. They need their parents to recognize that separation and divorce are adult solutions to an adult problem, and are not what they want at all. In some cases, teenagers will be relieved that a warring family has gone their separate ways so the fighting is over. In some cases, teenagers will be better off, either without that family situation or even the departing parent. But in the vast majority of families, teenagers need continuing contact with both parents. They need not to feel blame – young people always think that the family broke up because of something they did or didn't do, unless their parents have realized their need to be reassured on this. Teenagers need both parents to accept that while they are no longer partners, they are still parents and should remain so. They need to be loved unconditionally by both parents, not used as pawns in continuing conflict, and given free access to both. Teenagers need

to remain young people and not to become the confidant or support for their parents. Teenagers need help and support to manage new families if either – or both – parent goes into a new relationship. (For more advice on the ending of a family and the restructuring of a new one, see *Be a Great Single Parent* and *Be a Great Step-Parent*.)

Insight

Separation and divorce are particularly difficult for teenagers. Just at the time when they are pulling apart from their family and trying to stand alone, the safe foundation they want to jump from becomes risky and vulnerable. However well they may seem to be taking it, teenagers need especial support at this time.

School and homework

Steering your teenager through the minefield of school and qualifications, career advice and education, can be a nightmare. Young people can long for the short-term gain of just earning some money, or be beguiled by the story of how someone became a celebrity or an entrepreneur overnight, with no exams and no effort. They may see adulthood as a time of leisure compared with their school life and have no concept of how you keep a household going and where the money to do so comes from. They may also lose confidence in school or their place in it and truant.

What are your needs?
You need your teenager to be successful as well as happy – and you may see their happiness as located in their doing well in school and then in a job. You may also need your children to follow in your footsteps. Their teenage years might coincide with your midlife crisis, when many of us start thinking, 'Is this all there is to it?' For you to feel it was all worthwhile, you may need to see them taking a similar path, in order for you to feel justified. On an immediate level, you may need the security of knowing your child is safely supervised by being in school for most of the day.

What are your needs for your teenager?
You want your teenager to succeed, both for themselves and yourself. You want them safe and sometimes contained, out of harm's way. You want them not only to be learning but to have the opportunities for social interaction with friends at school.

What are my teenager's needs?
Your teenager needs stimulation. Left to themselves they may acquire a love of learning, and some certainly do have ambitions and ideas of what they want to do and where they want to go. But many feel jaded by the whole process of education and desperately need you to buck them up and give them direction and enthusiasm. They need to be themselves instead of your mini-me. However, your teenager needs you and their teachers to truly listen to what interests or inspires them and to guide them along a track that would be right for them. They need to have the long view – they are in the second decade of possibly ten; that's not the time to consider your life mapped out before you. They may need you to let them take risks – risks with unconventional goals, courses or work experience. Often, they need a gap year or the opportunity to go off backpacking to give them space to recharge or reflect, and to learn far more about the world and themselves than they can at home and in school. They may, however, need you to draw boundaries and insist that 'No, you can't leave school at 16' and 'Yes, you will attend school.'

Essential points to consider

▶ *An honest look at everyone's needs – yours and your teenager's – is the best approach to settling issues.*

▶ *At all times try to treat your teenager with respect, practise what you preach and get off the roundabout of circular argument.*

▶ *Chores are a necessary part of teenage development. Try to negotiate these as soon as possible and draw up a chore chart.*

▶ *Encourage your teenager to begin to understand about money by offering them an allowance – which teaches them responsibility – rather than just pocket money.*

> ▶ *Modern technology – the internet, mobile phones and video games – can be the new problem today's parents face, but equally technology can be benign and enormously beneficial. Ensure your teenager's safety and your peace of mind by negotiating a technology contract with them, and gain some confidence through using the technology yourself.*

Discipline – crime and punishment

Teens need to learn how to behave for their own sake, not just to do as you tell them. If you want to enlist their cooperation, discuss how much this may be for their happiness not your convenience – and if you're having battles, perhaps the reason is that it is your wishes and convenience you're regarding more than their wellbeing. Is your attention a reward for bad or good behaviour? If they've learned as children that the only time they do, and the only way they can, get your attention is by acting up, that's what they'll do – not only then but in their teenage years. Positive discipline, where you thank them, appreciate them and tell them you love them, focuses on positive behaviour; it expects it, looks for it, rewards it, fosters it. Negative discipline, where you object to what they do and say, complaining about their behaviour, actually reinforces all those things you hate.

Positive discipline:

▶ *takes account of young people's, as well as the adult's, feelings – 'I can understand you felt upset and had a right to feel angry. I just don't like it when you leave the room and slam the door.'*
▶ *encourages teenagers to take responsibility for their own behaviour – 'It must be disappointing for you that your favourite sweatshirt is dirty, but it is up to you to put it in the laundry basket.'*
▶ *allows teenagers to share decisions – 'I liked the way you came up with a plan for discussing our Easter holiday. We seem to have a disagreement about this weekend, so how shall we resolve it?'*

▶ *has self-discipline as its aim – 'I know you have to finish that homework before the end of the holidays. If you want any help, please ask, but now I know you're aware of what you have to do, I'll leave you to decide when you'll do it.'*

Insight
Noting, acknowledging and praising the positive always works better than focusing on the negative.

PROVOCATION AND YOUR REACTION TO IT

Since your teenager may well be deliberately targeting you – prodding and pressing the buttons they know will get a reaction – you need to use all the techniques we have already discussed to keep calm in the face of provocation. It's understandable you may occasionally blow up, so forgive yourself the infrequent loss of control. Your aim is to use the strategies and techniques we've already covered, and a few more, to turn arguments into debates.

One technique to avoid at all costs, even when it is really tempting, is any form of physical action. Hitting out or manhandling as a method of enforcing your wishes is a poor choice when you're dealing with young children, and worse than useless when applied to teens. The use of force is an ineffective form of discipline for the following reasons:

▶ *It teaches kids that might is right. If you, who are stronger, bigger and have more authority than they do, are justified in making them do what you want, that logically means they can apply the same test too. When they are stronger, bigger and have more authority, either when dealing with younger children or when they grow up, they too can throw their weight about.*
▶ *It makes them too angry and humiliated to reflect on what they did wrong. When you enforce your point of view, even when their actions were wrong, a power-play simply leaves them thinking about your use of strength. Their own embarrassment and an intense desire to get back at you or make you feel what they are feeling is all they will think about.*

- ▶ It doesn't give anyone space to put it right. Punishment has a way of wiping out the offence. Hit a young person for bullying, lying, playing truant and why should they make amends or change their ways? Your action has wiped the slate clean – until next time, when you're right back where you started.
- ▶ It escalates. Hit out, and where do you go from there? Hitting harder? Punishing more? And what if they hit back?
- ▶ It builds up resentment and has a time limit. Use smacking as your method of disciplining your children and one of these days you'll find they have the size or strength to hit back. And since you demonstrated a lack of respect for their personal space and integrity by hitting them, they may display the same lack of respect to you.

We often punish our children, of whatever age, because we are scared of what will happen if we don't. We think that not applying limits will mean they get out of control, or we believe that we will have failed as parents if we don't draw firm lines. But, the main problem with punishment as a tool to help young people become socialized is that it doesn't work. What should we do instead? We could try problem solving.

Problem solving – a six-point plan

When you hit a point of disagreement or conflict, the first thing you need is calm. Call a time-out and agree you'll work through a six-point plan:

1 Focus on what they need

Young people need flexibility and to be allowed to rebel, but they also need rules, consistency and structure. The trick is to make these rules something that they agree to and understand. Say: 'These are the rules, take it or leave it', and they'll probably leave them. A system that runs on negatives – don't do this, no doing that, you shouldn't, mustn't, can't – is far less likely to be effective than one that has positive values as its basis. Focusing on pointing out what they did right, rather than what they did wrong, and asking them to do what you want rather than what you don't want, is far more likely to come up with the goods.

It's also important to be generally affirming about your adolescent. Don't only praise or thank them for specific actions, when they've done something. When anyone only gets a stroke after particular events, their self-esteem becomes tied to activity; they get the idea that they must do something to please you and that your pleasure is dependent on their fulfilling tasks or actions. Instead of an overall sense of self-worth, they'll only feel good about themselves when getting praise and be dependent on other people's view of them, not on their own self-image. Teenagers need your time and attention; your good regard and praise – but praise for themselves, not yourself. Parents frequently bask in the congratulations and admiration of others for their child, as if nothing their child does or is, is by their own efforts – it's all down to them. You may be proud of your children and you may have good reason to feel you have a lot to do with their achievements, but let them take the credit for themselves. Being proud of them too often comes across as pride of ownership – as if it's you who should take the praise for whatever they've done, not them. Being proud for them puts the achievement squarely where it belongs – in their hands.

> **Insight**
>
> 'Love is never having to say you're sorry' was perhaps the stupidest movie catch phrase ever. Love means saying sorry, please and thank you. Frequently!

Case study – Brandon's story

Brandon feels his father never really appreciated him. 'I can't tell you how much it has always made my blood boil to have my father introduce me and say, "Didn't I do a good job?" The things I'm most pleased and proud about myself are things I've really had to work out for myself, often in the face of his objections and manipulation, so he didn't do a good job at all and it's most unfair of him to try to claim the credit. Of course, I do understand what it's all about. He feels he was a lousy father – he was a lousy father – and he's desperate for me and anyone else to forgive him and say he is all right. But that isn't the way to do it and it more than infuriates me, and always has. In fact, if he'd only stop and let me be myself, he and I may be able to build a better relationship. As it is, ever since I was 13 years old we've been at loggerheads.'

Let young people own their own bodies. It can be hard, as a parent, to see or accept the boundary that separates you and your child. After all, what seems to be just a few scant years ago, they were a twinkle in your own eyes and then tiny specks of your own body. For nine months, they occupied their mother's body and it can be very difficult to let go of that sense of connection, of their being an extension and a part of you. This shows in what may seem, to the adult saying it, as joking or loving remarks and habits. 'Put a sweater on, I'm feeling cold!' may seem a harmless and affectionate bit of family banter, but what it also says is that you think you speak for them, answer for them and can act for them, for example: 'Paul wants to be an astronaut', 'Mum I haven't wanted to be an astronaut since I was five!', 'Don't contradict your mother, Paul!' or 'She takes sugar in her coffee', 'Dad, I'm not dumb and I've been having my coffee black without sugar for ages', 'Don't be cheeky!' None of these may matter individually but they add up and deny them their own feelings, thoughts and choices.

Young people need privacy. Reading their diaries or listening in to phone calls, discussing them with their teachers or others behind their backs, only underlines that you don't trust or respect them or feel that they are capable of making decisions or choices. Encourage their autonomy and show respect if they're having a hard time. They are far more likely to come to you for help and support if you've given them the chance to try on their own than if you won't let go.

Of course, finding out what they need calls for all of your listening skills. Asking too many questions is often felt as intrusive and controlling. You can show an interest without it appearing to be an interrogation, using openers and reflective and active listening.

> **Insight**
>
> Reading their diaries or their blogs, however public they may seem to be, may be felt by teenagers as a trespass and a violation.

2 *Consider your own feelings*

Accept that anyone hates to be made redundant; by acknowledging your teenager's freedom, you are making yourself redundant. If you are going to succeed in letting go – by not rushing to answer all your teenager's questions and fixing all their problems for them – you need to feel needed, wanted and essential in other parts of your life. Parents often feel guilty about doing things for themselves; they feel that it deprives their children and makes them selfish and bad parents. In fact, the more you are able to take your own feelings and needs into account, the more you may be able to give your teen what they really need from you.

3 *Ideas-storm*

Ideas-storming is a game or technique that really helps you solve problems and come up with solutions. It has the added bonus of giving participants a good laugh and drawing people together. Try this exercise for a quick demonstration on how it works. Get a sheet of paper, give yourself five minutes and write down as many uses as you can think for a plastic drinking straw.

Done? Did you think of using it as a hairpin, or a piece of jewellery, or a quill pen? What about as an automatic pot plant watering device, or half of a pair of chopsticks or a gambling chip for a game of poker? Some of the ideas you might have come up with would be sensible and practical, some might work and some would be fanciful. The point about ideas-storming is that sometimes, when we let our imaginations run riot, we find that the most unlikely solutions could work.

In a ideas-storming session, everyone is allowed their say and no idea is out of bounds. Elect one member of your group to be the recorder and another to be time keeper. The recorder lays out a large sheet of paper. Explain the problem – for example, you need a way of stopping the arguments about what time your teenager comes home on Saturday nights. It is important to be clear about the problem. If you are vague, contradictory, or are only seeing the difficulty from one point of view, you may find it harder to reach a resolution. Saying you want a way of enforcing curfew hours, for example, is unlikely to get much cooperation from your teen. Since the real problem, most of the time, is the argument caused by your difference of opinion, focus on that. ANY solutions can then be put forward. Set yourself a time limit – 20 minutes is usually enough to get the creative juices going – but not so much that people run out of steam. At this stage, what is most important is that the solutions need not be sensible, workable or even desirable. Get every single person to jump in with as many ideas as they can, and write every single one of them down *without comment*: 'Let us stay out all night', 'Stop worrying', 'Put them in leg irons', 'Send a chauffeur-driven limo' – at this point every solution should be recorded, with no criticism or complaint.

The recorder should function also as a facilitator, pulling anyone up who pours cold water on anyone for their remarks, or tries to discuss them at this juncture. You'll find out why silly suggestions are welcome in ideas-storming when you go on to the next stage. Once the time limit is up and you've put all your ideas down, take a break. Then, start at the top of your list and talk over each one. Don't dismiss anything out of hand, but do ask everyone what they think about it. Why not, in this instance, accept the 'stop worrying' solution? Think about it and then explain why you'd find this hard or impossible. Explaining your point of view allows you to think it over – there is just an outside possibility they might be right – or gives you the chance to have them listen to how you feel. Chauffeur-driven limos may be out of the question, but what about money for a taxi? Staying out all night may be unacceptable, but if half the problem is that they go out with friends who live a long way away, why not let them stay the night with them?

The key to ideas-storming is that, hidden among all the jokes, dross and rubbish, you are likely to find a gem of a solution that you might otherwise not have discovered. Done properly, it also allows the whole family the chance to feel brought together in the search for a solution. Young people can be responsible, caring and sensible – if allowed to be so. The final benefit is that a solution that had been genuinely created and agreed upon by everyone becomes theirs. Most of us want to kick against rules that have been imposed upon us from above. When the solution is something we have had some input into knowing is necessary, we own it. It's our rule and we have a vested interest in making it work.

Ideas-storming works because:

▶ *everyone has, and everyone knows they have, as much right to speak out as anyone else*
▶ *everyone has, and everyone knows they have, as much chance of having their solution taken seriously as anyone else*
▶ *it's fun*
▶ *it helps you think of difficulties as challenges that can be overcome, not problems that can't be solved.*

Insight

Ideas-storming is effective and efficient. It's also enormous fun which gives you all an incentive to do it – often!

4 Have a family round-table discussion

Adults often use family discussions as a way of telling their children what they have decided to do. It isn't, however, a true family round-table unless you listen as much, if not more, than you talk and unless young people are given as much space and respect to have their say as adults. Round-table talks may not always be what you need. There will be plenty of times when simply having the time and space to talk with and listen to someone else in the family is important. Try to make a point of allowing every member of the family some time to simply talk and be heard by you and by the other adults. A family parliament is an ideal way, not just of keeping in touch, but also of pulling everyone together. It's above all a good technique to try if you are having problems and need to clear the air and one that, if used regularly, can head off disagreements. If you feel that your teenager is too young to give their views, or that you are uncomfortable about listening to them, this may be a difficult exercise for you to become accustomed to. It may seem false or awkward to think about sitting round a table actually explaining your views or listening to someone else's, but however silly all this sounds, the fact is that it can be enormously helpful.

The difference between a dictatorship and a democracy is the assembly. In the days when city states were small, all the members entitled to vote would come together to voice their opinions and vote. As populations became bigger, those with a vote would use it to put their choice of elected member into a senate or parliament, to discuss and legislate. You can run your family as a dictatorship, where only the adults have a say, or you can claim you're presiding over a democracy where your children are too young to be able to make choices. If you do, don't forget what usually happens in such systems. The oppressed peoples either overthrow the state in bloody revolution, or emigrate and never come back. There are three main rules to make a family round-table discussion work:

i *Owning what you say*

The most important rule is that everyone has to 'own' what they say. That means, everything you put forward has to be your own thoughts and feelings and you should acknowledge them as such, using 'I think' or 'I feel'. No one can say 'So-and-so says...' or 'Everyone knows...' or talk about what other people do or what you think they think. You can talk about how other people's behaviour affects you, by saying 'When you do such-and-such, I feel...', but the aim is to put your point of view, not to criticize or attack other people. Remember, the key is confronting problems, not people.

ii *Equality*

Everyone, from oldest to youngest, is to have an equal turn to speak and to be heard. You might like to go round the table letting each person say one thing, to start. Then take turns to add to the discussion. You can use an object handed round to signify whose turn it is to speak and ask everyone to keep the rule about only talking when they have had it handed on to them. It helps to appoint one person to act as the 'facilitator' for a family round table, and to have each member of the group take it in turns to play this role. The facilitator ensures that everyone takes it in turns to speak and not interrupt.

iii *Consensus*

The eventual aim of your discussion is to find a space where everyone feels they have been heard and appreciated, and have heard and appreciated everyone else's point of view. There should be no winners or losers, but an all-round agreement on the outcome. To that end, no one is to be shouted down for what they say. Discuss the points rather than arguing with the person. Set aside time for the discussion and allow everyone a chance to speak, as many times as they like.

5 *Draw up a contract*

Having ideas-stormed and discussed, you need a clear way of keeping track of the agreed changes and how you're all going to make these changes. To do that, you should draw up a contract.

The idea is to write down exactly what everyone has said they will do. The key is that it shouldn't be one-sided, with one person or a few people asked to make an effort or making changes and other people acting as usual. Work out a fair exchange and one you can all agree. Make a precise record, including:

▶ *what you've all agreed to do*
▶ *how you agree to do it*

▶ *when you agree to do it by*
▶ *for how long you have agreed to do this.*

Everyone should sign the contract and have a copy for themselves. You could pin up the original somewhere you can all check it out, such as on the fridge in the kitchen.

6 Follow up

Review the contract and the agreed changes regularly. If the terms are not being met, discuss why and whether the contract needs to be redrawn or whether something needs to be adjusted.

There are several very good spin-offs to this form of discussion. One is that it means you no longer have to be – you no longer should be – in the position of policing your family. If two or more of your children have an argument, they should bring it to the round-table discussion – but it's their responsibility, not yours, to sort out. If one of the younger members of the family and an adult has a disagreement, it's up to the ones involved to settle it, not the role of one adult alone. This puts a stop to one parent feeling they have to mediate between the other parent and children, when they should be having their own dialogue, or one parent being cast in the role of disciplinarian when the argument may be between the other parent and teen. Another benefit is that if agreed changes are not fulfilled, you have every right to insist.

Insight
Always tackle problems, not people.

YOUR TURN

Think of an issue in your family you'd like to resolve. Now fill in below:

▶ *Focus on your teenager's needs – what might they be?*

▶ *What could you do to fulfil some of those needs?*

▶ *What could you do to help your teenager fulfil some of those needs?*

▶ *Consider your own feelings – what might they be?*

▶ *What could you do to fulfil some of your needs?*

▶ *What could your teenager do to help you fulfil some of those needs?*

▶ *Ideas-storm with your teenager what you could all do to find a solution and fill in your agreed ideas.*

▶ *Draw up your contract and add it here.*

Follow up, revise and change as required.

THINGS TO REMEMBER

▶ *It might help if you can accept that a lot of the time your arguments with your teenager are not about a particular issue. They come from your feelings of rejection and loss as your teenager begins the process of separating from you.*

▶ *There is no 'one size fits all' way to resolve dilemmas with your teenager. With each dilemma, you need to negotiate and compromise and yet still hold to your important boundaries.*

▶ *Pick your battles; don't give the same weight to the trivial as you would to the important. You will 'win' more arguments if they are about something you have a good reason to insist on.*

▶ *When you have a disagreement or a conflict, stay calm, call a time out and use this chapter's six-point plan to resolve things.*

There will be so many issues for you and your teenager to sort out, but the principle is the same for all of them. Ask:

▶ *What are your needs?*
▶ *What are your needs for your teenager?*
▶ *What are your teenager's needs?*

8

Helping your teenager to fly

In this chapter you will learn:
- *how the circle of dependence affects everyone*
- *how to encourage independence*
- *how to let go*
- *what parents fear, and their anxieties about letting go.*

Separating and pulling away

The task of adolescence is to separate – to pull away from your parents, develop your own character and independence and learn to manage on your own. So, the task of parents of adolescents is to support this happening. Just as teenagers may struggle with the skills to manage their new job, so we as parents may find it hard too. Parents of children are there to protect, to socialize, to guide and teach. Parents of teenagers are there to encourage, to provide a safety net and to be facilitators.

But that doesn't mean that a teenager who makes the leap from being a child to being an apprentice adult turns their back on their parents and rejects help or bonds. When you consider the journey from childhood to adulthood and beyond, you can see that your children need love, reassurance and support at all stages – they just need it in different ways. The skill of being the parent of a teenager is to let them go, so they can choose to come back. Keep too tight a hold and they will fight back to be free, and that's when they may move away altogether.

Change and adjustment

As children move from dependence to independence, their needs change and parents can adjust to this. There are balances to be struck. Instead of protecting and guiding, now you act as a consultant so that they can make their own decisions. It can be hard when you feel the decisions they make might lead them into danger, for example, when they want to go out with friends involving issues about drinking, driving and being in unsafe areas after dark; or if the decisions affect their future, such as when you feel they are not taking school work seriously enough. Standing back to let them assess risk and safety can be difficult, but it is necessary if you are to help them grow up. If parents are over-protective, young people don't learn to assess risks for themselves. They continue to have the same attitude that children have – that parents will be there to bail them out, and that it can't be all that bad, anyway. Every time you do rescue them and protect them from experiencing the consequence of their actions, they continue with the idea that something or someone else will always be responsible. On the other hand, if you simply hand over the reins before they are ready, the mistakes they make may lead them to feeling that they are incompetent and will never manage. As with so many things, it's a drawn-out process – little by little, step by step. It has to be progressive and it needs to go at the pace of your teenager, not to suit you. If you find yourself saying, 'You're not ready for this' when your teenager asks you if they can go into town to spend the day hanging around the shops with friends, go to a late night party or on holiday with their mates, ask yourself this: who's not ready – them, or you?

Insight
> Submit any problem to the ACT test; what's happening to you around this, what's happening to your child, and what tools do you have to resolve it?

Circle of dependence

There is a progression that lasts throughout life, and, perhaps reassuringly (and maybe confusingly) it isn't a straight line but a circle. It's called the circle of dependence. The circle of dependence has three major stages – dependence, independence and interdependence. We all go round that circle.

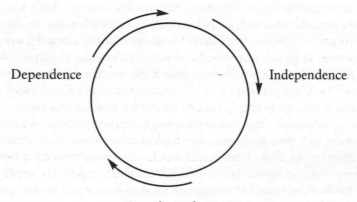

Dependence — Independence

Interdependence

THE CIRCLE WHEN WE ARE BABIES

We start as babies who are entirely dependent on parents and other carers for all of our needs. Babies can't help themselves at all, so as a parent you're responsible for keeping them healthy and safe – warm, fed, secure. It's your responsibility also to keep them feeling loved and stimulated – to play peek-a-boo, to give them toys (even when they throw them out of the pram!) to encourage them to learn how to walk, talk and develop physically and intellectually. You're in charge – totally. And while this can be scary, especially at first, and wearing, it is also very satisfying. You know where you stand and you know the buck stops with you.

THE CIRCLE WHEN WE ARE YOUNG CHILDREN

Young children are less dependent but still in need of a lot of emotional and practical support. They might be able to dress themselves and tidy up their own toys but they still need you to draw and hold lines – to say, 'That's what you're having for tea whether you like it or not' or 'It's time for bed.' During childhood, parents and children begin to experience conflict as children develop their own tastes, and a need to assert some sort of control over themselves and what is around them. That's why there are tantrums and arguments – it's your child trying to say 'Why can't I choose? Why can't I have it my way?' Children need you to be responsible because at this stage they aren't always able to recognize the consequences of their desires. Staying up late would be lovely – except it leaves them tired and bad tempered the next day. Only eating chocolate and fried food would be grand – except it leaves them overweight and possibly at risk from all sorts of health problems. The trick is to work out what your child really needs and fulfil those needs, as you understand is best. So sometimes, it does help to let children choose and have some control – being allowed to carry the full glass of water to the table, even if they may spill it. Your aim is to encourage the struggle – to help them try things out in safety and learn how to manage. They need protection and guidance, but they also gradually need more and more opportunities to try things out for themselves. Giving them appropriate opportunities to try out their skills helps them develop, not only the practical skills but the sense of being able, capable and worthwhile. It also helps defuse conflict. If much of the head-to-head tussles parents and children experience is about the child pushing boundaries, judge when it's the right time to be flexible and advance the frontier to defuse that argument.

TEENAGERS AND INDEPENDENCE

Teenagers need independence as well as the support of their parents. If you've begun handing over some of the reins when they are a child, negotiating when and what to let go of when they are a teenager may be easier. Not only will they be more used to the idea of earning such responsibility but also of the need to show you they can manage. But even if you've kept a tight hold up to now, it's never too late to start and the teenage years are when you'll have to begin to let go. Teenagers need to show to themselves, their family and the world at large that they can fly on their own. This can result in desperate and painful scrapes as they hurl themselves into various escapades and come down to earth with a bump. What they need from you, just as what they needed when they carried that full glass of water, is validation and encouragement. They need you to say: 'You can do it' and 'Is there anything you need from me to help you do this on your own?' If they can't manage, they need you to say: 'Never mind. Here's the cloth to clear up. Try again when you're ready. What have you learned and how can you do it better next time?' Being laughed at by someone saying 'There, I told you you couldn't do it' doesn't help. It doesn't make them any more careful. It doesn't make a parent any more loved or respected or needed if a teenager feels incompetent and incapable – it just makes them feel angry and let down.

Independence is something that needs to be won. It doesn't feel quite as satisfying if it is handed over on a plate. So while your job is to gradually draw back and allow your teen to take over, you will almost always find they will fight and demand and kick against you. Teenagers often demand more responsibility than you judge they can handle. This is likely to be because it's important to them to feel they are taking and winning their freedom rather than having it tamely handed over. It is up to you to be the adult and to hold fast against their insistence of taking charge when it is too early. But it may also be because you find it hard to judge the rate of change and may be lagging behind what they can and need to do. It's a difficult call, especially when you consider how painful it feels as a parent to see your children no longer need you in the way they did.

Insight

Sometimes it hurts to let our children go and for that reason we rein them in when we should be allowing them some freedom. Always ask yourself – whose need is this really fulfilling, mine or theirs?

THE BEGINNINGS OF INTERDEPENDENCE

Adults form interdependent relationships with others. Once we move through the fiercely independent stage of adolescence, we start on the next phase of the circle of dependence, which is interdependence. One of the signs of maturity is to recognize that it's okay – it isn't a sign of weakness but one of strength – to link up with, and even need, someone. Teenagers make fitful forays into this in their early relationships, when they may load everything onto one person who becomes the centre of their focus, pushing friends, interests and necessary tasks such as school work to the side. But one important aspect of interdependence is that it's mutual and reciprocal – as some teenage relationships certainly are, but some are sadly not. Interdependence tends to be part of a network, so that it spreads out from the couple at the heart of one interdependency, to encompass their family and friends. Interdependence isn't exclusive but inclusive and it's what allows you to be yourself at the same time as welcoming a close partnership with another person. Adults need to retain the ability to be independent at the same time as embracing and employing interdependence.

OLD AGE AND DEPENDENCE

Old people become more dependent on others again. As we age, we may gradually return to needing the support of others, to the point of being dependent on them. One of the difficult situations parents may be trying to manage is a balancing act between letting their teenagers go at the same time as becoming more involved in caring for their own parents – reeling one set in as you're seeing the other set run. Having to take over some of the responsibility you always saw your own parents managing for themselves, at the same time as needing to revise how much slack you cut your children, can be confusing and frustrating. It often means you have to think carefully about the roles that each person in your life plays and either wants or needs to play.

THE ROLES WE PLAY

We all play various roles in life – mother to one, while lover to another, father to your kids while being a friend to your peers. The three basic and important roles we play in life are child, adult and parent.

The child is the learning part of us: dependent, vulnerable, curious and exploring. An adult is the grown-up part of us: rational, reasonable and assertive – the ideal self who is dependable and mature. The parent is the caring part of us: nurturing, guiding, concerned, and responsible. Parents can also be controlling and critical. All three roles are natural and appropriate, in the right place and time and with the right people. We usually expect to be children when we're young and to grow through becoming adult to being a parent. What is significant is how we can take on and change these roles all the way through our lives, depending on who we are with and what situations we find ourselves in.

The child

Children should be children when they are young; they should have the time and space to learn their craft of childhood, adolescence and eventually adulthood, while being cared for by parents. Children should be like cats – into everything, patting and prodding and finding out how it ticks. That's what children do and should do, and it's our job as parents to make sure their curiosity doesn't kill them. It's neither a helpful nor healthy experience to be put in the position of taking on adult or parental responsibilities at a time when we should still be in child mode. When families go through crises – illness, loss, separation – children do sometimes end up not only becoming adult before their time but even of parenting their parents. It may seem admirable and necessary, but it's not good for the wellbeing of either child or parent.

The adult

Similarly, adults should be adults, taking on responsibility and recognizing that the buck stops with them. That can be wearing and boring, which is why it's perfectly appropriate for adults sometimes to go and play in the snow or run barefoot through the wet grass; sometimes we need to let our inner child out. But you should do it only when it's both healthy and suitable – constantly playing the child to your partner's adult or a child to your own children is putting a burden on them, and not allowing you or them to function to their full potential.

The parent

Then come the times when you are the parent; looking after your children, guiding and protecting them and taking decisions on their behalf. That's not always comfortable. Sometimes, you have to risk the anger or even apparent hatred of your children when you're doing your job and taking charge. The temptation sometimes is to switch roles – to become a friend rather than an adult, and act as if you're adult to adult, letting them be in charge of their own destiny, before they are ready. That makes for a quiet life. It isn't doing your job, though. You should be giving them respect and treating them as people who are approaching adulthood and letting them have chances to take the reins little by little, but you are the one to monitor that progress.

Falling into roles

People tend to fall into the role that corresponds with the role the other person they're with is playing. So, if you act as a child the chances are the other person will begin to be parental. If you act as an adult, the other person may fall into being an adult too. If you go all parental, your companion may act as a child. So, if you feel the role the other person is playing – your own parent being manipulative and acting as a needy child, your partner not taking proper responsibility, your child being parental – the first thing to note is what role you have fallen into. Are you taking on the parent role to your parent? The adult-to-child role to your partner? The child role to your child? Stop playing that game. Concentrate on expecting your parents and your partner to be adults, and for you to be a parent to your child; you should find by not colluding, you can turn the situation round.

The stages of childhood

Children need love, reassurance and support at all stages but some of their emotional needs change at different stages of development. Understanding some of the key stages children go through can help us to meet their changing needs. For example:

▶ *young babies need attention, stimulation, nurturing, food, warmth and love*
▶ *older babies need security, the chance to build strong bonds with particular adults*
▶ *infants need social skills and to learn how to deal with anxieties*
▶ *toddlers need to learn new skills and test the limits to their power*
▶ *juniors need to learn how to fit in with their own age group and make sense of the world*
▶ *adolescents need privacy and the chance to forge their own, separate identity.*

THE CHANGE TO ADOLESCENCE

You've done the babies, toddlers and juniors bits. Now you're in, or about to be in, the adolescence bit. And you can see, as children move from dependence to independence, their needs change and so your skills do too. It's your job, as parents, to help guide your children towards greater independence – to fly by themselves. As young teenagers, perhaps they fly like a kite, with you holding on to the string and letting it out little by little. Sooner or later, you'll have to let go and watch them wing away like birds.

There is a delicate balance, for example, between allowing them to take appropriate risks and making sure they are safe. Letting them take appropriate risks is saying, 'Yes, you can learn to drive and I may even agree to your having a motorbike.' Making sure they are safe is saying, 'Only on the condition that you take proper instruction and show me you can drive safely over and above passing your test and accept it's one strike and you're out. If I think you are not driving safely you lose the privilege until you are older and can show me you can do it properly.' Striking the balance between risk and safety can be difficult, but if you are over-protective, children don't learn to assess risks for themselves. On the other hand, if you give up and say, 'Oh, you can't tell teenagers what to do, can you?' you abrogate your parental responsibility and leave them vulnerable. As in so many things with teenagers, it's often a case of discussion, understanding, negotiation and compromise. Don't forget the key rules for negotiating are:

▶ *talk when everyone is calm*
▶ *gather information*
▶ *listen to your child's views, as well as letting them know what you need, and why*
▶ *be clear about what is (and is not) negotiable*
▶ *pick your battles*
▶ *make an agreement*
▶ *build in reminders for agreements*
▶ *review boundaries regularly*
▶ *have fun together.*

Insight

Teenagers don't want and certainly don't need you to be a friend. Be friendly by all means but you are their parent and should keep that in mind.

STARTING TO LET GO

One of the first stages of letting go is to make it clear you're happy for your teenager to go elsewhere for help or feedback. You like to feel yourself the final arbiters of your child's life – the one they turn to for help and advice, for opinions and views. Sometimes, you feel this is important, to make sure they are learning attitudes of which you approve. If you are religious you may not be comfortable having your child taught in a school that does not value faith, just as if you are not religious you would be uncomfortable having your child learn in an atmosphere in which faith came first. Other times, you feel this because you want to remain first in your child's heart – to be the people they come to, even if and when they may prefer or best be served by hearing another voice. Helping teenagers learn for themselves means sometimes having the trust in their good sense and in your previous upbringing, to encourage them to listen to other people too. Teenagers really benefit from being able to access adults and their peer group at school and in after-school clubs. They need to have friends and to know they can talk to other family members, the parents of friends, and consult professional support when they like and when they need to, and that you will be happy for this to happen.

> ### Essential points to consider
> ► *Your adolescent's journey is to learn independence and to eventually manage on their own and separate. As a parent, you should help and support this in all its stages.*
> ► *We all play the three roles of child, adult and parent in our lives. What is important is how and when you take on and change these roles.*
> ► *Deciding what degree of independence to give your teenager depends on their maturity rather than age. There are no fixed rules and you need to gauge when your teenager is ready and can cope.*

When is the right time to let go?

When it comes to knowing when your teenager can take certain steps and takes on certain responsibilities, the fact is that one size does not fit all. Maturity can be more important than age when deciding on what degree of independence to give – one 13-year-old can be infinitely more advanced than another 15-year-old, in the same family. There is no rule book that parents can follow – instead you need to gauge what an individual child can cope with and is ready for, and discuss it with them. Equality is an important principle to keep in mind, however. We often feel that girls are more vulnerable than boys and so give daughters less leeway than sons, in spite of the fact that girls do develop more quickly and are often more self-sufficient at an earlier age than boys. The problem with giving your teenagers different rules because of their gender, not because of different abilities, is that it can lead to resentment and then to rebellion.

LANDMARKS AND ISSUES

You might like to have some landmarks and issues in mind before they come up, so you have some ideas already considered. But flexibility is an asset – think these through and be prepared to change if your teenager can make a good case.

When do you think your teenager should...?

- *be left in the house alone*
- *be given an allowance rather than pocket money*
- *be left in the house alone for a weekend*
- *travel on a train alone*
- *go on holiday with friends*
- *decide for themselves when to go to bed*
- *prepare their own lunch*
- *prepare an evening meal for the family*
- *babysit for younger siblings*
- *learn about contraception*
- *have a body piercing*
- *be given responsibility over the state of their own room*
- *do chores*
- *stay out with friends after dark*
- *go to a party where there will be alcohol*
- *have a party without your being there to supervise.*

There are no right or wrong answers – what you decide is up to you. You will find the boundary between what they can do on their own, and what they still need or want to refer back to you, will develop in fits and starts, bit by bit. One day they'll be insisting they can organize an expedition to Everest on their own, thank you very much. The next moment, they'll be asking to sit on your lap and have a cuddle. You'll sort it out between you because that's what being the parent of a teenager is all about: constant adjustment, constant change, constant discussion and constant fun. Dull, it ain't!

> **Insight**
>
> When you and another adult have talked through your list, it might give you some useful insights to talk it over with your teenagers too.

DO AS I SAY, NOT DO AS I DO...

'Do as I say, not do as I do' is probably the most futile statement to make to a child or young person. Children model themselves on the people around them. Even when they consciously reject everything you say or do, they will actually be following your lead. If you would like them to be diligent, hard working but give time to those around them, sensitive to other people's needs as well as having self-confidence and self-esteem, to avoid drugs or early sexual behaviour... you need to look to your own life. The good news is that teenagers love their parents and want their attention and approval. They are far more likely to turn out to be like you than you think. The warning you need to heed is that you need to be who you want to be, in order for them to be what you would like them to be.

It's not your fault, but it is your responsibility. The work is hard but the rewards are high.

YOUR TURN

Think about the roles you play: spouse or partner, child, parent, employee, friend... List as many as you can identify.

Next, write down beside each role the main aspects of each – for instance, as a parent you need to be caring and responsible; as a friend you can be carefree but dependable; as a lover you can be romantic. List all your various selves and skills – you may like to ideas-storm to find them all. Compare and consider.

And you wonder why you're tired, confused and occasionally fed up? Go give yourself a pat on the back and a treat!

THINGS TO REMEMBER

▶ *Your teenager's task is to learn independence, to manage on their own and eventually to separate from you into their adult life. Your task is to support this happening and to encourage, provide a safety net and be a facilitator at every stage.*

▶ *There is no rigid rule about when the time is right to introduce changes. You need to gauge things for your teenager and discuss with them when they feel they are ready and can cope.*

▶ *Teaching your teenager interdependence is just as important as helping them to independence. It's what allows them to be themselves, as well as welcoming the close partnerships and friendships they should have in their adult life.*

▶ *As a parent, you need to change during your young person's adolescence. Instead of protecting and guiding everything, you should become a consultant helping your teenager to make his or her own decisions.*

▶ *What your teenager most needs from you is validation and encouragement. They need you to say 'You can do it' and 'Is there anything you need from me to help you do this on your own?'*

9

....

Looking after yourself

In this chapter you will learn:
- *how parents can look after themselves*
- *how to 'fill your cup' by caring for your own wellbeing*
- *how to make your personal relationship work.*

Being a parent of any age child is a complex and tiring job. When you've teenagers in the house, it's even more exhausting. You might have thought that sleepless nights were something that happened only when you had babies or toddlers, so finding yourself still lying awake can come as a shock. It's a challenge, but that challenge can be constructive or destructive. It can be as fascinating, energizing and joyful as it is stressful and hard. What often makes the difference between struggling or managing is the attitude you bring to the situation. Whether you have a positive or a negative attitude frequently depends on whether you are prepared to look after yourself as an individual, and as a couple, as well as look after everyone else. A strong relationship is the bedrock of a functioning family, so being selfish occasionally and concentrating on the wellbeing of yourself and your partner can often be essential.

Your needs

If children are to get what they want and need from a family, it's vital that parents look after their own needs too. Parents often spend all their time looking after everyone else in the family and leave themselves to last. Instead of being generous and helpful, however, this can become counter-productive. It can be difficult and painful to give other people what they need if you feel nobody looks after you.

WHEN YOU HAVE UNMET NEEDS

Trying to fulfil people's needs for emotional support and attention is like trying to share a cup of tea or coffee. The state of your cup entirely depends on whether your own needs are being met or not. If you feel tired and resentful and ignored, that means your own needs for care and attention are going unfulfilled. When asked for help by someone else, it's as if your cup is empty and when someone asks for a sip, you have to say 'I'm sorry – there's nothing for me so there's nothing for you, either.' You may feel angry or guilty or maybe even sourly triumphant that you can't offer anything to the other person, because no one is offering anything to you.

WHEN SOME OF YOUR NEEDS ARE BEING MET

If some of your needs are being met, it's as if your cup is half full. You may be able to say, 'Well, you can have some…' but you'd have to add '…but there's not much for you and if I give you a sip there won't be much left for me.' Again, you may feel angry or guilty or frustrated that you can do no more.

WHEN YOUR NEEDS ARE MET AND YOU CAN OFFER HELP TO OTHERS

If your cup is full, you can say, 'Have as much as you want!' You won't feel giving something to the other person robs you. Instead, you have lots to spare and feel ready and willing to be generous and to pass it on.

It's easy to be overwhelmed by the competing needs in a family, especially if you have teenagers and younger children, all competing in their different ways for your attention and care.

You have to learn not only the difficult and new skills for dealing with teenagers, but how to dip from one level to the other, managing them at the same time as dealing with younger children. A parent's cup can become empty very quickly and sometimes never fill up again. If you're running on empty, you have nothing to give to yourself and nothing for the other important people in your life. This can leave you feeling worthless and useless, and all of you feeling rejected, resentful and angry.

Having demanding teenagers in the family can strain the relationship between partners. When they were little, you could send them to bed and get some time for yourselves. When they were small, you could often manage all the questions and demands and still have time to spend talking things through with your spouse. Now they're teenagers, not only do they stay up and fill the house, and your attention, all the time but you may not have the mental resilience or agility to have anything left for your other half. To not only survive but thrive, a couple needs to make particular efforts to build their relationship and make it strong, but also to make time to enjoy themselves, together and separately.

Insight

Running on empty doesn't help you or your teenager. If for no other reason than to be a good enough parent, take the time to look after yourself.

The importance of looking after yourself

Treating yourself and looking after yourself isn't being selfish. It's being aware that you're important too and deserve to be cared for just as much as anyone else. Self-awareness means being in touch with your feelings and needs, it doesn't mean not caring about other people. The better you feel, the better you can help other people feel too. You owe it to yourself, your family and others in your life to do things – even small things – to make yourself feel good. Every little treat helps to fill your cup so you've got something to give out.

HOW DO YOU FILL YOUR CUP?

Take some time to work out what makes you feel looked after, cared for, rested and refreshed. It might be:

▶ *having a bath*
▶ *listening to music*
▶ *reading a newspaper, magazine or book*
▶ *gardening*
▶ *taking a walk*
▶ *being on your computer*
▶ *going to the gym or for a run*
▶ *going shopping with a friend*
▶ *planning a holiday*
▶ *phoning or texting a friend*
▶ *watching a favourite TV programme*
▶ *meeting a friend for coffee or a beer*
▶ *having a meal alone with your partner.*

MAKING TIME FOR YOURSELF

Work out what helps you and set aside certain times in the day and week to fill your cup. If you're having difficulty setting aside that time, ask yourself the following:

▶ *What gets in the way? All sorts of things can get in your way, either practical or emotional. Practical barriers may be lack of time or money, or anxieties about what your children may get up to if you went out. Emotional barriers may be negative beliefs about your entitlement, such as 'I don't deserve it' or 'It's selfish to think about my own needs'.*
▶ *How could you do it this week? Once you've identified the barriers, talk them through with the whole family to seek a solution. Letting other people know directly and clearly what you would enjoy and what you would like, starting with the word 'I', is an important tool in helping to get your needs met.*

For example, you would be able to negotiate a better result, if you called them together and said:

'I would really like to go out somewhere this weekend.'
'I'm exhausted. I need some peace and quiet.'
'How might we achieve this?'

▶ *What or who could help you do it? Partners, friends, family? Teenagers themselves may be only too glad to help you find and activate a solution, if you ask.*

GIVE YOURSELF PERMISSION

▶ *Sometimes you need to give yourself permission to relax or treat yourself. Even very small things you can do for yourself can help. The benefits will be that you relax, recharge your batteries, feel better about yourself and your teenager, feel better about life and more able to cope. Nurturing yourself helps you to take better care of your teenager. Sit down and work out what might really help you. A few ideas may be:*
  ▷ *Have the first 20 minutes after you get home from work alone, to get clean and chill out with a favourite music track.*
  ▷ *Reserve the last hour in the evening as adult time – children to their rooms, or else.*
  ▷ *Request no interruptions while you are in the bath – on pain of death.*
  ▷ *Have one night a month as an adult night in – children can go to relatives or friends while you have a meal and DVD of your choice.*
  ▷ *Have one night a month as an adult night out – a meal, a film, or just a drink on your own.*
  ▷ *Negotiate TV programmes throughout the week, but book some must-watch programmes for yourself.*

Insight
Having daily, weekly, monthly and occasional special treats planned and implemented helps you recharge your batteries.

Making your personal relationship work

Relationships need to be fed and watered and otherwise encouraged to grow and stay strong. Many parents find theirs coming apart at the seams because family life takes over. It can be wonderfully fun and heart-warming to spend most of your focus and time on bringing up your family but, as many couples sadly find out, if you only run your relationship through your children, when they grow up and no longer need you, the essential bridge between you can be gone and your relationship no longer functions.

One advantage you have is that you can remember what it was like to be together 'minus children'. When times are rough, with pressure on all sides, you can recall what brought you together and what has kept you together. But you can't get complacent and take it for granted. It's vital for you to take steps to strengthen your private, personal connection and you can do that in many little, as well as big, ways. You should try the following:

▶ *Talk. Intimacy is what brings people together, and you can only be intimate with someone you really know. Share your thoughts, your opinions, your tastes.*

▶ *Set good habits in the early days. Consider all the ways you show your feelings to your partner, by holding hands, hugging or kissing and telling them about your day, and resolve to continue doing so even when the honeymoon period is over. Don't let the presence of your children saying 'Yuck!' or your, teenager crying 'Gross!' put you off.*

▶ *Once your relationship has settled into a comfortable routine, keep reminding yourself and your partner what drew you together, what attracted you to them, and the way you felt in the early days of your relationship. Focus on the positive aspects.*

▶ *Make a point of doing something every day for your partner, and thank them out loud for anything they do for you.*

▶ *Regularly see your own friends and do something that specially and specifically interests you to maintain your own individuality*

*and social life. But share your thoughts, your ideas and your
enthusiasms with your partner so you both keep in touch with
this other side of yourselves, and never keep secrets.*

▶ *Be spontaneous. Relationships go stale and families get in
a rut because it all becomes so predictable. You may feel
you can't suddenly say 'I love you' because the children will
hear, or throw everything into the car and go out for a picnic
because the washing needs doing. Do it anyway.*

▶ *Make a big deal out of time together. Even if money is tight
and you're only spending the evening in eating sausage and
mash and watching TV, make it an event. Take steps to ensure
you'll be on your own, dress up and splash on the cologne,
turn the lights low and light candles and use the best china.*

▶ *Regularly look at your relationship and ask yourself and your
partner if you're satisfied, and if not what you could do to
improve things. If you feel it is healthy, look at what is making
it work and keep on doing those things.*

Essential points to consider

▶ *As a parent, you need to look after yourself, if for no other
reason than if you don't, you won't have the resilience to
care for your family.*

▶ *Remember the full cup of coffee; if yours is empty you have
nothing to share. You need to fill your cup up regularly to
have enough to go round.*

▶ *As well as being a parent you are also part of a couple.
Adults in a family need to make time to tend their own
intimate relationship.*

Insight
Treat yourself carefully and lovingly and let others do so too.

CARING FOR YOURSELF AND YOUR PARTNER

Most parents make a habit of looking after other people and often
forget to look after themselves, or to allow others to care for them.
It's really important that both adults recognize that they need and
deserve care, too, and that they should take the time and effort to

give themselves as much help as they are offering other people. It helps if you:

▶ *are as generous and patient with yourself and your partner as you may be with your children*
▶ *have realistic expectations of yourself and what you can do*
▶ *recognize that other people's problems are their responsibility, not yours; you can't fix everything nor should you try*
▶ *are positive with yourself and your family; give support, encouragement and praise, and accept it in return*
▶ *don't get stuck in a rut; change your routines as often as you can*
▶ *offload when you need to, but recognize the difference between complaining that makes you feel better, and complaining that just reinforces stress*
▶ *focus on one good thing that happened every day*
▶ *make sure you have some time to yourself at least twice a week when you can be calm and at peace, to have a bath, drink a cup of coffee, read a magazine or paper and where no one interrupts you*
▶ *take control of and responsibility for your actions; say 'I choose' rather than 'I should' or 'I ought to' or 'I have to' or 'I must'; If you don't choose to do these things, consider whether you should be doing them at all*
▶ *say NO sometimes – you can't do everything and you shouldn't be doing things you don't want to do. If you never say NO, what is your YES worth?*
▶ *be clear and direct; if you choose not to do something, say you won't, rather than making excuses*
▶ *say if you can't cope; it's far better to ask for help and back off than make excuses and let people think you're offhand, distant or indifferent*
▶ *give yourself permission to have fun – often*
▶ *make time; there are only so many hours in the day, but that doesn't mean you can't have some time for yourselves. Often, the only reason you don't is because you feel you don't have a right to it. MAKE time by planning ahead, knowing it's essential for you and everyone else.*

YOUR TURN

You and your partner need to look after yourselves. You should have some time to yourselves and some treats because you deserve it. You also can only function as a parent if you're not exhausted and running on empty.

Sit down and write out all the various things that would 'fill your cup'. You can list little things you could have daily (a cup of tea, a bubble bath, a chosen television programme), slightly larger treats you'd want weekly (a coffee with friends, a night at the cinema) or monthly (a shopping trip, a special meal out) – and whopping big ones (a big day out, a weekend break, a holiday) you'd love to have as the occasional special delight.

Small treat	Medium treat	Bigger treat	Whopper

Stick up the list and start marking it off. You want a tick every day, every week, every month for those small and medium treats. And every so often, you want to give yourself a tick for having had the 'Big One'. Because being a parent is a hard, skilled job. Well done for doing so well!

THINGS TO REMEMBER

▶ *Being a parent can be a complex and tiring job. What often makes the difference between struggling or managing is your attitude.*

▶ *A strong relationship is at the core of a functioning family. Be 'selfish' occasionally and look after yourself and your partner, as well as everyone else.*

▶ *Relationships need regular maintenance. Tending your relationship as well as your family should make your partnership stronger.*

▶ *Have realistic expectations of what you can and cannot do. Plan, make time for yourselves and take control of and responsibility for your actions.*

▶ *Being 'good enough' is the achievable goal, not perfection. You can't expect to be a perfect parent because there is no such thing. Be a 'good enough' parent, with 'good enough' teenagers. Relax and enjoy them – teenagers can be such fun!*

Taking it further

Following is a list of organizations providing help in p   _____
family issues.

Family Lives, formerly Parentline Plus
The national charity that works for, and with, parents. Family
Lives provides:

- *a free confidential 24-hour helpline: 0808 800 22 22*
- *a free textphone for people with a speech or hearing impairment: 0800 783 6783*
- *email skype or chat online through the websites*
- *groups and workshops*
- *information – as leaflets or downloads*
- *a helpful website www.parentlineplus.org.uk but soon to be www.familylives.org.uk with plenty of articles and tips and message boards to interact with other parents*
- *a website specially for parents of teenagers www.gotateenager.org.uk with a social network of parents of teenagers, message boards, blogs, interactive e-learning modules, web TV shows and more.*

Mumsnet
www.mumsnet.com
Offers a supportive community for parents on the web where you
can meet national and local mums and find out about local activities.

Black Parent Network
www.blackparentnetwork.com
Offers a wide range of information and support for black parents.

Race Equality Foundation (REF)
www.raceequalityfoundation.org.uk
Tel: 020 7619 6220

REF is a registered charity working towards better support
for Britain's black and minority ethnic communities. Runs a series
of parenting groups called Strengthening Families, Strengthening
Communities.

Fathers Direct
www.fathersdirect.com
The national information centre on fatherhood. It offers
publications to support fathers and their families. It also runs an
online community for fathers with help, advice, forums and features.

Positive Parenting
www.parenting.org.uk
email: info@parenting.org.uk
Tel: 023 9252 8787
Positive Parenting provides resources, parenting courses and
materials, and runs workshops for parents. It produces the
popular *Time Out for Teenagers/Parents* series of books.

Relate
www.relate.org.uk
Tel: 0300 100 1234
Offers relationship counselling and life-skills courses through local
Relate centres. Counselling is also available over the telephone, or
through the website.

The Trust for the Study of Adolescence (TSA)
www.tsa.uk.com
email: info@tsa.uk.com
Tel: 01273 693311
TSA is a national youth charity which carries out research, training,
and produces publications for parents and those working with
young people and parents.

Family Action
www.family-action.org.uk
501–505 Kingsland Road, London E8 4AU
Tel: 020 7254 6251

A charity offering home and community-based support to families in need. They run a network of family centres offering drop-in facilities.

Children's Legal Centre
www.childrenslegalcentre.com
For free legal advice on any topic relating to children, call the Child Law Advice Line (freephone) on 08088 020 008.
Offers information on all aspects of child law in England and Wales, particularly contact, parental responsibility and residence orders. A pre-recorded telephone service gives information on frequently-asked questions on a wide range of topics. A website and email response service is also available.

Citizens' Advice Bureau (CAB)
www.citizensadvice.org.uk
An independent organization providing free, confidential and impartial advice on all subjects to anyone. The address and telephone number of your local CAB can be found in the telephone directory. There is also advice online on their website.

Family Rights Group
www.frg.org.uk
Helpline: 0800 731 1696 (Monday to Friday 10 a.m.–12 noon and 1.30 p.m.–3.30 p.m.)
Provides a specialist advice and information service for families in England and Wales, who are in contact with social services concerning the care of their children, and their advisers and supporters.

NSPCC
www.nspcc.org.uk
Helpline: 0808 800 5000
The NSPCC can help with advice on keeping your child safe.

The Site
www.thesite.org
The Site is a website for young people with information about a wide range of local services, as well as discussion forums.

Youth Access
www.youthaccess.org.uk
Referral line: 020 8772 9900 (Monday to Friday 9.00 a.m.–
1.00 p.m. and 2.00 p.m.–5.00 p.m.)
Has a directory of youth advice, information, support and
counselling services for young people across the UK. This can be
found by ringing their referral line or by looking at the online
directory on their website.

ChildLine (now part of the NSPCC)
www.childline.org.uk or www.nspcc.org.uk
Freephone: 0800 1111
ChildLine, Freepost NATN1111, London E1 6BR.
Offers a free confidential helpline, open 24 hours.

National Youth Advocacy Service
www.nyas.net
Email advice for children and young people: help@nyas.net
Free helpline for children and young people: 0800 616101
Provides advocacy services for children and young people up to the
age of 25. They provide specialist help in children's rights, children
in care, contact issues, education and youth justice. They have a
network of advocates throughout the country and their own legal
advice helpline.

fpa (previously the Family Planning Association)
www.fpa.org.uk
Helpline: 0845 122 8690
The fpa is a registered charity working to improve the sexual
health and reproductive rights of all people throughout the UK.
The fpa works with professionals and the public to ensure that
high quality information and services are available to everyone
who needs them.

Brook Advisory Service
www.brook.org.uk
email: admin@brookcentres.org.uk
Helpline: 0800 0185 023

A charity that provides free and confidential help on contraception and abortion to under 25s.

Terence Higgins Trust
www.tht.org.uk
Helpline: 0845 12 21 200
Helpline and services for anyone concerned or affected by HIV/AIDS. The trust provides information on welfare rights, legal services, employment and housing as well as counselling and support.

Families and Friends of Lesbians and Gays (FFLAG)
www.fflag.org.uk
email: info@fflag.org.uk
Helpline: 0845 652 0311
Provides information and support for parents of lesbian, gay and bisexual young people and their families. They also have local parent support groups, a newsletter, publications and a helpline.

Lesbian and Gay Switchboard
www.llgs.org.uk
email: admin@llgs.org.uk
Helpline: 020 7837 7324
LGS provides advice and support for lesbian and gay people, and parents.

The Community Legal Service
www.clsdirect.org.uk
Tel: 0845 345 4 345
Can help you find the right legal information and advice to solve your problems. You can get help through a network of organizations, including:

Family Mediators Association
www.thefma.co.uk
National helpline: 0800 200 0033
Can put you in touch with trained mediators who work with both parents and children.

National Family Mediation
www.nfm.org.uk
Tel: 0117 904 2825 (Monday to Friday 9.30 a.m.–3.30 p.m.)
An umbrella organization for local family mediation services and which can provide details of local services in the UK.

UK College of Family Mediators
www.ukcfm.co.uk
Tel: 0117 904 7223
The college can help you to find a mediator. They can be contacted at:
3rd floor, Alexander House, Telephone Avenue,
Bristol, BS1 4BS.

Relationships Scotland
www.relationships-scotland.org.uk

Cruse Bereavement Care
www.crusebereavementcare.org.uk
Helpline: 0844 477 9400
Promotes the wellbeing of bereaved people and enables anyone bereaved by death to understand their grief and cope with their loss. The organization provides counselling and support, information, advice, education and training services.

PAPYRUS (Parents' Association for the Prevention of Young Suicide)
www.papyrus.org.uk
Helpline: 0870 170 4000
Provides information and advice for parents, teachers and healthcare professionals. Aims to raise awareness of young suicide, and many members are parents who have lost a child to suicide. They produce a range of publications and materials.

British Association for Counselling and Psychotherapy
www.bacp.co.uk
Tel: 0870 443 5219

The association can suggest a counsellor in your area. Write to:
BACP House, 35–37 Albert Street, Rugby, Warwickshire
CV21 2SG.

The Institute of Family Therapy
www.instituteoffamilytherapy.org.uk
Tel: 020 7391 9150
The institute helps with family problems. Write to:
24–32 Stephenson Way, London NW1 2HX.

The Hideout
www.thehideout.org.uk
The Hideout is a site for young people worried about domestic
violence.

Teenage Health Freak
www.teenagehealthfreak.org
This website is used by large numbers of young people to get
advice about physical health and wellbeing. The site is full of
valuable advice and ideas.

The Advisory Centre for Education (ACE)
www.ace-ed.org.uk
General advice line (Monday to Friday 10 a.m.–5 p.m.):
0808 800 5793
Exclusion information line (24-hour answer phone):
020 7704 9822
Exclusion advice line (Monday to Friday 10 a.m.–5 p.m.):
0808 800 0327
An independent, registered charity, which offers information
about state education in England and Wales for parents of school
age children. It offers free telephone advice on many subjects like
exclusion from school, bullying, special educational needs and
school admission appeals.

Parents Centre
www.parentscentre.gov.uk

An information and support website for parents on how to help with your child's learning, including advice on choosing a school and finding childcare.

Connexions
www.connexions-direct.com
Advice line: 080 800 13219
Connexions provides information for young people aged 13–19, covering topics such as education and work, health, relationships and housing. They can also provide services by text and email.

beat (formerly the Eating Disorders Association)
www.b-eat.co.uk
email: help@b-eat.co.uk
Helpline: 0845 634 1414
A charity which provides information, advice and support around eating disorders such as anorexia, bulimia and binge eating.

TOAST (The Obesity Awareness and Solutions Trust)
www.toast-uk.org
email: enquiries@toast-uk.org
Tel: 01279 866010
A voluntary organization that provides support and advice to parents of children who are bullied, due to being overweight or obese. It also provides information about healthy lifestyles.

Talk to Frank (formerly National Drugs Helpline)
www.talktofrank.com
email: frank@talktofrank.com
Helpline: 0800 776 600
Provides free and confidential information and advice about drugs. Also has a 24-hour helpline.

Release
www.release.org.uk
email: ask@release.org.uk
Helpline: 0845 4500 215

Release helps parents when their teenage child has been arrested or cautioned by the police for possession of a drug. They also provide support and legal advice about drug-related issues.

Parents Against Drug Abuse (PADA)
www.pada.org.uk
email: admin@pada.org.uk
Helpline: 08457 023 867
PADA offers information and support to parents of drug users.

ADFAM
www.adfam.org.uk
email: admin@adfam.org.uk
Tel: 020 7553 7640
ADFAM works with family members facing problems with drugs or alcohol, to help them gain access to a range of specialized services.

Tulip
email: tulip@hotmail.com
Tel: 0151 637 6363
A support group for parents who are experiencing (or have experienced) violence from their children.

Young Minds
www.youngminds.org.uk
Helpline: 0800 018 2138
Mondays: 10 a.m.–1 p.m.
Tuesdays: 1 p.m.–4 p.m.
Wednesdays: 1 p.m.–4 p.m. and 6 p.m.–8 p.m.
Thursdays: 1 p.m.–4 p.m.
Fridays: 10 a.m.–1 p.m.
This charity is concerned about the importance of children's mental health; the importance of recognizing when a child is troubled and providing adequate support for these children before their problems escalate out of control. They provide a helpline and information for parents and young people.

Mind
www.mind.org.uk
email: info@mind.org.uk
PO Box 277, Manchester, M60 3XN
Tel: 0845 766 0163
Mind is the leading mental health charity in England and Wales,
providing a mental health information service to people by
phone, email or letter. It offers support and understanding and
information on where to get help, drug treatments, alternative
therapies and advocacy.

Kidscape
www.kidscape.org.uk
email: webinfo@kidscape.org.uk
Helpline: 08451 205 204
Kidscape is a national charity which aims to prevent bullying and
abuse of young people aged 16 years or under, and which provides
support for their parents/carers.

Grandparents' Association
www.grandparents-association.org.uk
Helpline: 0845 4349585
Moot House, The Stow, Harlow, Essex CM20 3AG
The Grandparents' Association supports grandparents whose
grandchildren are out of contact with them or who have childcare
responsibilities for their grandchildren.

Grandparents Plus
www.grandparentsplus.org.uk
email: info@grandparentsplus.org.uk
Tel: 020 8981 8001
Grandparents Plus provides information about research,
resources and support for grandparents and those working
with grandparents.

The Child Exploitation and Online Protection (CEOP)
www.ceop.gov.uk

The centre works across the UK and abroad to tackle child sex abuse wherever and whenever it happens. Part of their strategy for achieving this is by providing internet safety advice for parents and carers and offering a 'virtual police station' for reporting abuse on the internet.

UK Parents Lounge
www.ukparentslounge.com
An online forums for parents.

Parents.com
www.parents.com
An online community for parents.

Homedads
www.homedad.org.uk
'The only UK support group for stay-at-home dads.' They have online forums discussing all the issues of being a dad at home with your kids.

Parent-teen.com
www.parent-teen.com
A US-based online magazine for families with teens with articles, forums, tips and ideas.

Urban Dictionary
www.urbandictionary.com
An online dictionary constantly updated and defined by users. It's probably the only way of keeping some check on what on earth your teenagers are talking about!

The Samaritans
www.samaritans.org
email: jo@samaritans.org
Helpline: 08457 909090

The Samaritans are available 24-hours a day to listen to people in distress and to provide emotional support.

Further reading

Hayman, Suzie, *Teach Yourself: Be a Great Step-Parent* (Hodder Education, 2010)

Hayman, Suzie, *Teach Yourself: Be a Great Single Parent* (Hodder Education, 2010)

Kreitman, Tricia, et al, *Everything You Ever Wanted to Ask About Willies and Other Boys' Bits* (Picadilly Press, 2002).

Kreitman, Tricia et al, *Everything You Ever Wanted to Know About Periods* (Picadilly Press, 2001)

Meredith, Susan, *Growing Up: All about Adolescence, Body Changes & Sex* (Usbourne, 2004)

Oh – and if all else fails, my own website: <u>www.agony-aunt.com</u>

Index

Image credits